Strange Country

The Clarendon Lectures in English Literature 1995

Strange Country

Modernity and Nationhood
in Irish Writing since 1790

SEAMUS DEANE

CLARENDON PRESS · OXFORD

Oxford University Press, Great Clarendon Street, Oxford OX2 6DP
Oxford New York
Athens Auckland Bangkok Bogotá Buenos Aires Calcutta
Cape Town Chennai Dar es Salaam Delhi Florence Hong Kong Istanbul
Karachi Kuala Lumpur Madrid Melbourne Mexico City Mumbai
Nairobi Paris São Paolo Singapore Taipei Tokyo Toronto Warsaw
and associated companies in
Berlin Ibadan

Oxford is a trade mark of Oxford University Press

Published in the United States by
Oxford University Press Inc., New York

First published 1997
First published in Clarendon paperback 1998

British Library Cataloguing in Publication Data
Data available

Library of Congress Cataloging in Publication Data
Deane, Seamus, 1940–
Strange country: modernity and the nation: Irish writing since 1790/Seamus Deane.
Includes bibliographical references and index.
1. English literature—Irish authors—History and criticism. 2. English literature—19th
century—History and criticism. 3. English literature—20th century—History and
criticism. 4. National characteristics, Irish, in literature. 5. Literature and history—Ireland—
History. 6. Civilization, Modern, in literature. 7. Nationalism—Ireland—
History. 8. Ireland—Intellectual life. 9. Colonies in literature. 10. Ireland—In
literature. I. Title.
PR8718.D44 1996
820.9'9415—dc20 96-24312

ISBN 0-19-818490-5

3 5 7 9 10 8 6 4 2

Printed in Great Britain
on acid-free paper by
Biddles Ltd,
Guildford and King's Lynn

For
Emer Nolan

Acknowledgements

The work and support of the following have been of inestimable value to me in the preparation of this book: Cormac Deane, Thomas Docherty, Tadgh Foley, Christopher Fox, Luke Gibbons, Declan Kiberd, David Lloyd, Marianne McDonald, Mairín Ní Dhonncadha, Edward Said, and Kevin Whelan.

I also wish to thank my graduate students at the University of Notre Dame; the staffs of the Hesburgh Library at Notre Dame, of the Royal Irish Academy Library, and of the National Library, Dublin.

I am also grateful to the Faculty of English at the University of Oxford and to the Clarendon Press for the invitation to deliver the Clarendon Lectures in May 1995; to Jason Freeman of the Oxford University Press for his patience, hospitality, and support; to Janet Moth for her copy-editing skills.

I will always remember, with fondness and gratitude, the extraordinary kindness and hospitality of John and Christine Kelly during my stay at St John's College, Oxford. Among many others at Oxford, I would also like to thank Richard McCabe, Roy and Alice Park, Val Cunningham, and Tom and Gitti Paulin.

Contents

ONE

Phantasmal France, Unreal Ireland
Sobering Reflections

FOUNDATIONAL TEXTS

I begin with Burke's *Reflections on the Revolution in France* (1790) because I want to read it as a foundational text for a particular description of a contrast and a contest between tradition and modernity that was to become routine in anti-revolutionary writing in Europe. This is a description which, I want to suggest, has a specific importance for Irish writing in the nineteenth century and beyond, although it is not confined either to Ireland or to Europe in its reverberations. To call a text foundational is not, of course, the same as calling it original. I am not claiming that Burke (or Edgeworth or Hardiman, two other authors I shall take as being foundational) is the 'first' Irish author in English from whom a whole tradition can be derived. That is a status that is more often assigned to Swift. A foundational text is one that allows or has allowed for a reading of a national literature in such a manner that even chronologically prior texts can be annexed by it into a narrative that will ascribe to them a preparatory role in the ultimate completion of that narrative's plot. It is a text that generates the possibility of such a narrative and lends to that narrative a versatile cultural and political value. In that sense, Burke's *Reflections*, as well as his other writings, especially of the 1790s, constitutes a foundational text. In Foucault's well-known phrase, Burke is 'a founder of discursivity'[1] and the *Reflections* is a text which opens a number of possibilities for the interpretation of earlier and the production of later texts that refer to it in a variety of ways.

For it is Burke who makes the annexation of Swift within the discourse of romantic nationalism possible. Swift had already been transformed into a heroic figure within the ideology of colonial nationalism; further, he had also become a species of cult figure in the folklore of an emergent Catholic nationalism when Burke's career was scarce begun.[2] But it is only after Burke's complicated defence of traditional society and his attack on the European Enlightenment, the French Revolution, and British colonialism in Ireland and in India that Swift's work becomes susceptible to the new ideological seductions of romantic nationalism. Swift thus becomes promissorily Burkean. Once viewed retrospectively from the Burkean position, his Anglicanism, like Burke's, can be understood to be a characteristic anti-revolutionary adherence to a spiritual politics that has its roots in a specific national tradition. Coleridge articulated the Burkean–Anglican politics in even greater detail between 1809 and 1829. From an English point of view, Swift and Burke are among his predecessors in the formulation of a powerful version of romanticism that is allied to the intellectual renovation of a national church. However, from an Irish point of view, the renovation of tradition remained more closely attached to the notion that the renovation could only be desired, the more so because there was no state, no social or political apparatus to support it. It was a romanticism that needed the spectacle of ruin to stimulate it to an imaginative intensity that would be the more impressive precisely because it derived from a history that had been lost, displaced, a history that had no narrative but the narrative of nostalgia. Nostalgia was the dynamic that impelled the search for the future.

However, it is merely reductive to assign to Swift and Burke a generalized hostility to a version of 'reason' and to read them as evincing a bitter hatred of the modernity that reason promoted. For what is most interesting about them is the discrepancy between the conventional nature of the politics to which they adhered and the extraordinary rhetorical innovativeness of their attacks upon its adversaries. Swift's defence of the Anglican Church and of the Irish Anglican élite has a narrower range and ambition than Burke's defence of European and British civil society, and his defence of the Irish Catholic community against that same Anglican élite group. But the mode of defence is, in each case, so radically disturbing and disturbed that the position to be defended is ultimately appealing only because the enabling conditions for its success are shown to have disappeared. It is not merely a nostalgic lament for the traditional pieties and the values that they produce. It is a lament for an idea of the traditional in which nostalgia is a constitutive element. This is a social and political vision that has potency precisely because it is a lost cause; lostness is central to its meaning, not just an emotive aspect of its appeal.[3] But it is Burke who gives to this lament a specifically historical character. He provides it with a tragic date, 6 October 1789, which is at once the beginning of the modern world and the end of the old one. It is a culminating moment in a process of subversion and the originating moment of that subversion's new-found legitimacy. Swift identified an impasse in the British–Irish relationship; Burke expanded that local instance into a crisis in the relationship between two modes of civilization.

READING THE REFLECTIONS

I want to argue that the *Reflections* can be understood as a work in which two dominant discourses are deployed—one cultural, the other economic. The first discourse is centred around the events of 6 October 1789 and has the French Royal Family, especially Marie Antoinette, as its most fertile emblem. The second is centred around the French finances and the possibility of their recovery through the kinds of fiscal reform that had been initiated by Calonne and Necker. Its central emblem is the new French currency, the *assignats*, issued against the security of the recently confiscated church property. These two discourses are to be understood as inversions one of the other. That is to say, there is a sense in which each field—culture and finance—enjoys autonomy. This autonomy is predicated on the assumption that the language of sensibility and the language of calculation, appropriate to each respectively, are not merely separate from but wholly opposed to one another.[4] The opposition is emphatic, at one level, cancelled at another. For part of the argument for tradition is that it provides a felicitous convergence of the two discourses, whereas part of the argument against modernity is that it divides the two schismatically and disastrously from one another. However, the opposition is itself a structural feature of an ideology which both governs the work—as an assumption—and is produced by the work—as a revelation. It is an ideology of the traditional culture—its capacity to endure as a set of universal truths and to survive changing circumstances by a series of modified reforms that fortify rather than weaken that durability. Inevitably, this also involves an ideological version of modernity—its lack of historical sense, its refusal of habitual practices, its disabling tendency to abstraction, its aesthetic of distance, and its global pretensions.

That ideology takes a specific generic form or, more accurately, a generic mix that gives the *Reflections* its peculiar character and that helps to explain what I am suggesting is its foundational relationship to later political and literary writings in Ireland. The mix has two elements—one is that set of conventions that we find in political pamphlets, the other the set of conventions that we find in travel literature. When the relationship between these two is grasped, then it is possible to observe the suasive force with which the autonomy of the cultural and the autonomy of the economic are both asserted and denied. It is in the tremor of relationship and separation between these zones that the *Reflections* achieves its ambiguous status as a highly polemical work replete with exaggeration, propaganda, and contradiction on the one hand, and, on the other, as a classic analysis of the nature of revolution and its melancholy connection with the condition of modernity.

The *Reflections* as a work of travel literature has clear connections with the vast and preceding corpus of travel literature in the eighteenth century—to go back no further. It resumes the conventional debate—first elaborated in the dispute between Locke and Shaftesbury—about the function and the technique of travel writing.[5] Shaftesbury argued that travel literature was a disreputable form of discourse when it was given over to exaggerated accounts—often by unreliable witnesses—of the barbaric strangeness of the customs and practices of others. A version of pulp fiction, it was, in this mode, designed merely to cater to a popular taste for the exotic and the extravagant. On the other hand, there was a kind of travel literature which, while acknowledging the differences in custom and practice between various societies, also revealed the uniform disposition of human beings to achieve a rationally benevolent form of social organization which, underneath its appearance of difference, was ultimately comprehensible to and in accord with the principles of a universal human nature that had been revealed more fully in European than in other societies. This is a long debate, in which the notion of a universal human nature was often seen to be at odds with the revelation of human difference and just as often found to be perfectly reconcilable with it. Swift, Montesquieu, Hume, Diderot, and Goldsmith are most notable among those who engaged with these issues.

Travel literature favoured the epistolary convention that permitted the author to adopt various modes of address to a correspondent who could occupy a number of roles—as the Gentle Reader, as an internal fictional presence, as the recipient of the narrator's enlightening information and influence. In the *Reflections* Burke addresses his correspondent, Depont, as someone who is expecting congratulation but must receive instead a rebuke, for he is, like the reader whom Depont represents, someone who does not understand the scale of a revolution that has transformed France into a condition unprecedented in the history of Europe. The new France is foreign to the traditional Europe to which the old France was central. In addition, the epistolary convention allows Burke to indicate that his work is hurried, spontaneous, more dishevelled than he would like. The rhetorical pretence allows the contrast between inhuman system and human disorder to operate as a formal as well as a substantive element in the text.[6]

I am not here concerned to unravel the various complexities of travel writing; merely to state its abiding concerns. It is, however, important to note that what we may call the Benevolist school was most emphatic in its claim that differences could be reconciled in such a way that the rationality and the benevolence of human nature could be proven or exhibited—whether travel took place in time or in space, in relation to societies in the past or societies that were geographically spread all over the globe. This is important because of the central role that Burke—among others—was to assign to Rousseau and his role in the French Revolution and in the production of modernity.

Travel literature was, of course, a mode of political critique and as such is not entirely distinct from political pamphleteering. It attacked corruption, fanaticism, irrational behaviour and practices, institutions, and individuals and made use of the mask of foreignness to bring these charges home. But it operated within what we may call a narrow philosophical range. Practices were either to be admired because they were rational or natural or both together; or attacked because they were neither of these things. The point to be defended or promoted in political terms was what Hume called 'civil liberty' and the most threatening enemies to its preservation were the Catholic–Protestant duo of superstition and enthusiasm respectively. Essay Nine of Hume's *Political Essays* discriminates between the enduring bad effects of superstition on civil liberty and the more short-lived threat of enthusiasm—which in the long run he argues is favourable, both in England and France, to its realization: 'enthusiasm, being the infirmity of bold and ambitious tempers, is naturally accompanied with a spirit of liberty; as superstition, on the contrary, renders men tame and abject and fits them for slavery.'[7] This Catholic–Protestant contrast is central to much of the discussion of the respective careers of liberty in France and in England, during the Enlightenment, the Revolution, and for long after. Again, it is a contrast that Burke is to reorganize in his anti-revolutionary writings and in his writings on Ireland.[8] But I want to suggest further that travel literature was not confined to this crucial political debate on liberty. It envisaged another alternative to societies caught in the storm of wild enthusiasm or subjected to the sedative of superstition. After all, British society, certainly in Burke's conventional interpretation of it, had undergone precisely that vacillation in the seventeenth century and had, in the Glorious Revolution, achieved an exemplary balance between these destructive forces. The French Revolution had introduced another possibility. It had made a political reality of the utopian element frequently found—although by no means often celebrated—in travel literature, by claiming to produce a new society constructed according to entirely theoretical and secular models of what the human world could or should be.

Such utopianism had traditionally been characterized either as a form of superstition or as a species of enthusiasm. Equally, it was standard practice to excavate from that distinction another polarizing opposition—that between simplicity and complexity, an opposition usually seen as one in which complexity of human circumstance was read as a historical and moral condition far beyond the reach of any rational or theorizing formulation, while simplicity was portrayed as a reductionist attempt to deny both history and all the miscellaneous varieties of human experience in order to fit it within an impoverishing and despotic system.[9]

It is in the light of these considerations that I suggest Burke's *Reflections* can be read. Put simply, the *Reflections* claims that, after 6 October 1789, when the modern world appeared, France became the foreign country *par excellence*; that it differed from all other foreign countries that had previously figured in the fictions or reports of travel writing because it was now historically actual, a short distance away across the Channel, in the centre of Europe, and that it was filled with a missionary spirit to convert or pervert all Europe to its model. It was or had become a foreign country because its barbarous philosophy had destroyed all the foundations of traditional civilization and had gone so far as to produce an alteration in human nature itself. It had attacked throne and altar; it had attacked and humiliated traditional conceptions of sexuality and sentiment; it had converted a society into a plebeian mob; most of all, it had raised theory to an unprecedented position of power in European politics and social thought. France was a new territory—the territory of theory. Burke was the traveller making a report on its astonishing bad eminence in the world and urging that world to respond with all the galvanic force that it could call upon to prevent its universal triumph. The literature of travel and the literature of the political pamphlet were conjoined to produce a critique of the despotism of the new France and the emergence of a new world in which the human person, as traditionally understood, was a stranger.

France has always more or less influenced manners in England; and when your fountain is choked up and polluted, the stream will not run long, or not run clear, with us or perhaps with any nation. This gives all Europe, in my opinion, but too close and connected a concern in what is done in France. Excuse me, therefore, if I have dwelt too long on the atrocious spectacle of the 6th of October, 1789, or have given too much scope to the reflections which have arisen in my mind on occasion of the most important of revolutions, which may be dated from that day—I mean a revolution in sentiments, manners, and moral opinions. As things now stand, with everything respectable destroyed without us, and an attempt to destroy within us every principle of respect, one is almost forced to apologize for harbouring the common feelings of men.[10]

Here is a new territory—the territory of modernity. Against that has to be counterposed the territory of tradition. The inhabitants of each territory have to be distinguished, not merely as French and British, although that does often become in pamphlet literature and in literary journalism the shorthand description of them; they have to be distinguished as groups each of which conforms to a radically different conception of the human. In effect, the French, as a group, are identified with the barbarous and new; the British as a group, are identified with the humane and the old. Within those national groupings, Burke goes on to identify characteristic groupings, seeing them in hostile pairings, providing each with a history, embedding each in an ideological disposition, above all reading them as belonging to the *ancien régime* or to the modern world, symptomatic social formations that are rooted in a recognizable or unrecognizable territory that exists both in the dimension of time and of space. Such groupings are clearly traditional in many respects, although Burke's intimacy with Montesquieu's work enabled him to produce a more refined variation on the ready-made distinctions between national characters that was integral to the formation of European nation-states.[11] The difference in his formulation of national character lay in his conception of its relationship to a territory. Although the influence of climate or geography was real, national character was more deeply formed by a territory that was felt to belong to a historical community. The relationship between character and territory was the more profound because it was traditional. When that traditional sense of kinship was replaced by a theory, when territory was defined in abstract and spatial terms, then the relationship was weakened. This weakened relationship was characteristic of modernity.

There might indeed be historical explanations, derived from French history and the French experience, why the French national character should have produced the theory of cosmopolitan modernity. But, in effect, these were beside the point. The French had broken the sound-barrier. They had ruptured historical time and produced a messianic revolution. In that context, national character became for Burke, and later for others as various as Coleridge, De Quincey, Southey, Croker, a synecdoche for traditional politics and a refusal of revolution.[12] Burke confers upon the English (now the British) national character, a specificity which, in some formulations, it had once lacked. The lack of specificity, however, had been one of its virtues. Hume had argued that precisely because the English were freer, because they had the advantages of a mixed constitution and therefore were not subject to the uniformity of disposition that was taken to be (at least since Montesquieu) one of the symptoms of a despotic culture, they were more individuated, gloried more in eccentricity and difference, than did other, less fortunate, European nations.[13] Burke reorganizes that description, regimenting its elements more sternly, emphasizing both the uniqueness and the universality of the national character, identifying its eccentricities as a symptom of deeply grounded communal fidelities rather than as an expression of individual licence. He plays a highly predictable variation on the theme of the national character's 'measured disorder',[14] but, by claiming that its flexible humanism has become almost anachronistic in the newly emergent modern world, gains for it a nostalgic appeal that makes it all the more endearingly vulnerable. To make the contrast with the new France more startling, he seeks to identify those social constellations in France that had altered the very notion of traditional social cohesion by deliberately giving to rancour and vanity the place formerly assigned to instinctive fidelity and love.

The constellations are well known—the men of letters, the new moneyed interest, the cabal, the mob. Their victim, representing throne and altar, the emblems of public fidelity and reverence, is the French royal family which represents private affections and fidelities and is also the family of the European tragic tradition in the theatre. Thus, we see three central groups—the family, the cabal, and the mob—participating in the story of the march from Versailles to Paris and the subsequent events of that evening of 6 October. The particularity of the event enhances its status as an inescapably symbolic moment in the whole history of European civilization. For all the events referred to in the *Reflections* are carefully chosen as synecdoches for a wider condition; this is true even of the quotations from Cicero and Horace, the references to Aristotle, the English Revolution of 1688—the whole infrastructure of citation. The narrative is cast in oppositional mode—chivalry overcome by brutality, heroine and hero of high estate brought low, affection overborne by heartlessness, chastity threatened by rape—the permutations of the description are multiple, once its larger resonance is admitted. Most of all, it is an event that is at once legible and illegible, because it is simultaneously a confusing, chaotic sight and a re-enactment of a tragic spectacle before a European audience. It is apocalyptic; yet it is also recognizable. The protocols of tragic theatre have been transferred to the realm of public politics and are discernible behind the furore of the anarchic present.

Hence the force with which Burke can portray the Queen of France in particular, along with her family, as comparable to a tragic protagonist in an Aristotelian tragedy in which pity and terror would be evoked in the breasts of those still humane enough to be moved in the traditional manner by what Europe has, since classical times, understood to be a primary feeling of sympathy and awe. In addition, the imagery of stripping, employed as an interpretative strategy for the central action of tragic drama, has particular reference to the great English tragedy of *King Lear*. In short, these chivalric passages, as we may call them, produce, out of the Greek–English combination, a representation of Marie Antoinette as a Queen Lear figure, almost obliterating her husband the king, as the central figure in an apocalyptic moment of nakedness and destruction.[15] It is important that Burke begins his apostrophe to Marie Antoinette with a memory of having seen her at Versailles as a young princess who was the cynosure of all eyes, who was viewed as a figure in whom a whole series of traditional and chivalric emblems was recapitulated. In contrast, he exclaims that he would have 'thought ten thousand swords would have leaped from their scabbards to avenge even a look that would have threatened her with insult'.[16] For the revolutionary way of looking, sexually threatening, is a way that sees her as a woman, as someone who is a body (exclusively that) rather than a figure—in the various senses of the word. There is a traditional mode of looking that is specular. In that mode, a person is seen as an emblematic figure in a hierarchical system. But the revolutionaries have a different way of looking at the world, especially at women. Their mode is speculation. Speculation indicates looking, thinking, and gambling. In speculation, a traditional emblem loses its fixed value and becomes vulnerable to risk. Burke exploits the financial meaning of the word when he attacks the revolutionary economy as a form of gambling, wild and empty in its conversion of real wealth into the confetti of the new currency. He exploits the sexual meaning of the word in his development of the imagery of stripping in relation to the French queen and the royal family. By speculation, the body is not only stripped; it is reduced to a material and vulnerable condition. This is the final step in the process of desacralization.[17]

Further, the plea that is recurrent within all of this passagework, insinuated time and again as part of Burke's attack on Richard Price and the English Dissenters who have abused the biblical imagery of the appearance of Christ in the temple—the moment when a new world is inaugurated, blaspheming thereby the sacred text's meaning—is that the actuality of this event in Paris is so fierce and astonishing that it appears almost phantasmal. Were it only a stage drama, a spectacle, the audience would be moved to tears. But it is an actual historical event enacted on the Parisian stage and, amazingly, the audience cannot weep for the real as it would more readily have for the fictional.[18] Once more, the distinction is between a spectacle in the theatrical sense and a spectacle in the political sense.[19] The distinction is blurred because people have not learned to look in the appropriate manner and, therefore, cannot see. But, of course, part of the ideological nature of Burke's representation of the event is rooted in the claim that the victims of it belong not to ideology but to nature—as do those witnesses who sympathize with the victims—while the perpetrators are wholly ensconced within the ideological world that had been theorized into existence by the *philosophes* and acted out by the mob. This leads naturally on to Burke's famous characterization of the connection between the actuality of history and the authenticity of feeling, paired against the phantasmal nature of theory and the inauthenticity of feeling that he would, in the following year, in *A Letter to A Member of the National Assembly*, attribute to Rousseau. It is in this connection that the relationship between the actual and the phantasmal extends to include the financial; through it, the division between the discourses of sensibility and those of calculation is both overcome and reaffirmed.

Revolutionary finances, based on the issue of the *assignats* against church land, belong in the world of the phantasmal. A paper currency replaces the traditional coinage; a traditional estate is vaporized into worthlessness by an act of vandalism. Gold coin, stamped with the head of the sovereign, the *louis d'or*, is converted into a paper promise; solid land is no longer worth the paper on which it has been transcribed.[20] All the minute discussions of the state of the French national debt, the various attempts at reforming the tax base, the calculation of the potential wealth of France against its strained financial situation, are—like the story of the Versailles march—elements in a narrative that is posing the specific and the actual against the vague and the phantasmal. In that sense, the two narratives—the cultural and the economic—are interlinked. Their separation into two autonomous realms is indicated by the manner in which Burke ascribes to the cultural—centred on the royal family—the priority in the political and social system. The economic or financial is derivative from that, not prior to it.[21] It is a system founded on landed property and the integrity of corporate bodies. These corporate bodies are both a mediating influence on potential despotic power and subject to a form of analysis different from the actual source of power itself, which is invested in the monarchy. This is the part of the *Reflections* in which the genre of travel concedes to the genre of the political pamphlet. Yet, while remaining distinct, the two narratives remain interwoven by the ideologically charged metaphor of a transaction between the real and the phantasmal, one converted or perverted into the other, which is analogous to the historical distinction between the *ancien régime* and the revolutionary state.

Here I want to exploit the importance of this distinction as integral to Burke's attack on Rousseau and the philosophy of benevolence. His famous or infamous *ad hominem* argument against Rousseau in *A Letter to a Member of the National Assembly* relies on the distinction for its full effect.[22] For it is not merely a matter of Burke's claiming that there is a wounding contrast between Rousseau's preaching universal benevolence to humankind and his treatment of his own children. It is, additionally, an intensification of the charge that revolutionary philosophy is phantasmal *because* it is global, that it lacks actuality because it is not anchored in specific persons or places. It is an attack on cosmopolitanism—on any political philosophy which denies the actual, formulated by Burke as that which is immediate and local. The difference is in the distance— Rousseauistic benevolence travels abroad and refuses to stay at home. It is the new traveller of the modern world—not a person, not an observer, not a composite of attitudes and views, but an idea that has reached an astonishing degree of abstraction, a portable virus that is highly contagious.

Ironically, it is this very distinction between patriotism and cosmopolitanism, between the relationship to those close to and those distant from us, that is anxiously addressed on several occasions by Rousseau himself. It is a distinction vital to the political thought of both writers and, by extension, to the issue which it seeks to clarify. In fact, Burke's attack on Rousseau and on modern philosophies of benevolence is no more than a reproduction of what

Rousseau himself attacks in *Emile* when he defines the false cosmo-politan: 'Distrust those cosmopolitans who go to great length in their books to discover duties they do not deign to fulfil around them. A philosopher loves the Tartars so as to be spared having to love his neighbours.'[23] Nevertheless, for all his misconstrual of Rousseau's position, Burke is determinedly redefining national char-acter as a necessary counteragent to what he wishes to characterize as a theoretic form of benevolence, as an emotion that has to travel light rather than stay at home, anchored in the specific gravity of the local and domestic situation. He is not denying the universality of human nature, nor is he asserting, in line with Shaftesbury and Hutcheson, that melodramatic instances of barbarous custom undermine that belief in any serious way. But he is now saying that what was once agreed to be universal human nature has been compelled to retreat, as if in a siege, within the national limits of the British state. To the degree that the British remain faithful to that old conception, they are still participants in authentic human nature. What has happened is that the Gulliverian traveller, the person who has been consumed by an idea and transmogrified thereby into an ideologue whose ambit is the whole world at the expense of those people and things that are nearest and should be dearest to him, has replaced a genuine with a false conception of the universal. Through the power of Rousseau's rhetoric, the French and their supporters have been persuaded that personal eccen-tricity—understood as the coincidence between the inner voice of conscience and Nature—can become the foundation for a concep-tion of the human. Eccentricity, stimulated by personal vanity, has become the interior space to which the whole exterior world is referred for moral evaluation. Cosmopolitan faith in humankind is the political consequence of a pathological condition which used to be understood as enthusiasm and is now sophisticated by Rousseau into an alliance between inner light and Nature, rechristened as global fraternity. As such, it is a condition that cannot accept reality; it must replace it by a phantasmal world and then announce that the phantasmal is the real. This is the basis of the ideology of the modern—an inner conviction of one's own election to the real, a species of dissent engrossed into a world politics through the corruption of sentiment. Such sentiment is phantasmal; its opposite is actual feeling. In such a politics, everything becomes reversed once that initial reversal has been achieved or accepted. The public becomes the private and the private the public. The validity of civil liberty is surrendered for the celebration of personal licence. Theorized by Rousseau into a political and moral philosophy, this condition has only one mode of existence for its survival. It travels. It cannot linger in the actual. It cannot stay at home. Its home is always abroad in the world of desire and abstraction. Further, this theory is even more specious and dangerous than the theories of rational progress promoted by the *philosophes*, precisely because it is, at base, a reconstruction of the modes of social relationship that constitute society.[24]

It is these modes that Burke chooses to defend by adopting, in the *Reflections*, a particular distinction between the realms of culture and of finance. By asserting the centrality of the French royal family and, further, by claiming that it is a universally human response to sympathize with it, he involves the family itself, as a social unit, within the precinct of that universalism. It is not a particular institution like the moneyed interest, the intellectuals, the clergy, the aristocracy, the mob, or the financial institutions of the state. It does not share in their historical contingency because it evokes—as a focus of feeling and of reverence—the primary feelings from which these others derive their prestige or their scandal. It is, nevertheless, subject to assault. The French Revolution has attempted to make the transhistorical feelings, out of which civil society as such emerges and through which it is legitimized, anachronistic. France, by attacking the royal family, and by placing fidelity to the nation (or the state) above all immediate familial ties, is attempting to give to primary and universal feelings a history that exposes them to the contingency of circumstance. Britain retains for the family and therefore for those feelings their universal, transhistorical status. Therefore it is in Britain that the universal feelings of humankind are now, through its respect for the family, located and confined.

The endurance of this set of primary feelings, for which the family is the basic expressive unit, is attested to by the endurance of the British national character. Because it gives no credence to atheistic intellectuals, because it does not permit a rigid separation between the landed and the moneyed interest, because it nurtures the alliance between the church and the state, the British national character is, in essence, anti-revolutionary. More, it founds itself on primary feelings out of which these other attitudes and political habits grow. It forms such habits and is formed by them. It is a closed system, autonomous in itself although besieged in the revolutionary era. Such besieging in fact enhances its autonomy while simultaneously permitting it to cope with the charge of provincial, exogamous enclosure by ratifying its claim to be preserving, within the walls of the national culture, all that is universally and primarily human, all that is being denied and laid waste elsewhere.

But this Burkean construction of a specifically British national character that is coincident with what we may call the *ancien régime* conception of a universal human nature, did not, like the institutions of the British state, quite extend to Ireland—even though he would have much wished to see the conditions for its development available there, especially in the fraught conditions of the 1790s. His Irish writings involve, of course, a well-known assault on the ill effects of the role of what came to be called the Protestant Ascendancy there and its nurturing of the penal system that made Ireland into a confessional state in which the mass of the population was excluded in most important respects from the advantages—as he understood them—of the British constitution.[25] I will not dwell on the detail of this critique just now. Suffice to say that Ireland was, in his view, that part of the British polity most vulnerable to the radical ideas of the Enlightenment and revolution precisely because it had never known under British rule the virtues of the ancient civilization that had collapsed in France. The bigotry of the Protestant junta was such that it could not contemplate the admission of Catholics into full citizenship, thereby treating a traditional society in such a way as to threaten the endurance and validity of the idea of civil society that Britain, more than any other European country, exemplified. Ireland was being treated as an irredeemably strange country—one in which the faintest reaction against oppression was regarded or described as sedition against the state, in which the mass of the people were regarded as foreign to civil society, in which power had never learned the intricate lessons by means of which it could have become authority.

There is, in Burke's view, an analogy between the Jacobins in France, the East India Company in India, and the Ascendancy in Ireland. None of them commands the assent or the affection of the people whom they dominate. Even more, they make a virtue of the lack of affection, of the lack of those ties that would give a political system intimacy. What is different in France, however, is that the failure of sympathy and the atrocities that accompany it has been theorized into a political philosophy that claims to legitimize such behaviour and to rob traditional conceptions of human sympathy of all their force. However, the point I want to dwell on here is that the consequence of such a philosophy and of the behaviour that it valorizes is such that the people and the territory victimized by it are transmogrified from a recognizable into an unrecognizable condition. Civil society disappears and is replaced by barbarism, yet by a barbarism that defends itself in the name of or in the language of civil society. This is what makes these territories phantasmal. They are unreal and yet real, the more real because they are unreal—like Paris. They are foreign, yet their foreignness is defined by the contrast they make with what is native and natural. In the modern world they represent, the moral person, the agent of civil society, is travelling in or observing a wilderness, a landscape that is at once unreal and perfectly recognizable. Burke is anxious to embody his critiques of British rule in Ireland and India in specific groups or persons—the Anglo-Irish Ascendancy, the East India Company, Warren Hastings—to point up the fact that the system as such is defensible, and only its corruptions indefensible. In the same way, the old French system deserves support; it is only those who corrupt it, like Rousseau, or the revolutionaries, who make it seem indefensible.

It is on the basis of this analysis, using the conventions of the political pamphlet and those of travel narrative, that I suggest modern Irish writing, even the notion of there being a 'tradition' of Irish writing, is founded. For over a century after Burke, the same ambiguity prevailed—between the representation of a country that is foreign and unknown, in which the conditions are phantasmagoric, especially to the English reader, and a country that is, at the same time, part of the British system, perfectly recognizable and part of the traditional world that the French Revolution had overthrown. Reality will be restored to that phantasmal country only through the introduction into it of that kind of civic stability which is characteristically British. The long and complicated struggles to effect the dismantling of the penal laws in Ireland, the alliance between the Irish Catholic Church and Burkean politics, the to-and-fro between Protestant fears and Catholic ambitions, and, above all, the destruction of the United Irish movement in the years 1797–8, involving the removal by force from Ireland of the spectre of French political principles, accompanies the foundation of that curious 'national' literature that emerges almost perfectly with the Act of Union.[26] It is a literature remarkably free of the discourse of theory. More than that, like much English literature of the period, it is remarkably hostile to such a discourse, always featuring it as abstract, systematic, and deeply involved with atrocious violence. But if the dismissal of this discourse, like the dismissal of the United Irishmen, from the literature and history of Ireland, is almost complete, it achieves its maimed success by finding for it a substitute that nevertheless often retains within itself the shadow of that absent discourse. The substitute is provided by the revised Burkean category of the national character, one that governs the strategy, highly appropriate in Irish conditions after the Union, of producing a convergence, or a narrative of the attempted convergence, between cultural and economic realities. The linkage between these is fraught with difficulty, but the prognosis is that an alteration in one or both will lead to a modernization of the Irish condition and thereby to its release from a bedevilled history.

AESTHETICS, ENERGY, NATIONAL CHARACTER

The basic premiss of what I have to say is this; that the definition of a territory as foreign or native involves the definition of a condition—wholly civilized or barbaric, or transitional—that defines its inhabitants. Second, that the appropriation of a territory understood to be foreign involves a species of therapeutic discourse in which that condition, usually understood to be extreme, is in some sense normalized. Third, that the process of normalization depends on the success of a system of representation in which all that is extreme is brought under narrative control by an observer, traveller, story-teller, whose function is to communicate to an audience that shares her or his values a sense of the radical difference of the other terri-tory or condition and, at the same time, however contradictorily, to claim that this territory and condition, once relieved of the circum-stances or causes of its extraordinary condition, can be redeemed for normality. But to effect such a process a particular kind of agency is required. That agency makes itself available in literary discourse more readily than in any other because it is, in effect, an aesthetic activity—one that also derives from or perhaps is fundamental to a Burkean counter-revolutionary politics. It is the aesthetic of the actual—an aesthetic which refuses the inclusion of distance and impartiality or disinterestedness as integral to its structure. And that aesthetic is conjoined with its political counterpart, the attribution to a community of a psychology that celebrates the actual, that remains immersed in the local, the folklorish—or, more impor-tantly, refuses the theoretical.[27] The psychology of the Irish commu-nity—in its national form—markedly and dangerously narcissistic in some respects—is created as a form of energy that is in need of appropriation, external control, so that it can become politically sober while remaining aesthetically vivacious. Its vivacity is repre-sentable in the novel more than in any other form, partly because of its adherence to the quotidian, partly because its political condition is representable as a civic inadequacy that can be overcome when that folklorish world is translated into the quotidian register of realism.

Vivacity itself, however, needs a history. Energy needs a narra-tive. The narrative had its strategies ready-made; in effect, they were inescapable. These were strategies rooted in the historical actualities of sectarianism, class, gender, and race, but efflorescing in stories of communities that had been deformed by these actualities and yet might be reformed by the rediscovery of the conditions in which that previously unrepresented energy—unrepresented both in the political and in the aesthetic sense—could be controlled within a recognizable regime of representation. Burke repeatedly character-ized Jacobinism as a form of fierce and destructive energy that had pitted itself against the solidities and stolidities of traditional so-ciety—its anchorage in a landed aristocracy and a stable national character. But, in addition, to make the contemporary story of energy versus mass effective, there had to be a governing and ex-planatory metanarrative, the story of stories, organized to take account of the requirements of the political present by a persua-sive account of the political past. Burke laid the basis for this metanarrative for Ireland by his campaign in favour of a relaxation of the penal laws with the aim of thereby attaching Ireland more closely to England and reducing Ireland's vulnerability to the French disease. Even his extreme distress at the recalcitrance of the Ascend-ancy and the ignorance of the British government with respect to Ireland is itself a recurrent feature of the historical narrative. So the history of Ireland and Britain in relation to France in particular, with 1798 and the Union as its turning-points and the forthcoming 1829 Emancipation as one of its culminations, coincides with a Burkean programme—the history of a consolidated effort, frustrated by prejudice but implacable in its direction, to recruit Irish Catholics into the Union with the help of the Catholic Church while appeasing the endless fears and bigotries of Irish Protestants.

But in literature, at least up to Emancipation, this historical narra-tive, while it survives as a kind of armature within which different works are produced, is given what we may call an allegorical form that re-presents the historical narrative as a rational account that is constantly threatened by the competition of irrational energies. These energies are differently distributed, although the rational ac-counting is universally assigned to an English source while the energies of excess and disruption are equally assigned to Irish sources. Thus, Irish energy and Irish national character, in all their uncontrolled forms—delinquent, violent, obsessive—were some-times assigned to the Anglo-Irish Protestant landowners and their ancillary supporters. But they were also, of course, assigned—espe-cially in pamphlet literature—to O'Connell and his Catholic hordes, and to his creation of the Irish Catholics as a decreasingly deferential political nation. This was a narrative, or series of narratives, that complicated the serene overview of the historical analysis to which, nevertheless, much of this writing owed its ultimate comprehensibility. The Anglo-Irish were, time and again, portrayed as anachronistic and all their wild and wasteful energy consigned to the past, as a force that would unsettle the present and also as a force that had anyway expended itself as a political or economic possibility. The regime of such anarchic energy was to be followed by an exercise in frugality, prudence, sobriety—social controls that were increasingly to be exercised by the Catholic Church and by the British government. The Catholics, on the other hand, had to undergo what John Barrell has, in a different but adjacent context called 'a civic emancipation' from destructive libidinal energies, the consequence of having had no power rather than too much.[28] Each grouping—and there are subsidiary groupings within these larger communities—has to be sobered down, one so that it can leave the political stage, the other so that it can enter upon it. Alternatively, in their mutual and new-found sobriety, they can perhaps find a new alliance—expressed as the 'national' marriage in many novels—that will allow for a reconciliation at the social and cultural level and for a solution at the economic level to the problem of ownership of and inheritance to the land—the actual territory of Ireland. The stories of such writings, although heavily laden with the rhetorics of healing, annealing, recovery, compromise, balance, were also equally laden with the rhetorics of subjugation, oppression, and degradation. The latter rhetoric was often too potent to be overcome by the former.

One of the curiosities of this rendering of the Irish situation is that the language of balance and compromise between opposing positions, supposedly favoured in English discourse, becomes, when applied to Ireland, the language of the half-made, the half-baked, the incomplete, the Anglo-Irish, the English–Irish, the hyphenated status of the colony that cannot, precisely because of its hyphen, ever achieve the fullness of being either one or the richness of being a combination of both: 'Suffice it to say . . . the discontent of the half-subdued, drew down the suspicious severity of the half-established,

and the subjugation of the former, effected by degrees the degradation of the latter.'[29]

The degradation of the Anglo-Irish and of the native population,
most pronounced, according to John Wilson Croker in the period
between 1715 and 1745, is a condition of mutually assured destruction unless some external element is introduced to prevent collapse.
The political form of that element is of course the Union. It would
appear, in the literature of the period, that the Irish condition is one
of abeyance—between a natively English colonial grouping that has
gone to the bad by becoming more Irish than the Irish themselves
and a native population that has never become sufficiently English
to reach the good and must be educated into doing so.

In claiming that Burke's texts of the 1790s are foundational, I am
entering into an alliance with the general view that this period in
history had of itself and has had ascribed to it ever since. The French
Revolution was widely understood to be a beginning or an end or
both. To distinguish between what we may call the revolutionary
and counter-revolutionary positions in relation to beginnings and
endings, we might distinguish, at the simplest level, between the
contrasting sanctifications of the new and of the old—new and old
languages, new and old attitudes, new possibilities and old certain-
ties. However, one of Burke's innovations, effected in the name of
tradition, was to bring into the arena of political and aesthetic discourse beliefs and habits that had previously been the more potent
precisely because they had not—in his account—been articulated
before. This is a practice that he believed to be a necessary
counteragent to the radically new, invented discourses of the Enlightenment and its revolutionary inheritors. The position is paradoxical, but unavoidably so. Burke is at once historicizing the British
state as the outgrowth of a series of processes and events peculiar to
it and going beyond the historical and contingent by claiming that
the mixed constitution of Britain has evolved from a complex process of which the national character is both generator and product.
His various and much-cited definitions of 'prejudice' and 'custom'
are exemplary instances of the forgery that is necessary for the
production of a self-consciously traditional language. Once defined,
'prejudice' is no longer 'prejudice'; in its subjunctively original con-

dition it operated by not being susceptible to definition or in need of it. Once 'prejudice' becomes a concept it has lost its original status, its pre-conceptual force—which is the after-effect of its having been conceptually defined. To go back to that pre-conceptual stage is, of course, impossible. Any ideology of homecoming, especially any national ideology that defines itself in terms of *Heimatlichkeit*, is undermined by the very enunciation that is necessary to defend it. This is the case, *in extenso*, for the whole Burkean armoury of terms and claims for that instinctive, intuitive, unconscious element or composition of elements that constitute the pre-revolutionary national character that had insensibly made the English Revolution no more than a stage in British evolution.

The *Reflections*, in this respect, bears all the marks of what Susan Stewart has called a 'distressed genre'.[30] Burke is a forger, an improver, somebody who distresses an object by making it look like an antique, as much as Chatterton, Percy, Macpherson, Scott, or any other of that host of writers who had claimed to be translating into written form material that had originally been oral (and thereby original or authentic). Stewart says:

Thus distressed genres often exaggerate a movement of time into space on several simultaneous levels. First, such a movement characterizes the transformation of the temporality of speech into the spatiality of writing. Second, the movement from time into space is often a device for the legitimation of territory and property, both private and national, by means of narrative or textual evidence.[31]

Burke is giving energy to property, which is naturally sluggish, giving alacrity to the natural sullenness of the British character, giving mobility to a system that is naturally static—all in the name of preserving all that sluggishness, sullenness, and immobility. He is making the antique fashionable by denying fashion and faddishness, claiming that the fashionableness of being British is an eternal verity to which fidelity must be reattested.

This is a brilliant appropriation of political folklore, presented as an anti-theoretical position. It is often read as a defence of the integrity of the organic and local community against the despotic encroachments of uniformity, especially of the kind imposed by an

ideologically driven state system. But the traditional interpretation
can be reversed. The most acute commentary on this practice of
annexing the past's unmediated orality and the interpretations that
exploit or are exploited by its mobilization of nostalgia as a political
force is provided by Nietzsche in his essay 'The Use and Abuse of
History' in which, as Paul Bové says,

> his discussion of this attractive communal image makes clear that the
> German state's disposition of cultural mandarins to valorize such antiquar-
> ian social values is in fact an appropriation of folk tradition meant to make
> them the province of the high cultural forces manipulated by the reaction-
> aries of the Prussian monarchy. These newly produced objects of historical
> knowledge go on to become the 'populist' base for an oppressive and
> absolutist state.[32]

Nevertheless, the Burkean forgery of the antique, of the pre-
conceptual in an ostensibly non-conceptual form, of the oral as
written, the folklorish as populist, is central to the national aesthetic
of Britishness as the anti-theoretical opponent of the cosmopolitan
and revolutionary abstraction that is the mark of the modern state.
The rhetoric of the *Reflections* manifests this vacillation between its
ambition to be a work of high conceptual definition and a work of
non-conceptualizable complexity by its variation between the long,
pseudo-Ciceronian sentence that inventories a mass of detail and the
short, proverbial bursts that sententiously abbreviate the wisdom of
the ages. For the proverbial form aspires to enunciate a universal
truth; the inventory aspires to indicate the depth of historical detail.
When the first operates as a summation of the second, we move
from the historical to the universal, from the non-conceptual to the
proverbial in a single operation, avoiding thereby the moment of
theory that lurks between. This is a variation that had been much
remarked upon by commentators on Montesquieu whose *Esprit des
lois* was similarly marked by abrupt manœuvrings between analytic
passages and sententious explosions.[33] But Burke refashioned
Montesquieu's rhetoric for a different purpose, making the variation
into an integral feature of the defence of the British state by converting his mentor's typology into an ideology that was the more effective for pretending that it was not one.

The connection between Burke's politics and travel writing begins to emerge more clearly at this conjuncture. In brief, what Burke manages to do is, first, to identify France as a country that has become foreign through the estrangement of theory and second, to identify Britain as the country that has become home to all that was traditional, pre-theoretical—despite the threat posed by the Dissenters, the East India Company and Warren Hastings, and the Protestant Ascendancy in Ireland. All of these were, like the Jacobins in Paris, estranging or threatening to estrange Britain from its heritage. Third, in travelling through the history of European political custom, emphasizing its age-old habits and attitudes, he is characterizing Britain (or England) as a community that no longer visits or revisits this temporal space in a disinterested spirit; instead, he is writing for England a biographical narrative, a national biography, in which the identity of the community is formed by its experience within that territory and in which that identity is threatened by any sustained excursion into the territory of theory. In other words, the *Reflections* is the first of Ireland's national narratives and the first political work in which the notion of a national, anti-modern narrative becomes a governing principle in its development.

Yet Burke's defence and articulation of the British national character, although it had a signal political importance in the circumstances of the 1790s, was not a novel procedure. The belief that the world of antique (classical) learning and humanism was in sore need of defence against the onslaught of modern science and, in the late eighteenth century, against the scorn of the *philosophes* for what they regarded as outmoded pedantry, had long been struggling to reassert itself. In addition, that belief had increasingly taken the forms that were to be seminal for the beginnings of sociology—sponsorship of the notion that 'History cannot be studied properly unless you know the geniuses of peoples, their customs, rites, institutions, laws, arts, crafts, and all products of the human intellect.'[34] Montesquieu had been influential in asserting the arguments for the complexity of social and political forms against the *simplisme* of more radical Enlightenment thinkers. But it was in Germany, particularly at Halle, that this belief finally took an institutional form. Its masterpiece was F. A. Wolf's *Prolegomena ad Homerum* (1795) and his lectures on 'The Encyclopaedia of Philology' in which he revived the study of the Classics.

He did so by identifying the central subject of philology as the Greek national character. Each subdiscipline had value insofar as it contributed to 'the knowledge of human nature in antiquity, which comes from the observation of an organically developed, significant national culture, founded on the study of ancient remains'.[35]

Similarly, Gibbon's work, a comparable blend of erudition and political philosophy, relied heavily on a valorization of the Roman republican character that had been undermined by a series of factors and events, leading to the construction of the empire and its eventual demise—although Gibbon devotes relatively brief attention to Rome, despite the title of his masterpiece. But, in addition, Wolf addressed himself to an issue that has a further bearing on Burke's writings. He claimed that Homer's text, as Europe knew it, had been altered and revised countless times since its first oral delivery; therefore, it could never be known in its true original form. The uproar that this caused in Germany and in Europe is legendary. But it is a claim and a procedure that is structurally akin to Burke's version of what Pocock calls the Ancient Constitution.[36] The unwritten constitution, an 'oral' original, survived solely in the emendations and interpretations of those—like the great common law lawyers—who had commented upon it and those politicians—like the Whigs of the seventeenth century—who had emended it. Burke, like Wolf, was the writer who was now clarifying its status by asking his audience to recognize that, in all its successive variations, it was an emanation of a national character that Burke wanted to define not only as British but also as the most central, because most fully developed, national character of the modern world as the Greek national character had been of the classical world. It is in that light that Burke's valorization of national character can be associated with the rise of German and European historicism.[37] National character contains within itself that theory of antiquity which, in its Roman political form (in France) and in its Greek literary form (in Germany) provided a basis, however frail and even illusory, for the revolution and the romanticism of the European bourgeoisie.[38]

Burke's anti-modernism is, then, closely allied to the revival of scholarship that is itself part of the so-called Romantic reaction to the sciolism of the Enlightenment. Yet it is true that, despite the foundational claim I am making for him here in relation to Irish writing, most of the writings of the first three decades of the nineteenth century in Ireland were specifically pro-modern. A standard theme, however varied in its inflections, is that Ireland, now emerging from the shadow of the penal era, recovering from the shock of 1798 and the aftermath of the French Revolution, rescued from the worst excesses of the Protestant Ascendancy by the Union, increasingly under the tutelage of Roman Catholicism, might now enter into modernity. However, in the inherited discourses the Irish exercised about themselves there was a measure of irretrievable contradiction. On the one hand, there was the long-standing and now newly organized discourse about national character. On the other hand, there was the discourse of cultural emergence, heavily dependent, like the first, upon notions of recovery, recuperation, re-establishment. A whole cultural tradition had to be revised; so too did the national character. For both were understood to have been damaged or degraded, occluded or deformed, by a long history of oppression. Yet, if national character were to be renovated in alliance with a new sense of cultural tradition, the benign definitions of the two had to be accommodated within a theory of modernity that was, in many important respects, hostile to them both. For both were read as having the characteristics of a native energy or set of energies that modernity, were it to be achieved, had to restrain. Modernity was a condition of control; character and tradition were conditions that the exercise of control threatened to denature by making them other than they were, by erasing rather than incorporating them. Ensconced within this ideology, much Irish writing had to ask the question whether indeed modernity were possible in existing conditions; and if it were not, whether the conditions were subject to change or whether they were so durable that they could not be reformed. This was an especially hard question to address, never mind answer, if the assumption underlying the question—that a cultural condition could be reformed or altered by economic development—was itself contradictorily allied to the belief that economic underdevelopment was produced by Irish national character. The contradiction is a symptom of an evasion. For the alternative—that underdevelopment was a structural problem produced by the colonial relationship between the two countries—indicated that only the demolition of that relationship could begin to clear the ground for a resolution of the vexed connection between cultural and economic discourses.

REFORMING THE NATIONAL CHARACTER

The question of national character and the avowed need to reform or reconstitute it is an English and European, as well as an Irish, obsession in the late eighteenth and early nineteenth centuries. In England, popular women novelists like Hannah More were especially prominent in a long and monotonous literary crusade to rescue English men from the snares of French or Frenchified women. For it was between the women of England and France that More found the contrast in national characteristics to be most pronounced. The published reminiscences of some of the leading *salonnières* of the French Enlightenment—Madame du Deffand, Madame de Genlis, Madame d'Épinay prominent among them—[39] and the welcome bestowed on Madame de Staël by the Whigs of Holland House (especially Sir James Mackintosh and other reviewers for the *Edinburgh Review*), provided a widely noticed context for More's portrayals of intellectual or 'French' women. Formidable conversationalists, fashion-conscious, licentious, and seduced by revolutionary ideas, they were depicted as characteristically corrupt products of a Catholic convent education and a libertine society. Their natural opposite was the British Christian wife whose virtues symmetrically corresponded with her French sisters' vices. More's standard plot was one in which a man had demonstrated to him the twin dangers of fashionable society on the one hand and a derelict and savage provincialism on the other. This was sufficient to persuade him—eventually—to embrace the charms of a Protestant housewife, stalwart in her faith, nationality and frugal habits. Thus, much popular fiction, especially by women, stressed the importance of Christian marriage, rescuing its happy pair (more usually, the male partner) from the dangers of atheistic Jacobinism. More's *Coelebs In Search of a Wife* (1809) is a paradigm of the search for the paragon of female virtue which provides the basis for so many of the plots in the novel of this period.

Madame de Staël, novelist and intellectual, much lauded in England for Napoleon's dislike of her and his censorship of her work, as well as for being the daughter of Necker, the former French Minister of Finances, was a crusader for a structurally similar, although politically different, reconciliation of rationality and intense feeling. She espoused a post-revolutionary marriage between the 'romantic' Europe of the north (Germany and England) and the 'rational' Europe of the south (France and Italy), with the *gravitas* of the one countering and blending with the gaiety of the other. It was from a fusion of these national characteristics that the new cosmopolitan and liberal spirit of a new European union would emerge.[40] Hannah More's widely shared hostility to the public role of women in French political and intellectual life blinded her to the specific, civilizing role assigned to women by many French writers. In his *Siècle de Louis XIV* Voltaire had reaffirmed the already conventional claim that France had been the first to transform itself from 'a barbaric to a civilized nation' through the agency of women. This was the boast of 'an aristocratic culture that based its claim of superiority on its transcendence of brute force for gentler virtues'.[41] Equally, de Staël, in sponsoring a new form of cosmopolitanism, was extending the French notion of civility as a modern version of the public sphere that included conversation, letters, and the dissemination of information through print culture that would liberate the various national communities from their parochialism.[42] Burke had recognized these features of the French social system in the *Reflections*, although of course he regarded them as dangerous and destabilizing agents of a kind of horizontal and synchronic exchange, interlopers on the territory of the traditional, vertical forms of transmission that were for him sufficiently and safely contained within the concepts of traditional family lineage and descent.

Thus, when we meet with the Irish national novel, it is not at all surprising to find that its interests and protocols are similar. It too is seeking to find some reconciliation between versions of the English and Irish national communities that would stifle the impact of the French Revolution. Such a reconciliation is most often envisaged as the provision of the ballast of English national character for the volatility of the Irish. But the brutal nature of the history that linked Ireland and England strained this project to breaking-point or left it in a twilit ambiguity, most especially in the writings of Maria Edgeworth, Lady Morgan, T. Crofton Croker, and many others. In particular, Edgeworth's Irish writings initiated an investigation into the relationship between Ireland and England that was grounded in a series of dyadic oppositions that no one before her had co-ordinated with a comparable skill. So effective was she in making these oppositional elements appear ultimately harmonious with one another that her fiction produces the illusion of having performed an analysis of the Irish situation when its real achievement was to have produced an analgesic version of the question of English–Irish relations.

Yet Edgeworth did not confine herself to a contrast between the different national characters of the Irish and the English; she duplicated that contrast in the distinction between the physical territories of Ireland and England, and in the dramatizing of those relations as an early form of imperial romance—one in which a 'utilitarian' adventure is undertaken in a romantic territory in order to conquer it, remap it, domesticate it.[43] Yet even in the narratives that describe this adventure there is an element of resistance, and not only among the Irish, to the conquering of the romantic territory; there is an element of resistance in Edgeworth herself. For the 'utilitarian' rationality that she sponsors has both a normalizing and a disenchanting effect. In its ambition to produce prosperity out of poverty, it might also produce uniformity out of difference; it might threaten tradition by erasing its irrational and unproductive practices—the very identifying features of Irish 'tradition'.

All the Irish novels are, in one form or another, educational tracts—like those of so many of the counter-revolutionary writers such as More, Mrs Elizabeth Hamilton, and Sarah Trimmer and also of the radical novelists like Mary Wollstonecraft, Godwin, Bage, and Holcroft. As a form, the novel has rarely been more didactically inclined than in the last decades of the eighteenth century.[44] The social virtues Edgeworth promotes are similar to those recommended by Hannah More for the ideal English woman in her *Strictures on the Modern System of Female Education* (1799). Her Enlightenment values are specifically 'Protestant', although she does not use the word in More's more aggressively sectarian manner. Further, the role of her ideal female is to 'civilize' an unruly or lovable male by letting him see the twin dangers of fashionable society on the one hand and derelict provincialism on the other. The sexual relationship is, in other words, a micro-version of the political ideal in her novels. The Frenchified frippery of high society and the rapscallion anarchy of Hibernian society are the extremes between which this ideal and English sobriety must steer. Marriage is the conventional means and therefore the woman must embody that English–Christian ideal since, according to the received wisdom, she would give to it its moral tone. Despite the sectarian realities of the Irish political situation, Maria Edgeworth does not give much emphasis to religion in her novels, a factor which may have contributed to the decline in her popularity after 1817, when the religious revival in England, and its extension to Ireland, was well under way. In place of the Christian element, Edgeworth places sober, industrious, rational thrift, best represented by Florence Annaly in *Ormond* and most sharply contrasted with the spendthrift lunacy of the Rackrents or the dishonest connivings of a Jason Quirk. She is, *au fond*, a provincial writer in the English 'Protestant' tradition of Hannah More, in which thrift (and its sexual analogue, chastity) is a supreme virtue and recklessness (and its sexual analogue, promiscuity or licentiousness) a radical vice. The moral scheme of her fiction stays within those limits.

Her Irish novels, therefore, may be seen as documents in the 'civilizing mission' of the English to the Irish. Yet the process was a two-way one, since the English idea of its own ('British') national character was involved as well. For British national character, recently renovated by Burke as an anti-revolutionary concept, still retained, in Edgeworth's fiction, the characteristic traits of the Enlightenment ideal. It was sober, industrious, rational, and liberal in its attitudes while remaining steadfastly anti-Jacobin in its aims and purposes. Edgeworth's Irish, in their political disaffection, tend to be Jacobites, not Jacobins. The contrast between Corny O'Shane, King of the Black Islands, in *Ormond* (1817), or Count O'Halloran in *The Absentee* (1812), and the Annaly family and Lord Colambre (from the same novels respectively) is a perfectly innocuous one in that period. There is nothing revolutionary in these Gaelic remnants. They are, rather, nostalgic figures whose archaic loyalties must be transposed to modern conditions. But the real conflict emerges in the presentation of the Protestant Anglo-Irish figures like Lord and Lady Clonbrony or, more memorably, Ulick O'Shane in *Ormond* and the whole Rackrent family in *Castle Rackrent*. Ormond's marriage to Florence, on the other hand, is the perfect national marriage in that it reconciles English, Irish, and Anglo-Irish elements in a sweet, if schematic, accord.

The fact that Maria Edgeworth chose to write about Ireland does not make her a Romantic novelist, but it does help to preserve her reputation as a serious one. She was not the first novelist to have chosen Ireland as her 'scene'; but she was the first to realize that there was, within it, a missionary opportunity to convert it to Enlightenment faith and rescue it from its 'romantic' conditions. She defined that opportunity, as did so many others, as an educational one. Irish national character was to be brought to school. In other words, the utilitarian faith in pragmatic reason, when faced with the intractability of the Irish situation, found in the concept of national character a saving resource. The alternative to this would have been to query the basis of the colonial relationship itself. Edgeworth believed that Ireland was backward, unenlightened, poor, ill led, even romantic, not because it was a colonial culture, but because it was Ireland. Her fiction concerning it is, on that account, regional. She does not, like Walter Scott, in the first chapter of *Waverley*, claim a universality for her fiction which would rise above regional or antiquated manners,[45] a claim that helps to distinguish the historical from the regional novel. The power of her analysis of the Irish situation depends on her version of national character, even though the reality she ascribes to this makes the 'moral' of her novels—the exercise of a redemptive rationality and responsible authority—inoperable. In that sense, her fiction is not an analysis but a symptom of the colonial problem the country represented.

It could hardly have been otherwise. One consequence in Ireland of the French Revolution had been the easing of penal restrictions on Catholics in an effort to deflect them from Jacobinism. Another had been a reconsideration and, ultimately, a demotion of the Anglo-Irish from their position as governors of the country. In this respect, the government in London had followed the advice so urgently pressed on it by Burke in his last years. But it had acted too slowly and too brutally. In killing off the Jacobin threat in 1798, and in raising the hopes and fears of both Catholics and Protestants by its policy of union, it had, in effect, undermined its authority by exercising its power. Ireland had now been transformed into a 'national' country; the struggle was an internal one for the leadership of that national consciousness, fought out between Catholic and Protestant in the name of 'national character'. Edgeworth represents this as a battle between the Enlightenment and Romanticism, between Protestant and British values and Catholic and Irish values. The essential point, though, is that her Irish Protestants have to be recuperated from a long degradation which has led to their impoverishment and irresponsibility. So restored, they will redeem the other Irish from their native and unreliable, if endearing, romanticism.

In what did this romanticism consist? To the extent that Edgeworth introduced Irish manners and speech, and made of them an antiquarian's or folklorist's delight, she was romantic. Similarly, her treatment of the political and economic conditions of Ireland, although realistic in many ways, is also governed by the conviction that they are exotic—that is, the consequence of quaint Irish behaviour rather than of colonial conditions. Further, as in many romantic novels, the spectacle of shattered estates, ramshackle buildings, and anachronistic attitudes and personalities is surveyed from the counter-revolutionary perspective of nostalgia for the antique, the pre-modern, the regrettably lost past of the old world. Her Ireland, so romanticized, is also a place which offers itself for improvement and reform, and her Irish are a people who would benefit greatly from these medicinal measures. But the ready-made romanticism of Edgeworth's fiction is unique, not in itself, but in its fusion with the eccentric version of utilitarianism that, under her father's implacable influence, is offered as a remedy for its failings.

There were, in this period, three dominant forms of utilitarian thinking. The first, egotistic utilitarianism, associated with Bentham, is founded on the natural selfishness of the individual and its operation is based on the assumption that selfish and social interests will, by cosmic coincidence, co-operate with one another. The second, altruistic utilitarianism, associated with William Godwin, is rooted in the belief that the human person is, by nature, benevolent. In following his nature he does good to others and pleases himself. The third kind, universalistic utilitarianism, is associated with Shaftesbury and Hutcheson in the eighteenth century, and with John Stuart Mill in the nineteenth. It proclaims that human happiness lies in the welfare of humankind as a whole, and attempts to make the good and the beautiful one. It aestheticizes morality to make it the more appealing and extends the horizon of human duty to the world at large, rather than restricting it either to the self or to immediately neighbouring others. If Maria Edgeworth is a utilitarian, she is of none of these three kinds. What differentiates her utilitarianism from the other versions is her historical sense, her attempt to give at least parity to the historical processes that produce certain forms of behaviour and her assumption of a universal human nature that is already in place, anterior to such processes. This is a precarious undertaking, because the first of these elements is always liable, when under stress, to fold back into the second.

Nowhere in her fiction do we find a belief in the natural benevolence or malignity of human nature. Instead, she offers the historical view that national communities are the product of general and long-enduring conditions. It is easy to see, therefore, why she adverts so often to the idea of national character. The national characters of the English and Irish are different because their historical experience has been different—even though the statement can be reversed to say that the respective historical experiences have been produced by the difference in the national characters of the two national groups. But, even if this determinism is ignored—although it cannot be erased and will continue to reappear—can these national characters be assimilated with one another by making their historical experience similar? It would seem that her answer to this must be a positive one and the means she supports for bringing it about would centrally include the destruction of absentee landlordism and its replacement by benevolent, responsible leadership. In effect, this is a genteel version of the old plantation policies of earlier centuries. Such leadership, however, is hard to find because it must come from a formation that is independent of or other than that of the national character. It may have the improvement of Irish conditions as its aim, it may have English tradition as its example. But where does it come from? Is it something independent of historical conditions in its origin but hospitably received within them on its appearance? Edgeworth is in fact saying that the English system, if transferred to Ireland, would work better because it is—radically—a more rational and benign system than any Ireland has produced. English national character is, therefore, more in conformity with human nature than Irish national character. She is meeting here the same impasse as those of her contemporaries who contrasted the English and the French and decided on the superiority of the English on the grounds that the English were more 'natural' than the French. Why this should be remained mysterious, although it seemed sufficient to many to posit a historical explanation of some kind—for example that the French were (or had been) Roman Catholic and authoritarian in their religion and government and that the English had been Protestant and free. This only defers the question Edgeworth avoids. For it is less answerable than the questions about the French national character. It is the question about the Anglo-Irish. Why had they failed to bring to the Irish the benefits of British rule? What had happened to their national character? It is not satisfactory to say that they had become more Irish than the Irish themselves, for that would involve the admission that English character needed English conditions for its survival and would therefore make contingent on circumstances a concept which was, in its local or national disguise, universalist in its claim—that in deriving from history it also derived from nature. Burke had confronted this issue in his *Reflections on the Revolution in France* by claiming that the English had conformed to the imperatives of human nature throughout history whereas the

French, since 1789, had departed from them. However, Burke's proposition was inapplicable to Ireland; he himself had character-ized the Irish political system as unnatural. Edgeworth could only introduce history as the producer of the national character, then withdraw it again in order to admit national character as the pro-ducer of history. Any serious change in the prevailing political con-ditions that challenged her view of the Irish–English relationship would drive her ultimately into silence, caught in the hopeless con-tradiction on which her fiction was based.

For of course conditions did change, especially after 1817, the last year of her career as a novelist. Ireland did find leadership, in the person of Daniel O'Connell, a most improbable phenomenon in the Edgeworth scheme of things. Here was a national character with a vengeance. O'Connell was as anti-Jacobin as one could wish an Irish leader to be; but in every other respect he was impossible. Yet he was much more a utilitarian than Edgeworth. The sale catalogue of his library shows the division in his nature: almost half the books are devotional works of popular Catholicism; the remainder are utili-tarian works of various kinds.[46] That combination was as inconceiv-able to Edgeworth as was the Ireland of O'Connell's Catholic Association, of Pastorini, and of the sectarian conflicts of the 1820s and the Tithe Wars of the following decade.[47] Such a world was simply not susceptible to the nostrums of the Edgeworths.

Yet it is perfectly appropriate that it is Scott and Scotland that produced the historical novel for which Edgeworth had created the possibility that she herself failed to realize. For it was in Scotland that the new discourse of sympathy had emerged, as a local ex-tension of and refinement upon the theory of benevolence that had been formulated by Shaftesbury, Hutcheson, Diderot, and Rousseau, with important contributions by Hume, among others.[48] Its most notable text is Adam Smith's *Theory of Moral Sentiments* (1759), although it is the expanded sixth edition of 1790, the year of the *Reflections*, that is regarded as the more complete (it contains the important part VI, 'Prudence, Beneficence, Self-Command'). The standard version of the 'Smith' problem, so-called, is that there is a real or apparent disjunction between Smith the moralist of the *Theory* and Smith the economist of the *Inquiry into the Nature and*

Causes of the Wealth of Nations (1776).[49]. The problem has its local aspect too; Smith could be said to have produced in these works, as well as in his *Lectures on Jurisprudence* of 1761 and 1766, and in his *Lectures on Rhetoric and Belles Lettres* (1751), an account of the union of Scotland and England which effected a conciliation between the two on the grounds of commerce, sociality, politeness, and aesthetics. His work is the theoretical grounding that makes Walter Scott's novels possible; it is all the more timely because the Ossian controversy highlighted the relation between the devastated Gaelic order and the British state in an unprecedented fashion. Whatever one might say of the relation between aesthetics (or sensibility) and economics in Smith's works, it is plain that he, with the other giants of the Scottish Enlightenment, was able to found the notion of a civil society on a doctrine of social sympathy which was predicated on a concept of distance.[50] There was the famous Stoic distance of the 'impartial spectator' in moral matters; there was the distance of the state from the self-regulating economy in the commercial sphere; there was the polite distance of the historian from historical events, adapted in preference to a proximity that would not allow for the overview that enabled the history of society to be written. This is exactly what was not available to Burke or Edgeworth. Neither could conjugate the relationship between the traditional, understood as a mode of sensibility or energy, and the modern, understood as a system of discipline and frugality. Burke wanted to prove that this had still been possible in France in 1789, but the revolutionaries had destroyed all hope of it. Edgeworth wanted to show that there was a conceivable balance between 'native' or 'wild' energy and a new regime of beneficent, frugal landlordism. But Irish economic and political realities made such a balance little more than a fictional convention that had evolved in England for other purposes. For Ireland, before and after the Union, could not be conciliated as Scotland was. The divisions were too deep, the antinomies too strong. The culture lacked a theory of society and would continue to do so, precisely because theory had been identified as inimical to its preservation. Burke both founded and disabled Irish romantic literature; it differed from its English and its European counterparts because it could form no articulation with social or political philosophy.[51] Even the separation between the United Irishmen, armed with Enlightenment concepts, and the Defenders, deriving from the traditional, popular culture, was a symptom of this situation.[52]

For Edgeworth, above all in *Castle Rackrent*, had to confront a version of the Burke problem—the reconciliation of sensibility with economics. This was an issue that involved her, as it did Burke, in a chronological anxiety. Put simply, it meant that sensibility, understood as traditional modes of feeling that were threatened by the revolutionary dismissal of them, had to be assigned to the past. It was important to decide how recent that past was. For Burke, it was recent indeed—prior to 6 October 1789. For Edgeworth, it was prior to 1782, the year of Ireland's achievement of a measure of parliamentary independence. But this recent past, as far as the history of feeling went, was also immemorial. The argument, such as it was, wanted to claim that feeling of this kind had always been there; that it had endured all of the vicissitudes of political change and it still endured, although now under unprecedented threat. In the new political and economic climate, some way had to be found to preserve it; otherwise it would be destroyed by becoming, or by seeming to become, anachronistic. Yet, in *Castle Rackrent*, as in the *Reflections*, feeling is understood not merely as sensibility, but as an embodied form of political obligation. Thady Quirk's feudal loyalty to his delinquent Rackrent masters needs to be redirected towards more responsible rulers; the year 1782 is offered as a moment in which that redirection might finally begin to happen. The Rackrents have forfeited their place in history; their unfortunate tenants must now be rescued for history by the introduction of a more rational and prosperous economic regime.

But, as in Burke, the account of the destruction of the economic world and of the world of traditional political affection is immensely more powerful than the account of how it might be redeemed. Traditional feeling is identified in both these texts with a condition of enervation which leaves it defenceless before the dramatically less chivalric but determined activity of the new revolutionary agents or of Jason Quirk. Burke wrote of the need to galvanize the inertia of traditional sentiment to make it competitive with the *élan* of

Jacobinism, which he defined as a principle of energy. But he and Edgeworth can only offer a vision of the traditional society as one given to inertia, a mass that lacks the impelling energy that it needs for survival. In Edgeworth, even more than in Burke, Irish peasant society is presented as little more than a feudal residue, a ramshackle collection of antique attitudes and remnants, utterly devoid of the economic skills that would make it a serious political presence. The condition of such a society is pathological. It has the capacity for political obligation but nothing to which that obligation might be given, except the phantasm of Jacobitism.

For Thady and his ilk, even Jacobitism is not an option. They simply have the habit of subservience; their only criterion of excellence is an index of their failure and the failure of the political system they inhabit. It is the criterion of 'generosity', of the master's readiness to spend money, even when he does not have it, to buy drink when his house is falling apart, to engage in any activity—litigation, politics, the savage exploitation of women—in order to cut a dash in the neighbourhood. Of course, these are not social activities as such; they are obsessive forms of behaviour that find their pale explanation in the hospitable concept of national character. Even if we concede the possibility that *Castle Rackrent* is to be understood as an oblique narrative in which Thady's role is dubious, hypocritical, or ironic, and even if it is further conceded that this is a novel written about Ireland for an English audience and that it is therefore committed to a representation of the country and its people as exotics and eccentrics, it is still a work of startling incoherence. All its surrounding apparatus—preface, glossary, footnotes—parades its anthropological ambitions as an 'objective', external account; all its rhetorical devices, however subtle or unsubtle they may be thought to be, parade its claim to insider status, as a subjective, intimate narrative. But ultimately the work's attempt to reconcile these organizing discourses, and its attempt to reconcile the worlds of economic rationality and feudal affection, are abandoned for whimsical and cryptic questions that seem to hope their opacity might be taken for profundity. Yet the discrepancy between the work's ambition—to achieve verisimilitude, 'realism'—and its realization of that in a strange, fractured, and unstable narrative, is *the* symptomatic discrepancy of the nineteenth-century Irish novel. Indeed it is so potent a discrepancy that it hardly seems accurate to describe as novels those works that are plagued by it and structured around it. Edgeworth, in a sense, founded the historical novel; but, with her, it lost its initial definition and became a 'national tale'. But that too lost its definition and became an aborted national tale, one that did not readily achieve that happy ending so characteristic of Walter Scott's fiction. For, within that fiction, there is inscribed an end to history— that is, an end to the bitter relationships between England and Scotland and a final reconciliation of which marriage is the stock analogue. This is not available to Edgeworth or any of her Irish contemporaries or successors.[53] The excessive, uncontrollable nature of a history that is not yet finished, that has not been sufficiently domesticated within the forms of novelistic verisimilitude, needs a countering analogue—not marriage, with its ideal of balance, compromise, equality, shared affection, but something unbalanced, improvident, self-enclosed, extreme. Alcoholism was the most favoured alternative.

ALCOHOL AND TRADITION

Let us take one of these questions from the end of *Castle Rackrent*, as a further point of departure. Edgeworth's editorial appendix provides a prescription for Ireland after the Union and the disappearance, as she predicts it, 'of the few gentlemen of education' to England. It is that 'The best that can happen will be the introduction of British manufacturers in their places.'[54] Were the novel to end so, it would be in some degree a coherent appendix to the narrative, even if it operates at some distance from it. But she goes on, in a final sentence, to ask, 'Did the Warwickshire militia, who were chiefly artisans, teach the Irish to drink beer, or did they learn from the Irish to drink whiskey?'[55] Like so much else in this novel, the question admits of no clear answer. Maybe it is a shorthand way of asking if the English in Ireland were seduced by the native inhabitants into a degrading fondness for whiskey—or if the English improved or could improve the Irish by teaching them the milder delights of beer over whiskey. It is perhaps related to the peculiar interrogatory form of this novel's subsequent interpretations—does the success of Jason Quirk, the passing of the Rackrent family, that is both Gaelic and Anglo-Irish, spell the end of feudalism in Ireland, thereby clearing the way for modernity, or is it a reprise of the old Irish question of the repossession of the land by the 'natives'? Does Thady approve or disapprove? Does Thady consciously know whether he does either of these?[56] After all, the novel does, in a seminal way, chart the decline of a form of delinquency that was characteristic of at least a ruling sector of the Irish polity. It would seem thereby to participate in the debate about the recovery from the defects of a class's or a nation's character and its replacement by something more sober, more modern. So, what does the question mean? To put it in a wider context, a very wide one indeed were it to be pursued throughout the century, it is a question that refers to one of the standard objections to the Irish and their national character—their propensity to drink alcohol and the need to teach them control—a task much advocated by Protestant evangelicals but only effective on a wide scale in Father Mathew's temperance crusade in the 1830s and again, more successfully, at the turn of the century, when the Catholic Church put its formidable weight behind it. Although there are many instances in Irish novels and Irish travel writing in which the issue of the excessive indulgence of the Irish in alcohol is discussed, I want to take a slightly more recondite example from another text that is or was also widely regarded as foundational for the Irish literary tradition, this time in the Irish language—James Hardiman's *Irish Minstrelsy* (1831).

In the first volume, the first section is devoted to Turlough Carolan, the most famous of the Gaelic poets of the eighteenth century, 'our national melodist'. In the prefatory note to Carolan's poems, with their accompanying translations, Hardiman takes issue with the antiquarian Joseph Walker's description, in his *Historical Memoirs of the Irish Bards* (1786) of Carolan 'as a reckless reveller, whose genius required the constant stimulus of inebriating liquors to rouse it to exertion'.[57] This Hardiman denies, as a slur on Carolan's 'moral character', but goes on to say: 'It is not, however, pretended that he was a mere water drinker. On the contrary, he always delighted in cheerful society, and never refused the circling glass. Perhaps few individuals ever heightened "the feast of reason", or enriched it with "the flow of soul", in a greater degree, than Carolan.'[58]

At the same time, Hardiman is lamenting the failure of the Irish to commemorate Carolan, the 'national bard' famed abroad, ignored at home. Even though there had been a 'musical commemoration in Dublin in 1809, with the impetuosity natural to Irishmen, [it] was held twice in the same week, but never since repeated'.[59] So Carolan drank quite cheerfully, but did not need drink to stimulate him. The Irish ignore him, but celebrate him, typically, twice within one week and then never again. One further item—Hardiman tells the story of Carolan's skull being dug up when his grave was opened to bury with him a Catholic priest whose (mysterious) dying request had been that he should be buried with the bard. The skull was thereafter kept in a niche above the grave. But in 1796 a northern Orangeman rode up, asked to see the skull and, on being shown it, discharged his pistol at it, shattering it, and rode off, damning all papists. 'This brutal act', Hardiman avers, 'could be perpetrated only through the demoniac spirit of party rage which then disgraced this unhappy country.'[60] In these passages, Hardiman is trying to negotiate between Carolan's character and Carolan's reputation; similarly he is negotiating between national character and national reputation. He is denying excess and yet asserting vivacity. He is speaking of a period in history from which the country has recovered, marked by party rage, and a historical condition from which the Irish still have to recover—their limp lack of self-confidence in failing to celebrate their national genius. This latter point is itself part of a long-running series of references in Hardiman's editorial apparatus to the contrast between the Scots and the Irish on the issue of celebrating literary reputation. The Scots are good at it, the Irish not. Burns's reputation exceeds that of Carolan and yet—going back here to the Ossian forgeries—it is Ireland not Scotland which is the true home of the Celtic spirit in Britain. All through the late eighteenth and well into the nineteenth century, Irish commentators had fought the Ossian battle over and over, denying to the Scots the primacy they claimed in the Celtic hierarchy, insisting instead that it was the Irish who had been the original founders of the culture of which Scotland was a derivative. Yet because of the Irish failure to recognize and commemorate their own achievements, the Scots had almost won the battle of public relations on this score.[61] The English scholar Robert Wood was one of those who had noticed the connection between the arguments over Homer and Ossian, affirming the commonplace that an original text underwent radical changes in oral and print transmission.[62] While this was to be increasingly recognized as true also for the Irish sagas, Hardiman was less inclined to admit its bearing upon poetry and songs, even if these survived only in manuscript or in oral tradition. Authenticity in the Irish texts had to be asserted in order to reaffirm priority, and priority was more easily claimed for poetry. For, claimed Theophilus O'Flanagan in 1808, 'It is a fact, universally acknowledged, that the most ancient historical accounts, and legal institutions of the earliest associations of men, were committed to the sacred and enchanting custody of versification.'[63]

Hardiman's selection of Carolan is followed by what he calls a 'Bacchanalian Addenda' in the preface, in which he returns to the question of the Irish, their national character, and alcohol. The three pieces that constitute the addenda ('Why, Liquor of Life!', 'Ode to Drunkenness', and 'Maggy Laidir') are described respectively as 'a tolerably good specimen of our jovial effusions', 'an ingenious satire on our extra-jovial propensities', and 'a lively description of an Irish merry-making of the olden time. Taken together, they exhibit some striking features of national character.'[64] Thereafter Hardiman launches into a defence of the Irish as having had the reputation 'in former times' for temperance and sobriety. Now that they have the opposite reputation, he claims (citing one Samuel Madden) the reasons are not, as prejudice has it, to be ascribed to 'Pope and popery' but to 'the baleful impoverishment of the country, to the oppressed and degraded state of the main body of the people'. However, now the change has taken place:

Since the relaxation of the penal laws, great and general amendment has taken place in Ireland. Habits of intemperance have gradually declined among the middle classes of society, but unfortunately, still largely prevail

over the lower orders. Here they will also disappear, when, on the aboli-
tion of the impious remnant of that degrading code, security shall be
increased, and property extended, the latter flowing like the blood from the
heart, and revolving to its source, continually preserving and invigorating
the entire system.[65]

In the notes to 'Why, Liquor of Life!', the first of the three poems,
he repeats this diagnosis of the Irish propensity to whiskey and goes
on, in a passage reminiscent of Edgeworth's final remark in *Castle
Rackrent*:

In the use of this enticing beverage, even our English friends frequently
become 'Hibernis Hiberniores', when they visit Ireland. During the late
wars, the English soldiery, when ordered hither, felt delight at the anticipated idea of cheap intoxication in Ireland; and Paddy, with characteristic
hospitality, always took care to soften down their prejudices by copious
libations of his 'liquor of life', which too often proved to them the liquor of
death, by too frequent potations.[66]

In the note to the last of the three poems ('Maggy Laidir'),
Hardiman returns to the Scots theme. The Scots appropriated 'the
ancient saints of Ireland', some of its music, and in particular this
song. There has been some success in restoring to Ireland 'a few
purloined ascetics', but it is only in recent times that an effective
effort has been made 'to rescue our national melodies from
Scotland, and oblivion. The Irish origin of Scotch music has been
admitted by the best-informed writers on the subject.'[67]

   Thus, we have a strange sequence: alcohol, national degradation,
national vivacity, recovery of national Gaelic tradition, claim to
primacy over Scotland, and the English soldiery drinking Irish whiskey. What connects these items is the pursuit of modernity within
the Union, even though that pursuit is dependent for its success on
recovery *of* the past, in one light, and recovery *from* the past, in
another. The question is, though, are these compatible recoveries?
For the issue of alcohol is not merely a cultural one, in the restricted
sense. It has its economic aspect too. Indulgence in alcohol is one
item among many in the thick archive of national habits that are
presumed to produce poverty and violence and/or are produced by
them. It is linked to the project of so revising the national character

that it becomes economically fit for recovery and no longer prone to violence, while not so altering it (since part of the argument is always that national character is a *donnée*, inalterable) that its unique features are lost. But the problem Maria Edgeworth's fiction initially broaches, although it does not define it, is the relational problem of England and Ireland, of the *mœurs* of one and of the other entering into an alliance that will not be mutually degrading and might be mutually beneficial. All of her Irish novels that deal with Ireland after *Castle Rackrent* are optimistic, although not unsubtle, exercises in the exploration of the prospects for an improving alliance. Yet *Castle Rackrent* is the ambivalent and most memorable precursor to a form of fiction that she eventually had to abandon when the protocols of representation available to her were finally exhausted and the Ireland that she had wanted to see healed seemed to be more than ever traumatized.

Castle Rackrent can be read in this light, although the cryptic nature of the work will by no means be resolved in it. First, the novel's historical juncture—published in 1800, just before the Act of Union was passed, written probably between 1797, the year Burke died, and 1799, the year after the great rebellion of 1798, claiming it is a tale of the years before 1782, when Ireland achieved a measure of parliamentary independence, claiming too that this Ireland has now passed away and has been succeeded by something different and/or better—is one of its most obvious contextual meanings. Second, it is a novel about a region that is part of the British dominions but wholly unfamiliar to the readership in England. Third, it is a novel about a landed family, told by a retainer whose whole value-system is, or seems to be, based on loyalty to his masters and pride in their family name. Yet it is also a story about the takeover of that ancestral family by his own son, Jason, a takeover to which Thady apparently refuses his approbation. Provided with a glossary and commentary, written in dialect, ventriloquized into Thady's mouth, the novel insists endlessly on the difference of all conceivable conditions in Ireland—from the linguistic to the economic. This is a land of alterity that has been overtaken by a revolution (1782) that has—by implication—normalized it, or has begun the process of normalization. It is, in a way, the opposite of Burke's

France, even more so if we remember that Edgeworth, for all her prescriptions for the improvement of Ireland, gave primacy to a highly Rousseauistic 'education of the heart'.[68] This is especially cryptic since the improved Ireland has, we are told, emerged since 1782—as indeed it had in many respects even though the frailty of that economic system was to be exposed in 1801 when 40,000 people died of famine. The replacement of the Irish landlords whose anticipated flight after the Union is mentioned at the close of the novel, by British manufacturers is all we get of 'improvement' and its prospects. Instead, the work concentrates almost entirely on the past regime. Its second part, which relates the tale of Sir Condy and which gives Thady a participant's as well as a narrator's role— thereby intensifying the ambiguity of his position—brings that regime to a close.

The text is, nevertheless, full of elisions and obliquities. It is not— like Jonah Barrington's *Personal Sketches of his own Times* (1827–32)— a celebration of the hard-drinking Irish gentry of the period between 1760 and 1782, when 'a kind Irish landlord then reigned despotic in the ardent affections of the tenantry, their pride and pleasure being to obey and support him', although it bears a notable resemblance to that work.[69] In fact, the rapscallion delinquency and the financial incompetence of the landed gentry is part of the after-history of their disappearance. With them went a certain *joie de vivre*, an *ancien régime* wildness that more polite and civilized times could only look back to with nostalgia. That wildness was, of course, also an important ingredient in the alliance between despotic landlord and obedient tenant, especially when the lord's despotism is described as being enthroned in the hearts of the tenants rather than in the institutional system of power. In effect, both Edgeworth and Barrington have in common the belief that those days—and with them a certain vitality of a natural and instinctive kind—have been replaced by an altogether more prosaic world. For Edgeworth, this would seem to be a gain, for Barrington a loss. Yet even in Edgeworth's case the gain is ambiguous. For there is, after all, a preference for the 90-year-old Thady's feudal sentiment towards the Rackrent family as against his lack of fatherly affection for his son who destroys the economic basis for that feudal relationship.

Indeed, feudal sentiment is all. No other relationship—certainly not the relationship of marriage, which is a cruel and vindictive bargain at the expense of the wives of the Rackrents—competes with it. In addition to the unhappiness of these despotic and commercial marriages, the Rackrents are hopelessly barren—perhaps an instance of the demographic blight that mysteriously afflicted the landed gentry in Britain and Ireland at the end of the eighteenth century.

Is it then possible to see in Edgeworth, as in Burke, a tremulous accommodation between two discourses—one dominated by the language of sensibility, feudalized and given to nostalgia for a vanished past—and the other by the language of calculation (here presented in the legal terms of financial arrangements, rents, debts, interest, loans, mortgages, etc.), with no conciliation possible between them? The failure of conciliation between feudal loyalty and financial wisdom is represented by obsessions that are ruinous—drink (Sir Patrick), law (Sir Murtagh), gambling (Sir Kit), drink and politics (Sir Condy). Obsessive delinquency is as much a sign of lovableness as it is a sign of futility. The only economic advance is made by Jason, but in him it is not associated with anything that could be called ethically admirable or affectionately attractive. Edgeworth refers at the close of the novel to Arthur Young's famous *A Tour in Ireland* (1780)—itself possibly much influenced by information supplied by Burke. It was, she says, 'the first faithful portrait of its inhabitants', and she goes on to claim for her own 'sketch' that its 'features . . . were taken from the life, and they are characteristic of that mixture of quickness, simplicity, cunning, carelessness, dissipation, disinterestedness, shrewdness and blunder, which in different forms, and with various success, has been brought upon the stage or delineated in novels'.[70] These self-cancelling pairings are themselves indications of a puzzle—the character of the people, already established as a cultural stereotype, yet none the less unaltered in any substantial respect, it would seem, by having been drawn from 'the life'. Any given hundred pages from Irish writing of the first three decades of the nineteenth century—perhaps even including writing about Ireland from this period—could be shuffled a dozen times to ensure the proper conditions for stochastic trials and it would still be almost impossible to find the epithet 'national' used to denote any-thing other than some powerful form of incontinence either in behaviour, habit, or feeling. The odd thing is, that it is precisely such forms of incontinence that are more usually identified with 'life'; anything more controlled and sphincter-tight is likely to be under-stood as the consequence of strenuously careful cultivation. The control of life is a requirement of civilization; but then civilization, when successful in its controls, may lack vitality. The antithetical pairings that Edgeworth discerns in the character of the Irish people are replicated, even produced, within her own system of cultural economy. It is itself the very disease of which it pretends to be the cure.

TWO

National Character and the Character of Nations

THE NATION AND THE FAMINE

There is a vast body of writing in the nineteenth century on the character of nations which is scarcely distinguishable from the equally vast literature on national character.[1] Even though the two are intimately linked, they are significantly different discourses with significantly different purposes. The character of nations is thematized repeatedly in nineteenth-century writing as the explanatory element in the story of a progression from the narrow ambit of the national place into the new territory or space of the state. National character, on the other hand, has no comparable progressive expansion. Instead, it is often featured as a controlling voice in a recalcitrant community narrative that refuses, with decreasing success, to surrender its particularities, to yield itself either to the state or to any comparable transnational, or 'universal' goal or condition. Those who remain in thrall to the spell of the national character see such a universalizing history as an impoverishing process that eliminates traditional practices and customs and, with them, those resources (strong communal feeling, imaginative flair, independent, even eccentric, personality) that are vital to the preservation of the native community's distinctiveness. Its largest ambition is to formulate a coherent idea of a nation and to keep that distinct from the idea of the state, even if or especially when the state is claimed to be either a fulfilment or transcendence of the nation. In Ireland, this conflict is usually engaged on Burkean terms, even though these terms are constantly undergoing modifications in relation to the historical contingencies of the moment.[2]

The Famine was the cataclysm that enforced a radical reconsideration of the question. In one view, more widely canvassed in the nineteenth century than it has been since, the Famine ended the possibility of Ireland's conceiving of itself as a distinct nation in the traditional sense, since one of its most remarkable effects was to alter the national character and with that, the whole question of the national territory and language.[3] Ireland was now more susceptible than it ever had been to reorganization and rational reform.[4] The Famine resituated the relationships between land, language, and national character and cast the Irish, as if by destiny, in the role of a traditional people who had failed to survive in the Malthusian, Darwinian universe of economic law and its racial–cultural counterpart, the character of nations.[5] No longer Scythians, Carthaginians, a people of oriental origin in an occidental empire, once historically important, they were now a vestigial remnant of the Indo-European system, overtaken by catastrophe and bypassed by progress in equal measure, their absurd claims to exceptionalism now finally chastised.[6] They were ripe now for integration within the system of empire and capital. Such integration did eventually take place, but it was a complicated process, hampered at every turn by the attempts, from Young Ireland to the IRB (Irish Republican Brotherhood) to the Irish Revival to the Catholic Church, to assert some form of Irish exceptionalism that would retain the category of national character as a defensive strategy against state secularization and all its accompanying alienations.[7]

Even though the Famine fatally weakened any argument in favour of Ireland's being a beneficiary of the Union and immeasurably strengthened the case for some form of independence, it was still difficult to maintain the position that a traditional culture had been destroyed while making the integrity of that culture the basis of a claim for political independence. The difficulty was, nevertheless, overcome by an intensification of the claim to Irish difference, an intensification largely achieved in the literature of the Irish Revival by the remarkable feat of ignoring the Famine and rerouting the claim for cultural exceptionalism through legend rather than through history. The modernization of Irish society after the Famine was, therefore, accompanied by the archaicizing of the idea of Irish culture. These are not entirely opposed processes, although they never lose their conflictual and contradictory alignments. The archaizing impulse was itself part of the modernizing process, although it was also an inhibition to it. For modernity is not only a sequence of enlightenments characterized by progress; it is a sequence that depends upon a constant return to and re-reading of the past that depends upon the paradigm of rebirth, renaissance, recovery of which the modern becomes both the beneficiary and the culmination. It is not, therefore, surprising to find that in Ireland a modernizing process should be accompanied by this kind of cultural annexation of a distant past. For it is obviously one means by which the idea of Irish modernity can be liberated and a peculiar distinctiveness claimed for it. This is true of almost all modernist movements.

But in Ireland there was the difference that the country had just endured one of the most apocalyptic disasters in modern history. This immediate past had to be negotiated, either by being ignored or by assigning the Ireland that had disappeared then to the ancient Ireland of legend. The rupture between the traditional and the modern culture could then be dramatized as the characteristic national experience, with neither the loss of the old nor the entry into the new complete. That transitional condition was understood to be one of incoherence, caught between two languages, Irish and English, two land systems, also Irish and English, two civilizations, one vivacious and wild, the other organized and dull. If the national character were to be preserved, it must be seen as surviving this rupture, despite all the attendant damage. The cultural politics of the next half-century was dominated by the need to find sufficient emblems of adversity in which this tragic transition could be exemplified. The most successful of these emblems was the poet James

Clarence Mangan. He was not only a great transitional figure; he was one who had effected the transition into modernity by representing, in his life and in his work, the experience of breakdown and the overcoming of breakdown by exhibiting, within both, the classic features of the national spirit. In him, the national character survived; in him too, the national character almost expired. The construction of Mangan as a tragic and deformed writer, magnificently gifted but incomplete, permitted the Famine to enter into the cultural arena as an event from which recovery could be achieved by the sublation of Mangan into the revival's notion of the incomplete, the nearly 'great' writer whose deficiencies could later be repaired by another writer's completeness and greatness. The legend of the Irish writer who would transcend the limits of the disfigured national fate was one of those by which the Revival encountered the ill effects of the Famine.

In general, there is a structural kinship between the ways in which writers are interpreted (besides Mangan there are others, like Thomas Moore and Edward Walsh) and the ways in which the land itself is construed. The land, the territory, the soil of Ireland, the native property system under which it was once possessed, the foreign system under which it is now possessed, the collapse that derived from the latter, the recovery that will follow from the reinauguration of the former system, are central elements in a discourse that seeks to overcome the experience of a disastrous transition by asserting that there is a national spirit, of which both writing and landownership systems are embodiments, that will or should survive and prevail. With such survival will come recovery. The Revival's later apotheosis of the west as the site of the immemorial Irish culture is a telling example of this assertion, as is the Yeatsian extraction of the Irish peasantry and the Anglo-Irish Ascendancy from their specific histories into an ideology of anti-modern Irishness.[8] The west became the place of Irish authenticity, the place that was not yet subject to the effects of administrative, governmental rules and laws, and which therefore preserved among its population the national character in its pristine form or, at least, in such a state of preservation that the pristine form could be inferred from it. It was not only geographically distinct; it was historically precedent to the rest of the country which, especially in Dublin, had been reduced to a colonized space of the imperial administration. This emphasis on the west as a national place, as the site of a deep authenticity, was intensified by the political question of the land, from the Famine to the Land War, in which the western counties played a crucial role. The repossession of language and of land and the dispossession of both are the intimate themes that link the political and the literary campaigns for recovery from the early nineteenth to the early twentieth century, from Catholic Emancipation in 1829 to the secure foundation of the Irish Free State a century later.

Thus, central to the nationalist position were the claims that (a) Ireland was a culturally distinct nation; (b) it had been mutilated beyond recognition by British colonialism; and (c) it could nevertheless rediscover its lost features and thereby recognize once more its true identity. In order to hold the mirror up to nature it was first necessary to hold it up to legend; the reflection would represent Irish nature in the form of its heroic national character, pursued with great energy in the cultural field, even as its *alter ego*—the commercial, the economic, the religiously conformist version of the contemporary Irish—was derided as a betrayal of that heroic face, even though it was its inescapable companion. The literature and politics of the Revival era are dominated by this apparent contrast, producing as a consequence various analyses of paralysis (Joyce) and degeneration (Yeats), both of which seek a conclusion in the verdict that Ireland, star-crossed as ever, failed to achieve modernity because of that schismatic divide. But it could be argued that it was in virtue of the literary construction of such a divide that modernity was achieved at all. For modernity defined itself as the new emerging from the old; it needed the presence of archaic elements in order to articulate its difference from them. Still, it was indeed a modernity that was obliged to retain, as the price of cultural autonomy, a strong admixture of the archaic or, more benignly, the traditional. This took many forms—the Revival, the Irish language movement, a constricting version of Roman Catholicism, and protectionist trade policies among them. These were the stigmata of identity, the marks of the nation and its sufferings, reminders to the emergent state of its origin in the nation, resisting its secular arrival even while enabling it through that very resistance. The conditions for sustaining these forms of resistance continued to disappear as the nation became the state, yet the state could only assert its Irish identity by engaging in the struggle with the archaic forms that helped give birth to it. This is a story that largely belongs to the twentieth century, but it had its opening chapters in the nineteenth.

It was then that one of the story's most obsessive preoccupations was announced and achieved its first articulations. The issue of representation had to be central for a culture that wished to defend its autonomy on the basis that it had not been and could not be represented in colonial–imperial forms and must therefore find alternatives more suited to it. This immediately historicizes the question of representation. If its various modes are specific to particular societies or historical moments, then its universalist claims are laid open to question; further, it is possible to think that all systems of representation, if they are so specific in their genesis, must be systems of mis-representation, since they are agencies of power and therefore have an interest in misrepresenting the powerless.

Even before the Famine, the various formulations of the Irish national character had emphasized the existence of a natural relationship between the people and the land that had been deformed or distorted by the violent expropriations of the seventeenth century and the penal legislation of the eighteenth. Burke's reading of the French Revolution had given added impetus to the fear that land confiscation and the subversion of traditional beliefs were the characteristic opening acts of a revolutionary regime; since Ireland had undergone this process a century earlier, the Burkean alarm was that the consequences of that experience might now have a revolutionary effect. In addition, the conviction that there was a prevailing deformation in the Irish social and political system extended into other areas as well, although the relation between land and people remained the exemplary deformed condition from which others arose. Yet if that conviction of deformity were to be articulated, it obviously had to avail itself of existing discursive conventions, basic to which was the convention of speech. But speech itself was problematic, not only because of the degraded status of the Irish language but also because of the connection between it and the Irish mode of speaking the English language. Irish English was not only a dialect or patois; it was one that was consistently characterized as suffering from deformity—excess, illogic, mispronunciation. It was a language that lacked rational order and was therefore incapable of providing an acceptable analysis of the condition of the people who spoke it. For to represent their speech as deformed was also to represent their account of their social and political condition as deformed. Verbose, inaccurate, melodramatic, unreliable, in sad need of some form of sobriety, Irish speech and the Irish political condition required a rational articulation that was beyond the capacity of the national character to produce. Irish eloquence became the index of Irish inarticulacy, speech removed from fact—blarney. Speech of this kind could not accurately define a condition; for Irish speech to be trusted, and for its account of the Irish experience to be acceptable, it must be subjected to the protocols of English speech and, in consequence, to the 'improving' English account of the Irish condition that accompanied the Union.

The sounds that issue from the mouths of the Irish—as speech, song, or wail—pose a challenge for those who wish to represent them in print. Similarly, what is taken in by those mouths—food and drink—poses a problem of another sort. Food is problematic, especially during the Famine, because there is so little of it; and drink is problematic, because there is so much of it. A starving or a drunken people obviously lack articulacy. They cannot tell their own story, nor can their story easily be told by someone else who has no experience of these extreme conditions. Indeed, it is a common narrative ploy to assert that Irish conditions cannot be represented to an English audience. What is taken in by and emitted from the mouth cannot easily be represented in print. The movement from an oral to a print culture is not simply a matter of translating folk tales or customs from the mouths of the people to the page. It involves an attempt to control a strange bodily economy in which food, drink, speech, and song are intimately related. Can a printed account in English represent the history that lives in the mouths of the Irish? This is a question to which the concept of national character attempts to provide an answer. But that concept cannot be mobilized effectively unless it admits a connection between itself and the territory of Ireland since, as Burke and shown, such a connection defines a historical and traditional community.

SPEAKING THE NATION: *THE COLLEGIANS*

National character, as a category, illuminates some of the connections between speech and land in their various representations, most especially when the possession of each is taken to be a matter of critical political importance. There is a way of possessing speech and land that is held to be 'native' to the Irish; and there is equally a mode of possession that is English. It is not merely a matter of claiming a difference between these. It is a matter of making one claim superior to the other or, alternatively, of eliding that difference and showing that the Irish can speak English as do the English and that they can, comparably, hold land according to English law.

However, if national character is to be altered, renovated so that it will allow the Irish to enter into the English world of progress and modernity, the consequence might seem to be that such a renovation might make the Irish indistinguishable from the English. In reforming the national character, national identity might be lost. It is, of course, true that the words identity and character are miscellaneously used in a diverse number of texts right through that century and beyond.[9] But there is, I suggest, a difference between them. In becoming a nation-state, England or France, for instance, could claim that the national identity had been preserved because identity was the condition attained by the national character when it became duplicated all over the globe via imperial expansion. Only privileged, successful versions of a local national character could claim a place in the evolutionary story of the character of nations—nations, that is, that were simultaneously particular in themselves but also universal in their global appeal. This, obviously, could neither apply nor appeal to the Irish; for them the character of nations, so construed, was profoundly oppressive. It assigned to them a national character that had no global future. To the extent that they tried to reform this character so that it might find an entry into the imperial adventure of modernity, they risked losing their identity. The risk was taken. The first step was to find a mode of representation for Ireland that would confirm its uniqueness and liberate it from the notion that it was a civilization doomed to extinction in the evolutionary history of nation-state formations.

The first requirement for the national character was to find a manner in which its speech might be represented. This was first engaged with as a conscious political and historical question by Maria Edgeworth, both in *Castle Rackrent* and in her *Essay on Irish Bulls*. It remained a charged issue in Irish fiction thereafter, undergoing its ultimate transformation in Joyce's work, where the idea of representing an already existing national character was replaced by that of forging the national identity through the act of writing.

If *Castle Rackrent* is set alongside Gerald Griffin's *The Collegians* (1829), the effectiveness of the national character as an agency for the production of the country's general history in the form of an exemplary, ostensibly 'private' or family, narrative is further vindicated. Griffin was ultimately upset that the villain of his novel, the half-sir, Hardress Cregan, should be more memorable and more likeable than the stalwart Kyrle Daly, the young Catholic son of a middleman farmer who eventually marries Ann Chute, the daughter of a landed family and the heiress whose fortune will confer respectability and ease, as well as freedom from sectarian identification, on her spouse. Griffin was right to be so worried, although his ethical or moral anxiety is perhaps too limiting in its version of the problem.[10] For the melodramatic form of his novel demands that the choice between good and evil be stark, and its ethical imperative— that control win out over excess—ensures that the history of past excess, embodied in Hardress, should be much more materially present to us than the yet to be written history of control ever could be. The good are pallid because they have, in the economy of this novel, no historical time; they are anachronistic, out of time, in a sense opposite to that which applies to the villains of the piece. Peter Brooks establishes the convention's norms and anxieties:

Melodramatic good and evil are highly personalized: they are assigned to, they inhabit persons who indeed have no psychological complexity but who are strongly characterized. Most notably, evil is villainy; it is a swarthy, cape-enveloped man with a deep voice. Good and evil can be named as persons are named—and melodramas tend in fact to move toward a clear nomination of the moral universe. The ritual of melodrama involves the confrontation of clearly identified anatagonists and the expulsion of one of them. It can offer no terminal reconciliation, for there is no longer a clear transcendent value to be reconciled to. There is, rather, a social order to be purged, a set of ethical imperatives to be made clear.[11]

The Collegians is, self-consciously, a national novel in the form of Romantic melodrama. Various people are identified as having the national characteristics of recklessness, vivacity, unsteadiness, lack of moral perception—excepting young Daly, who is the rational and noble emblem of the new type who is to inherit the Irish earth after Emancipation. The novel can indeed be read as an account of the newly emergent relationship between the national and the rational, with the rational understood to be that progressive condition that grows out of and surpasses the national. But this is not the revolutionary rationality of the system-maker. Rather the reverse: it is the rationality of control, of reform, of modified, educated improvement. Kyrle is controlled by his rationality and is thereby equipped to control what would otherwise be his national fate—epitomized by his Trinity College friend Hardress Cregan. The young Catholic beauty, Eily O'Connor, the Colleen Bawn, is murdered by the young half-sir Hardress (or at his instigation) after a secret marriage and his subsequent regret at a liaison that is both socially embarrassing and financially unwise—since only Ann Chute's fortune will redeem his property. Hardress is a version of the Rackrents; and the other HCs in the novel (Hyland Creagh, Hepton Connolly) are cut from the same cloth—duellists, hard drinkers, ruinous spendthrifts, sportsmen, and, most important of all, anachronisms: 'Mr Hepton Connolly was one individual of a species now happily extinct among Irish gentlemen. He just retained enough of a once flourishing patrimony to enable him to keep a hunter, a racer, and an insolent groom.'[12]

One of the features of Edgeworth's and Griffin's texts—as also of those of novelists like the Banim brothers, Carleton, Charles Lever, Lady Morgan—is the rendering of Irish speech as a mode of authenticity and as a claim to realism. But whatever the fidelity of this rendering, the function of dialect, most especially of a dialect that is marked by vigour, oddity, fierceness, malapropisms, grammatical fractures—is worth considering more closely than any dispute about its authenticity. Its claim to authenticity resides in its mere presence, not in its proximity or otherwise to the actual speech of Irish people. In *The Collegians* there is a correlation between certain physical characteristics and certain forms of speech. Kyrle Daly and his friend Hardress Cregan have servants, Lowry Looby and Danny Mann. Both these servants are physically deformed, although in different ways, and both speak a dialect that is, in Looby's case, endearingly attractive (or meant to be so) and in Mann's case coarsely repellent. Their dialect is, like themselves, inferior to the educated speech of their young masters. Because each speaks in this manner, each is manifesting a national characteristic—but that national characteristic is indissolubly allied with degradation. Looby has come down in the world: a cottier, he has lost what land he had in an agricultural crisis during the Halifax administration. Now he is a faithful retainer, exhibiting in his posture 'the effect . . . of habitual penury and dependance',[13] But from the outset Looby was doomed to misfortune. In his physique, 'It seemed as if nature . . . had laid the foundation of a giant . . . but . . . had been compelled to terminate her undertaking within the dimensions of a dwarf.'[14] He has 'the national talent for adroit flattery';[15] and before he became a servant he lost the chance to become a postmaster because of a superstitious belief. In this respect he is like his master, Mr Daly, father to Kyrle, who named a child of his 'North-East' in compliance with a popular superstition, again because the Dalys, otherwise sensible, 'were not wholly exempt from the prevailing weakness of their countrymen'.[16] Landless, superstitious, physically grotesque, illiterate, comically eloquent with a strong country brogue, Looby is an exemplary instance of the national character of the Irish, benignly viewed; one step back from his master, Mr Daly; two steps back from Kyrle Daly. Danny Mann, by contrast, besides being a hunchback, is marked 'by that look of pert shrewdness which marks the low inhabitant of a city, and vents itself in vulgar cant, and in ridicule of the honest and wondering ignorance of rustic simplicity.'[17] Mann's injury has been inflicted by Hardress: when they were younger, Hardress hurled Mann down a flight of stairs, injuring his spine. But the consequence is that Mann is Hardress's slave; he will do anything, even to the point of committing murder for him. He may be free of Looby's disabling superstition; but he has so internally secreted his own oppression that his savage fidelity is itself a form of superstition too. Both men are physically, psychologically, socially, and economically retarded. Their speech is geared to their conditions; one rural and innocent, the other urban and corrupt; one superstitious, the other cynical; one harmless, the other violent. Neither has undergone civic emancipation. Nor can they. They are no more than representations of a historical moment in the evolution of their respective masters. There is no question of psychological complexity here. These four male figures constitute a palimpsest of an evolving historical condition, with Kyrle Daly the most highly evolved in the direction of rationality and Hardress Cregan the most fatally, if attractively, still engaged with the emotional intensities of his forebears. The extent of evolutionary progress is indicated by the difference between a speech that is civil and one that is disfigured, between received pronunciation and dialect, analogous to the physical characteristics of the handsome masters and their deformed servants.

However, the most important dialect, the one that places the speech of the male quartet most luminously, is that of the Colleen Bawn, Eily O'Connor, herself. Even the fact that she has two names, one in phonetically rendered Irish, the other in English, establishes her as a person who summarizes in her name a historical process, a transition between folk origin and social respectability. Eily's birthday is St Patrick's Day; the celebrations on that day in Garryowen are as boisterous as one could wish: Garryowen, like Eily herself, has an Irish name, Garbh Eoin, meaning Eoin's garden, which we are told, because of the Garryowen boys, and because Moore, 'our national lyrist', has adapted the song 'to one of the liveliest of his melodies'[18] has made the place 'almost a synonime for Ireland';[19]

Eily's fateful meeting with Hardress takes place on Patrick's Day and in the course of it she and her father are rescued from the boisterousness of the Garryowen boys by Hardress. Her condition is, to say the least, overdetermined; her position is self-consciously allegorical. But the allegory extends itself to speech also. In the following passage, the links between speech, physical appearance, and a violent communal history are heavily marked:

It is true, indeed, that the origin of the suburban beauty was one which, in a troubled country like Ireland, had little of agreeable association to recommend it; but few even of those to whom twisted hemp was an object of secret terror, could look on the exquisitely beautiful face of Eily O'Connor, and remember that she was a ropemaker's daughter; few could detect beneath the timid, hesitating, downcast gentleness of manner, which shed an interest over all her motions, the traces of a harsh and vulgar education. It was true that she sometimes purloined a final letter from the King's adjectives, and prolonged the utterance of a vowel beyond the term of prosodaical orthodoxy, but the tongue that did so seemed to move on silver wires, and the lip on which the sound delayed

'long murmuring, loth to part'

imparted to its own accents an association of sweetness and grace, that made the defect an additional allurement.[20]

The links are telling. Eily is a ropemaker's daughter; the rope is associated with the hangman (Mr Daly calls Micil O'Connor 'a species of collateral hangman'[21]): in a country such as Ireland the association is inevitable; her beauty does not mask vulgarity; her speech is not the King's English: she filches from it, she breaks its orthodox rules, yet this defect is the more attractive for the sweetness of her voice. State violence, defective pronunciation of the King's English, female beauty, Irish accent: as with Looby and Mann, there is a politics inscribed in speech, a politics understood in terms of a degradation that cannot be represented in received English. For Eily's speech is not rendered in dialect, although we are to understand that the King's English undergoes some distressingly Irish mutations in her mouth. Eily has had a measure of education, through her uncle, the priest, Father Edward, who was educated at Salamanca in the penal era. But the 'moral entertainment' provided by her reading of Addison and Dr Johnson is insufficient to raise her, in appearance or in speech, to the status of Ann Chute, whose beauty is described in terms that indicate she is of the classical 'art' tradition (the Temple of Theseus, the Doric pillars of Trinity College[22]) rather than that of nature, like Eily. Degradation of speech, unruly behaviour leading to violence, tatterdemalion dress, the small variations in low economic status, the lack of personal or civic control, are all symptoms of Ireland's past and all have to be overcome—as in Kyrle Daly—so that the emergence of Ireland from its history can be completed. That history is represented at one level as something to be escaped from and finally resolved in the national marriage of Kyrle Daly and Ann Chute.

Despite the fact that history is represented as a retarding influence, manifest in defective speech, physical deformity, and in the violence that takes the lives of Eily, Danny Mann, and Hardress, it retains its dominance. Even the long perspective in which the story is cast, the better to persuade us that the bad old days are gone, does not disguise the inescapable reality of this unreal territory and its murky past. The novel's attempt to abandon a delinquent nationality for a modern rationality is a failure. What we may call the folklorish elements in the fiction, the authenticity of the Irish cultural and historical setting, is precisely what must be sacrificed for a marriage that will be economically emblematic of future success and that will be representable not only in the King's English but by people who speak the King's English. Irish history, the Ireland of Garryowen, the Ireland of the 1770s, the Colleen Bawn, duellists, exotic murder, shadowed by the hangman's noose, is a foreign country because it is a country foreign to the present of the 1820s. To travel in it is to wonder how it can ever be reformed into a proper and civil part of the United Kingdom. Catholic Emancipation was not merely a matter of the franchise and the penal laws; it was a matter of emancipation from the past into civic freedom from that dark, phantasmagoric unreality of earlier times.

In Boucicault's dramatic version of *The Collegians*, *The Colleen Bawn*, first performed in New York in 1860, the question of accent is even more prominent. But now there is a significant change in roles.

Hardress is no longer the squireen. He disapproves of whiskey, smoking, and, above all, of Eily's brogue and her frequent use of Irish chevilles—'asthore' and the like. All the obloquy that was formerly his is now transferred to the gombeen man, Corrigan. But by the close Eily is commanded to speak (or rather 'spake') in her natural accent, and the 'Brides of Garryowen', she and Ann Chute, are happily reconciled with Hardress and Kyrle Daly. The most significant alteration in the Boucicault play, and in the opera derived from it, *The Lily of Killarney*, is not in the roles of the characters so much as in the disappearance from these adaptations of the heavily upholstered prose of Griffin himself. For that is the form of the King's English that is ultimately dominant—self-consciously respectable, wearing its learning on its sleeve, even making its classical quotations, tags, and references a ground bass to the lighter Irish melodies of place names, personal names (Myles-na-Copaleen), and chevilles. It is writing with an accent, the accent of respectability, education, responsible and tender feeling. In this novel, it is crucially important that speech should not be deformed, for deformity of speech indicates moral, social, or political delinquency. This is a point exploited in the opera adaptation, especially in Danny Mann's recitative, where he makes the connection between physical and moral and emotional deformity clear in the standard way of the villain:

> Duty, yes, I'll do my duty,
> What is love and what is beauty
> To a rough misshapen creature,
> Crook'd in form and hard in feature?
>
> Hearts that melt in soft compassion
> Beat in frames of other fashion,
> I'll help the master where I can,
> No other law has Danny Mann.[23]

ACCENTS AND SOBRIETY

On the question of accent, we remember that Burke too had a brogue that occasioned much merriment and routine insults from his colleagues in the House of Commons; that one of the regular objections to his speeches, as to his writings, most especially the *Reflections* and those subsequent to it, was the extravagance of his rhetoric, the lack of sobriety in his prose that seemed deceitful, gorgeous, and Hibernian. In addition, Burke was well known for his melodramatic gestures in the House—throwing a dagger across the floor and thereby arousing the derision of the radicals especially.[24] The intricate melodrama of Burke's rhetoric was, of course, widely identified with the complex of privilege it was determined to glamorize, whereas his opponents, especially Paine, regarded themselves as the producers of a prose that was, by virtue of its simplicity and plainness, democratic in its form and appeal. The democratic identification was stifled in relation to Irish speech, for its corrective contrast was the speech or rather the prose of respectability, civility, control. Irish speech—accent, pronunciation, eloquence, blarney, malapropism, excess—has always been a matter of interest and dispute, heavily laden with prejudice and exotic benignity, condescension and disdain, in the reaction of those who regard it as something not simply foreign, but complicatedly so because it still retains a sufficient quota of the familiar to make defamiliarization upsetting.

We see a similar sequence of reactions to O'Connell's demagoguery, his violence of speech, his abundant but banausic rhetorical skills, counterbalanced nicely by the later admiration for Parnell's aloofness, hesitancy (if we may use the word), and landlordly penury of speech. These are sounds that echo in a highly political auditorium. The writers who reinvented Irish dialect as an indicator of a nationality that increasingly came to be moulded into the opponent of rationality ignited within that contrast others— between the richness of one, the anaemia of the other, the human warmth and sympathy of one against the calculating impersonality of the other. They were, in effect, attempting in variant ways to rewrite Irish history as a series of pasts that were to be escaped from or returned to, something to grow out of or to grow back into, something to be erased or something to be revived.

Irish accents, in their regional forms, have their periods of glory or of occlusion—the accents of the west or of the West Briton, or of

Munster, the accents of the Anglo-Irish, of Dublin 4, the accents of the north. In the Irish language a similar system of relations prevails. In it too, accent, dialect, and pronunciation attain different levels of prestige. One standard example is the contrast between the high prestige afforded the Munster dialect of Peadar O Laoghaire because it is or was regarded as the closest printed approximation to the *caint na ndaoine* (speech of the people), and the general derision reserved for the official state version of Irish, which is looked down on as a maiming of the authentic speech of native speakers of the language. In their turn, native speakers and scholars scorn the failures of pronunciation and euphony that afflict those who learned Irish at school and who lack those cradle fidelities to the language which are cherished so dearly in the hearts of purists. The Irish Revival takes much but not all of this linguistic politics on board and thereby produces another amalgam. But the central point here is that speech, like all the other excessive energies of the Irish national character, is encouraged throughout the nineteenth century to become more temperate or, conversely, more indulgent. The first attitude is a species of unionism, the other of nationalism; yet the division so described is altogether too curt, for there are mixings and overlappings between these traditionally polarized positions. But Irish speech *is* a political territory, exotic and bar-barous, at times indecipherable, surveyable only from the vantage-point of the traveller–narrator whose norm is Received Pro-nunciation of the King's English, a civil prose, unstained by dialect or rather by the clusters of apostrophes, clottings of consonants, and feverish punctuation that indicate dialect's dread and malformed presence, visible to the eye as audible to the ear. Abnormality char-acterizes both the speaker of Irish English and the speaker of the Irish language itself, whose status in English-language fiction and travel writing is scarcely that of a language at all. The speakers of these languages can be endearing, sentimental, loyal, savage, humorous, excessive—but they are never subject to the charge of being cool and analytic. Such a role is preserved for those whose language is the King's or Queen's English. Above all, it is a role never assigned to those who write or speak in the Irish language.

THE POLITICS OF MUSIC: THOMAS MOORE

But there is another mode in which the instability of the Irish national character and the discourse appropriate to it are registered. In Thomas Moore's 'Letter to the Marchioness of Donegal', affixed as a preface to the third number of the *Irish Melodies*, he identifies that mode as music:

It has often been remarked, and oftener felt, that our music is the truest of all comments upon our history. The tone of defiance succeeded by the languor of despondency—a burst of turbulence dying away into softness—the sorrows of one moment lost in the levity of the next—and all that romantic mixture of mirth and sadness, which is naturally produced by the efforts of a lively temperament, to shake off, or forget the wrongs which lie upon it: such are the features of our history and character, which we find strongly and faithfully reflected in our music; and there are many airs, which, I think, it is difficult to listen to, without recalling some period or event to which their expression seems particularly applicable.[25]

Moore's *Melodies*, and his own placement of them in relation to national character, co-ordinates national history, national character, within a political programme for Catholic repair and renewal. But his verses are a form of polite narrative that masters the wild and fierce music, which he and Sir John Stevenson were said to have emasculated, giving to it instead the 'correct' musical accent, far different from those accents that had been heard at the Belfast Harpers' Festival in 1792 and written down (although again imperfectly) by Edward Bunting.[26] The *Melodies*, like a number of later compilations of songs, cannot escape the problems raised by transmission from an oral to a print culture. The premiss is that the music that had existed for centuries had never been written down; when it was, the relation between that music and its pre-print form was generally considered to be deformed in some sense. In Moore's case, we constantly find ourselves reading the *Melodies* without the music; the music is supplied by memory. So he, like the others I have mentioned, appears in two forms—with or without the music—and the arguments are conducted on the lines of deformation: the words deform the music, the musical notation is inappropriate to the native forms. In such textual confusion, where does the claim to authenticity lie? Part of the answer is that the whole territory of Irish music, and by extension of Irish authenticity, is betrayed into print; and yet it is only through such betrayal that it can be preserved at all, for it is only through the medium of print that an audience can be found and established. If sympathy for the Irish problem within the Union were to be won, it had to be publicized and commercialized in a recognizable and attractive form. To that end, Irishness had to be sold as 'Irish national character'—a form recognizable precisely because of its complicity with, as well as difference from, the successful anti-revolutionary version of a syndicated British national character that Burke had inaugurated. The one element in that character that had to be erased was the revolutionary element; for once that appeared, the commercialization failed and Ireland became a territory as Other as revolutionary France.

Thus, the disputes about Moore's brilliantly syndicated versions of the Irish in his *Melodies* were inevitably political. Douglas Hyde's verdict on Moore epitomizes the hostility to him—a hostility more marked during the Irish Revival than before or since. Moore 'had rendered the past of Ireland sentimentally interesting without arousing the prejudices of or alarming the upper classes'.[27] But this is an accusation that applies much more accurately to Moore the melodist than to Moore the political writer. Moore seems to have been disgusted by the servility displayed by the Irish on the occasion of George IV's visit in 1821. Certainly for some years after his prose versions of Irish history manifest a much more acerbic view of his country's history than do the *Melodies*. Moore favoured the tactic of concealment, whether in *Lallah Rookh*, where the disguise is 'oriental'[28] or in *Memoirs of Captain Rock* (1824) wherein he frames within a polite narrative the fierce accents of the wild and temperamental Irish, with the well-tried device of an Editor, who is engaged on a missionary crusade in Ireland. When this Editor is given an autobiographical manuscript recounting the exploits of Captain Rock, a famous rebel leader of the 'poor benighted Irish', he discovers the significant detail that Rock was born on the day Father Nicholas Sheehy was judicially assassinated at Clonmel in 1776—an incident that Burke, O'Connell, and many others alluded to over the next sixty years.[29] The significance here is that Sheehy was hanged in order to cow the Whiteboy movement into submission on the standard grounds that agrarian disturbances were disguised forms of sedition. In such details, Moore offers an indirect apologia for the 'seditious' activities of the Captain and provides a much more sympathetic understanding of the chaotic state of Irish political life than that given in, say, Eyre Evans Crowe's story of agrarian disturbances in 'The Carders', in *Ireland Today* (1825). *Memoirs of Captain Rock* is an interesting narrative in that it recounts the history of Ireland in ironic mode, pretending that the Rock family has only been able to sustain its ancestral violence as agrarian rebels because of the co-operation of the British government's spectacularly cruel policies. It is, in effect, a rebel view of Irish history cast within the frame of an abortive Protestant missionary attempt to convert the Irish from their wildness and Catholicism—two interdependent conditions.

Still, it remains true that the horrors of the penal era and the brutalities of the Ascendancy are consistently narrated by Moore, as by Griffin and Edgeworth, even by the Banim brothers and Lady Morgan, as a history that is about to be overcome, as an inarticulacy that is now beginning to pass away and be replaced, however indirectly, by an increasing articulacy, even if it still shows marked traces of its inarticulate origin in the semi-civility of dialect. Since Ireland still had no institution that could plausibly be said to acknowledge its unique condition, printed discourse has had an especially important role to play in defining it and in providing a narrative for its resolution. It is a commonplace that organized movements, clubs, and societies—secret, learned, and otherwise—formed the matrix out of which various forms of protest and historical redefinition emerged into print. Since the days of the Volunteers, and even more since the organization of the United Irishmen through the press, the pamphlet, and the broadsheet, this had been generally recognized. Further, this expansion of print culture was regularly associated with the French Revolution. As late as 1831, Thomas Moore notes in *The Life and*

Death of Lord Edward Fitzgerald that 'The immense efficacy of clubs and societies, as instruments of political agitation, had been evinced by the use which the workers of the French revolution had made of them.'[30]

For such discourse, the central organizing cultural concept was national character, as it had been evinced in history and as it was displayed in the present. Increasingly, in the first decades of the nineteenth century, national character is an enduring category of collective existence that is expressed (although really constituted) within a series of miscellaneous narratives—travel literature, the political pamphlet, the novel, collections of music and folklore, and, in Moore's case, collections of ancient melodies, refashioned in contemporary poetic idiom, that have exchanged the wild harp for the civil pianoforte. The difficulty encountered by such discourses, although they all encounter it with varying degrees of emphasis and success, is the connection between the constitution of a national character and the development of the material circumstances that are appropriate to it or to its alteration and improvement. The assumption is that national character is independent of material conditions and yet that its full development or final extirpation is dependent on their restructuring. Obviously, the various contradictions that both bedevil and define the national character are not subject to resolution. The relation between material conditions and cultural identification is critical; generally, the view is that one or other must be altered drastically before any resolution is possible. But then that is not a resolution; it is a surgical procedure that will remove one of the two elements that, in their combination, constitute the problem and in their separation either stifle it or prolong it. Part of this issue is embedded within the very act of transmission itself, whether that be in musical notation, in type fonts, in the representation of dialect. The point is that the problem was not really altered by these newly adopted modes of transmission. They actually determined its shape—even though the problem remained as one that was understood to have had an anterior existence that was now, however imperfectly, emerging into newly communicable forms.

LAND AND SPEECH

Speech has its norms and abnorms; so too has land. If we look at the ways in which the island of Ireland has been figured in literary and political discourse, we can see, from the Famine onward, a terminological shift that indicates sequences of attitude towards the object that is nominated as 'Ireland'. Three terms are of particular importance—territory, land, and soil. 'Land' is the middle term in the sense that it always occupies the civic space in the ontological hierarchy the three constitute. 'Territory' I will call the term that belongs to the conception of Ireland as a state; 'land' belongs to the conception of Ireland as an economy, within the civic sphere; 'soil' is the term that belongs to a nationalist and communal conception of Ireland as a cultural reality that is not fully represented in the modes of articulation that are proper to the other two. In Isaac Butt's pamphlet *The Irish People and the Irish Land* (1867), he laments the fact that agrarian reform is more easily accomplished in India than in Ireland, because Ireland is not recognized as being sufficiently foreign:

And this is not done in the case of Ireland, just because we have the fiction of an identity with England. The owner of the soil is a 'landlord' not a '*zemindar*'—the occupier is a 'tenant' and not a '*ryot*'. I believe in my conscience, that if we had Irish or Gaelic names to express the relation, if the owner were a '*corbe*' and the occupier a '*kerne*', an English Parliament would not for one session tolerate the continuance of this wrong. Our misfortune is that English phrases are applied to relations that bear no resemblance to the things which the words describe in the English tongue.[31]

Butt's point is effective. All the legislation directed towards the reform of the land question in Ireland between the 1820s and the 1870s—the Sub-letting Act of 1826, the Incumbered Estates Act of 1849, Deasy's Act of 1860, the establishment of the Board of Works in 1831 and the extension of its powers in 1842 to cover drainage and fisheries—was founded on the conviction that the British system of legality must be extended to Ireland. We may begin from the fundamental and familiar concept of the contrast between custom and status on the one hand and contract on the other. The native land systems of both Ireland and India included certain elements of status defined only by custom, and therefore by no means precisely defined. But 'the British mind found incomprehensible a society based on unwritten custom and on government by personal discretion; and it knew of only one sure method of marking off public from private rights—the introduction of a system of legality'.[32]

Such Edgeworthian efforts ignored a cultural and agricultural reality. For there is a difference between the Irish battle for the land in the nineteenth century and the battle for the soil, even though the two merge and interfuse at various points. Soil is what land becomes when it is ideologically constructed as a natal source, that element out of which the Irish originate and to which their past generations have returned. It is a political notion denuded, by a strategy of sacralization, of all economic and commercial reference.

In an allied version, soil is what land had been when it was communally owned, by tribe, comunity, or nation. Soil is eternally possessed by a community; land is temporarily owned by an individual. The various migrations from one term to the other tend to enforce a polarization between the diachronicity of the systems of landholding and the synchronicity of the link with the soil, even though there is no escaping the fact that any such claim to synchronicity must ultimately give preference to some system of landowning that is rooted in history, however ancient. Still, it is part of the nationalist, as it is part of the imperialist, self-characterization to claim that the custom that was initially local and original has thereby also a claim to universal assent. The straining for ontological purity in this kind of discourse is one of its most notable and least attractive characteristics; it makes a virtue of a philosophical excess that is registered consistently as a rhetorical deficiency.

An analogous stress characterizes the movement from oral to print culture, from Irish to English language, from folklore to rationality. The basic paradigm is that of original possession to modern dispossession and then, in a second reversionary variation, of converting that dispossession into a repossession. The recovery of land and the recovery of speech through an act of repossession that will alter the established hierarchies of speech and landowning are intimately associated ambitions in the project of Irish nationalism.

LAND AND SOIL: THOMAS DAVIS

In contrast to the story of the struggle for the language, the struggle for the land and, indeed, the struggle with the land, is contrastingly marked by an inexhaustible series of references to its economic status—property, rent, productivity, upkeep, improvement, impoverishment, ownership, tenant right, landlord right, buying and selling, state purchase, redistribution, etc. The distinction is not peculiar to Ireland nor is it confined to versions, sacred and secular, of territory. It perhaps has its origins in the counter-revolutionary reaction to the re-division of French territory during the revolution when the traditional boundaries between the old provinces were replaced by divisions that were based on a mathematical and symmetrical model. Burke fulminated against this, but so too did French commentators like Rémusat and de Maistre. It was construed, not only as an assault on historically sanctioned pieties, but as a characteristically modern or secular reinterpretation of land as merely or exclusively an administrative or economic category. Stripped of its ancient associations, it entered into the world of the political economists and their peculiar idiom of measure and price, forgoing the idiom of presence and value. Nationalism was the two-faced ideology that could exploit both idioms, although in doing so it rarely interfused them. It could make the claim to authenticity in terms of the soil and make that in turn part of the concurrent claim to ownership of the land. This was an especially powerful claim in Ireland, where the relationship between landlords and tenants was so fraught and the relationship between the land and those it supported was so dangerously poised, especially after the agricultural collapse of 1815.

Thomas Davis's 1843 essay, 'Udalism and Feudalism', is the best-known statement of this positional manœuvring between the categories of land and soil. The argument is simple. There have been in Ireland as in Europe four systems of land tenure. The first, a species of gavelkind, communal, tribal ownership, was udalism. This was followed by the 'rank feudality of the dark ages';[33] that in turn was succeeded by the modified feudality of England and Germany; finally, there came landlordism. Feudalism had been militarily imposed on a udalistic Ireland in the seventeenth century; landlordism in 1688, marking an even worse stage both in its history and in the history of civilization.[34] For landlordism, in Davis's view, is the introduction into Ireland of a specific British version of modernity. It is not the modernity of the wage-earning city-dweller; but it has in common with that condition a profound alienation between those in authority and their minions.

In censuring the English system of wages, we much more condemn the rack-rent system of Ireland. Other things being equal, a system of tenancy is better than one of wages, for it is a step less in the scale of dependence; but a system of wages under the national aristocracy of England is better than a system of tenancy under the alien landlords of Ireland.[35]

The hatred between landlord and tenant is, in Davis's view, irremediable. It is a bitter irony that, writing just before the Famine, he should dismiss the two remedies for the land problem that the economic quacks and the landlords respectively recommended—emigration and extermination.[36] Yet he also dismisses one of the nostrums much favoured in Irish fiction—certainly in Edgeworth and Lady Morgan and a host of lesser writers—the return of the absentee landlord to his Irish estates to dispense economic wisdom and bring blessings on the head of a grateful tenantry by introducing various kinds of agricultural reform. This he calls 'pious Feudalism'. Davis's landlord is much more in the George Moore mould:

Is it not flat nonsense to represent the absentee recalled to this contentious and uncomfortable *province*, rejecting his religious and political prejudices, giving up London notions and Paris habits, and dealing out justice, economy, and seed oats to his *wondering* tenants, who . . . learn from him farming, quiet, loyalty, and Church-of-Englandism?[37]

What Davis envisages is a revolutionary return to the earliest system of land tenure Ireland had known—udalism. In desiring this, he reveals one of nationalism's strategies for the recuperation of the republican or socialist traditions—to rewrite utopia as Eden, to claim that what was originally in place was both compatible with human nature as such—('gavelkind is the law of human nature . . . was the universal law of mankind'[38]) and was characteristic of the nation as such. So antiquarianism has its political uses—as had long been recognized. In his essay 'Irish Antiquities', Davis praises the eighteenth-century scholars and fantasists Walker, Vallancey, and O'Halloran because they gave 'a dreamy renown to ancient Ireland',[39] besides making the path smooth for the music of Bunting and the national identifications of Moore's *Melodies*. But the French revolutionaries also had, however unwittingly, done what Irish nationalism was consciously seeking to do: 'Strange, unconscious antiquarians were Mirabeau and Danton, who treated primogeniture and landlordism as vulgar novelties, and restored the land to the people.'[40]

Part II of 'Udalism and Feudalism' is largely devoted to excerpts from various authorities about the state of the Irish peasantry as opposed to the condition of the people of Norway as described in a recent book; towards the close of part I, Davis explains that he has dwelt most on the economic benefits of udalism and small property, communal, ownership because these were the most questioned. The cultural benefits he claims are undisputed; the beneficial effects of the possession of a small estate 'on the family affections, on hardihood, on morals, on patriotism, are greater still; and the virtue and valour, the faith to God, and faith to country . . . are found in small states . . .'.[41] Thus Davis's form of cultural nationalism incorporates antiquarianism, radicalism, the Burkean love for the small platoon and hatred of Protestant Ascendancy, and an economic defence of the notion that the land is for the people, always was and always will be, despite the interventions of history, law, the British empire, and modernity. Only with the disintegration of these impersonal and interconnected forces will the national character be restored; only with that restoration will art flourish: 'We do not hope to see art advance much till national character is restored by the break up of two or three of the huge and hateful empires.'[42]

LANDLORDS AND SOIL: DAVITT, LALOR

Thomas Davis died in 1845 just before the Famine began; James
Clarence Mangan died in 1849 in the cholera epidemic that intensified its prolonged close. In those four years, the question of the
land of Ireland, its ownership, and the political and economic control over its produce, became, understandably, a highly charged
issue. Two writers in particular, James Fintan Lalor and Michael
Davitt, made the previously casual distinction between the land
and the soil of Ireland a governing element of their political analysis
of the catastrophe. In effect, ownership of the soil was interpreted by them as a national right; ownership of the land was an
individual claim. The solutions they provided were not realized,
even though the land system was indeed radically altered as a consequence of the Famine. In 1902 Davitt admitted that his 'plan of
Land Nationalisation' had failed: 'The plan was either disliked, or
misunderstood, or the principle on which it rested—national, as
against individual, lordship of the soil—did not appeal to the strong
human desire or passion to hold the land as "owner" which is so
inherent in Celtic nature.' [43] In addition, Parnell and the Irish Parliamentary Party had listened to the wishes of the tenant farmers,
'the preponderant political force in Ireland'. So 'the country has
remained . . . overwhelmingly for an "occupier ownership" of the
land as against the "national ownership" which Fintan Lalor pas-
sionately pleaded for after the great Famine, and which I have urged
almost in vain upon the acceptance of the Nationalists of my time.'[44]
Davitt is, of course, referring here to Fintan Lalor's famous letter of
19 April 1847 to Gavan Duffy, editor of the *Nation*, (which published
it on the 24th under the title *A New Nation*), and his article in the
first number of the *Irish Felon* newspaper (24 June 1848), in both of
which he warned the Irish landlords to commit themselves to Ireland, to their tenantry, and to the new Social Constitution that
he proposed for the country or to perish. What he called in the
1848 essay 'the first great Article of Association in the National
Covenant of organised defence and armed resistance' is described in
a famous passage:

On a wider fighting field, with stronger positions and greater resources than are afforded by the paltry question of Repeal, must we close for our final struggle with England, or sink and surrender. Ireland her own—Ireland her own, and all therein, from the sod to the sky. The soil of Ireland for the people of Ireland, to have and to hold from God alone who gave it—to have and to hold to them and their heirs for ever, without suit or service, faith or fealty, rent or render, to any power under Heaven. From a worse bondage than the bondage of any foreign government, from a dominion more grievous and grinding than the dominion of England in its worst days—from the cruellest tyranny that ever yet laid its vulture clutch on the soul and body of a country, from the robber rights and robber rule that have turned us into slaves and beggars in the land that God gave us for ours—Deliverance, oh Lord; Deliverance or Death—Deliverance, or this island a desert! This is the one prayer, and terrible need, and real passion of Ireland today, as it has been for ages.

Lalor's aim was, in one version, grandiose:

Not to repeal the Union, then, but to repeal the Conquest—not to disturb or dismantle the empire, but to abolish it forever—not to fall back on '82 but act up to '48—not to resume or restore an old constitution, but to found a new nation, and raise up a free people, and strong as well as free, and secure as well as strong, based on a peasantry rooted like rocks in the soil of the land—this is my object . . .[45]

In another version it was more specific. Lalor pleaded for what he called 'a combination of classes'. The movement for repeal of the Union was, he claimed, 'a question of the population'; but 'the land tenure question is that of the country peasantry'.[46] In merging them together in one enterprise he appeals to the power of the distinction between soil as a material–metaphysical possession and land as a political–legal entity. The nation is of the soil; the state is of the land.

'I hold and maintain that the entire soil of a country belongs of right to the people of that country, and is the rightful property not of any one class, but of the nation at large, in full effective possession, to let to whom they will on whatever tenures, terms, rents, services and conditions they will; one condition, however, being unavoidable, and essential, the condition that the tenant shall bear full, true, and undivided fealty, and allegiance to the nation . . . I hold further . . . that the enjoyment by the people of this right, of first ownership of the soil, is essential to the vigour and vitality of all other rights . . . For let no people deceive themselves, or be deceived by the words, and colours, and phrases, and forms, of a mock freedom, by constitutions and charters and articles, and franchises. These things are paper and parchment, waste and worthless. Let laws and institutions say what they will, this fact will be stronger than all laws, and prevail against them.[47]

From there, Lalor goes on to attack the landlords and recommend their removal and the assertion thereby of the rights of eight million people against the selfish interests of a class of eight thousand.

The laws of the land are, in this vision, dependent upon the rightful ownership of the soil. Soil is prior to land. It is actual and symbolic, the more symbolic because of its claim to sheer materiality. The romantic–nationalist conception of the soil, its identity with the nation, its ownership by the people, its priority over all the administrative and commercial systems that transform it into land, is the more powerful because it is formulated as a reality that is beyond the embrace of any concept. It does not belong to the world of ideas; it precedes the idea of the world as a politically and economically ordered system. This construct had great appeal for left-wing, socialist or proto-socialist activists like Lalor, Mitchel, and Davitt. It had equal appeal for those who identified the emergence of a bureaucratic, heavily administered society with modernity and espoused instead a conservative, reactionary vision of the nation, particularly of Ireland, as a territory not conducive to such rational-ized ordering. As in the instance of Burke, who regarded adminis-trative rationalization as an unnatural imposition of inhuman, geometric reason on the natural conditions of the traditional soil of France in the revolutionary period, Irish writers of the post-Famine generation and beyond rewrote the opposition to landlordism and to British rule as a characteristically national repudiation of modernity.

It is curious that Davitt should have believed that the 'Celtic' character's hunger for land should have made his dream of national ownership impossible. For the various figurings of national charac-ter that are produced in the late nineteenth and early twentieth centuries are generally concerned to portray the Celt as dreamy, imaginative, indifferent to the material world. It is appropriate that Lalor should speak in terms of classes and communities, peasant and town-dweller, because he wrote before the image of the Celt was fully formed. However, this very division between peasant and town-dweller, between one who is anchored in the soil and one who is tied to the petty disputes of politics and commerce, was readily recruited into the descriptions of national character that we find, contested indeed but confined within recognizable boundaries, in the writings of Yeats and Pearse, Joyce and Sigerson, William P. Ryan and Thomas MacDonagh. The apotheosis of the peasant and of the Celt readily allied itself with the notion that the soil was a sacred possession, mystically owned by the dispossessed (the peasantry) or disgracefully betrayed by the owners (the landlords).

NATIONAL CHARACTER AND THE INDIVIDUAL SELF: JOHN MITCHEL

The most effective, because the most influential, written response to the Famine was provided by John Mitchel, who saw it as an act of straightforward genocide.[48] At issue here is Mitchel's analysis of the relation of Ireland to the imperial system. He rereads the whole nineteenth-century story of gradual concessions to Catholic claims as no more than a strategic series of accommodations between the imperial interests of Britain and the recruitment of the Catholic landed and professional classes to their preservation. Catholic Emancipation, in particular, was an act that appeased this class of Catholics, turning them into 'West Britons from that day',[49] leaving 'the great multitudinous Celtic enemy'[50] more absolutely at London's mercy. O'Connell's great campaigns were disastrous for the Irish people; he 'bewitched them to their destruction';[51] his Catholicism blinded him to the church's hostility to freedom, his aristocratic background made him an enemy of republicanism. But, most of all, for forty years the 'open and noisy' Catholic Relief Agitation had pre-empted the 'secret and silent' Ribbon and Whiteboy movement that, in 'defiance of London Law, contemplated nothing less than social, ultimately political *revolution*'. It was for fear of the last that Britain had yielded to the first. It is at this point in his analysis that Mitchel produces his critique of the relationship between a state and imperial system and the individual. O'Connell was successful 'by virtue of being more intensely Irish, carrying to a more extravagant pitch all Irish strength and passion and weakness, than other Irishmen, led and swayed his people by a kind of divine, or else diabolic right.'[52]

O'Connell's individuality is, in fact, no more than an intensification of his corporate Irish identity or character. In his *History of Ireland* (1869), Mitchel attributes to the Irish Protestants a measure of that national character that O'Connell exemplifies. His description is perfectly recognizable to a reader of Edgeworth, the Banims, Lady Morgan, or Griffin. By the late eighteenth century,

there was recognizable in the whole character and bearing even of the Protestants, a certain dash of that generosity, levity, impetuosity, and recklessness which have marked the Celtic race since the beginning. They were capable of the most outrageous depravity and of the highest honour and rectitude: of the most insolent, ostentatious venality and corruption, as well as of the noblest, proudest independence. The formation of the modern composite Irish character is of course attributable to the amalgamation of the privileged Protestant colonists with the *converted* Irish, who had from time to time conformed to the Established Church.[53]

In an allegorical mode that had become almost *de rigueur* in Irish writing, Mitchel is assessing the weight of the relationship between the national and the individual. However, the entirely radical and new version of the recent events of Irish history from the days of the French Revolution to the Famine begins to exercise a refiguring pressure on the convention of the corporate character and its role within the historical sequence that is its manifestation and is also its progenitor. Mitchel is not yet quite capable of claiming that national character is constituted by those discourses that give it an anterior existence of which they are the later representations. But he is coming close to recognizing that, in Irish conditions, it is impossible to accept the division between the public and the private realms that is so widely accepted in Britain both as a political and an aesthetic 'truth'. Ireland cannot have an aesthetic of distance or of separation precisely because in it the operations of the imperial system of capital are so grossly visible and so fiercely coercive and brutal in their effects that no disguise, no system of ideological concealment, is possible. Yet, even when this is the case, the Irish analysis, variously conducted, still retains, as part of its dispute with this system, the notion of a national corporate character as both the site of resistance and also as the site of victimage. It cannot but be both. Mitchel, indeed, shares this bifocal vision of the national character with Marx and Engels, both of whom regarded the Irish as dependent on the English working classes for liberation and, conversely, as a potentially revolutionary force that would liberate their English working-class comrades.[54]

Part of Mitchel's importance is that he attempts to reconfigure this double role for the national character by producing a double narrative—the story of Ireland's ill-treatment and the story of his own—in which he attempts to escape the imprisoning category of the national by embedding Ireland's struggle against the British empire within the wider discourse of a 'Jacobin' revolt against the degradation of a society in which empire or colonialism was sustained merely by an economic system that was itself a commercial con-trick, a fictitious production of a fictitious money system. In doing this, he oddly combines elements from Burke's attack on the French revolutionary finances—now reassigned by Mitchel to Capital—with Burke's attack on the Protestant Ascendancy, with the literary constitution of Irish national character and the discourse of European degeneration. In combining these elements, he produces a composite form of the national allegory that becomes a startling account of revolutionary *ressentiment* and a nationalist critique of empire.

In the introductory narrative to *Jail Journal*, Mitchel pursues this identification in relation to himself:

The general history of a nation may fitly preface the personal memoranda of a solitary captive; for it was strictly and logically a *consequence* of the dreary story here epitomised, that I came to be a prisoner . . . 'The history of Ireland,' said Meagher to his unjust judges at Clonmel, 'explains my crime and justifies it.'[55]

But it is in the well-known Ego–Doppelgänger passage in *Jail Journal*, that the personal-national issue is most fully engaged. Doppelgänger is assigned the role of criticizing Ego's identification of his woes with those of the nation, of claiming that Ego's bitterness and thirst for vengeance has no other cause than his own sense of victimage. In response, Ego attempts to produce a political–philosophical position that, he wants to claim, is distinct from personal feelings, even though his personal plight is indeed the consequence of his having these convictions. In effect, he claims that his support of French republicanism in 1848 is a pragmatic matter; 'in the abstract', as he repeatedly says, he regards both monarchism and republicanism 'as being for the Western nations of Europe worn out',[56] most especially for Ireland. However, these political systems are sustained in their frail afterlives by the system of capital ('kept alive by the commercial world'). That in itself connects readily with his praise of France as the leading nation of the world—'Paris is the great moral metropolis of mankind'[57]—because, unlike the Anglo-Saxons, the French are not devoted to money-worship. Nor is the Ego's readiness to welcome a cataclysm that would break up the British empire and devastate Europe anything like what Doppelgänger calls 'a diseased longing for blood and carnage'.[58] France's mission to the world has nothing to do with its happiness; a nation, no more than an individual, has happiness as an end or goal. A nation must 'act with all the energy of its national life'; the truth it must speak it should 'utter in thunder'.[59] France, more than the United States, has given an exemplary lesson to the world, and still remains exemplary, because its revolution came out of the heartland of the *ancien régime*.[60] Ego is not a hater of England; he is a friend of the English people. What he hates is the English imperialist-capitalist system, the mill-owners and landlords and all those who operate a 'commercial world [that] is trading on fictitious capital'.[61] The soap-bubble of the national debt will burst; despite the fact that the extension of the national debt saved England from invasion and internal revolution, the price for this was paid by the Indians and the Irish—'the reeky shanks and yellow chapless skulls of Skibbereen!—and the ghosts of starved Hindoos in dusky millions'.[62] These are not accidents of the system; these atrocities are integral to it and the basis for its survival. Therefore, horrible as the violence of war may be, it is less horrible than 'the horrors of peaceful and constitutional famine':[63] 'Because the Irish have been taught peaceful agitation in their slavery, they have been swept by a plague of hunger worse than many years of bloody fighting, because they would not fight they have been made to rot off the face of the earth . . .'.[64]

Mitchel then goes on to invoke the spectacle of an Armageddon, calling on all Jacobins to take their place in the great battle that is to come. To Doppelgänger's objection that this is private revenge, not politics, Ego replies:

The vengeance I seek is the righting of my country's wrong, which includes my own . . . let Ireland's wrong be righted, and the wrong done to me and mine is more than avenged; for the whole is greater than the part. Now, Mein Herr, you have my theory of vengeance; and for such vengeance I do vehemently thirst and burn.[65]

The mobilization of the nation and of the individual within a concerted movement towards liberation through acknowledged violence from a system that uses unacknowledged violence is part of Mitchel's political programme. But it is not the most interesting part. Most of the objections to his fierceness and his revolutionary extremism—so-called—are anticipated by him in the Ego–Doppelgänger conversation. What is of more enduring interest is Mitchel's recognition that the colonial system is both an ally of and in some ways a retarding influence on the development of Capital; that this vacillation between the two systems has had disastrous consequences for Ireland, especially in the Famine years; and that there is, in such conditions, very little possibility of the self, the individual, ever gaining the opportunity even to indulge in the bourgeois illusion of the private self that can exist independently and autonomously, out of the tentacular reach of those systems that have actually produced the ideology of the private self as a disguise for their own operations. In Ireland, with Mitchel as with Burke, the aesthetic of the actual is inescapable—the actuality of a system that, in its disclosure, offers such unexampled and policed violence that no enchanted or enchanting distance can be gained from it. Most of all, such a system, so exposed, loses its most striking disguise—the pretence that it is not a system at all and that it is only those forms that oppose it, especially revolutionary forms, that deserve to be called systematic or theoretic and to be damned on that account.

Mitchel is aware of the power of propaganda, of media control, and of narrative—especially of a narrative that gains such a degree of consolidation that it becomes almost impossible to recognize the conditions and interests that gave rise to it. The first sentence of his introductory narrative to *Jail Journal* says it: 'England has been left in possession not only of the soil of Ireland, with all that lives and grows thereon to her own use, but in possession of the world's ear also. She may pour into it what tale she will: and all mankind will believe her.'[66]

In such a world 'Success is right and Defeat is Wrong'; in Ireland, this is a world dominated by the 'touching and sanctimonious tale of barbarian Celtic nature for ever revolting in its senseless, drifting way, against the genius of British civilization'. The tale might pass unchallenged if the 'last conquest of Ireland was indeed the final and crowning conquest'.[67] This is the time-frame that gives to much of Mitchel's work its apocalyptic and yet satiric force. Does last mean merely 'most recent' or does it mean a 'final' solution? In the case of Standish O'Grady, the apologist for the Ascendancy and the land-lords, the apocalyptic sense was not modified by satire, merely intensified by sarcasm or by anger.

TWILIGHT OF THE LANDLORDS: STANDISH O'GRADY

O'Grady has one story to tell—the standard nineteenth-century story of degeneration from a heroic past to a wretched present, a degeneration that is coincident with the decline in power of an aristocratic, landowning class and the rise of democracy and social-ism. It has affinities with Mitchel's account, most especially in its hostility to urban capitalism and the new global systems of finance that accompanied it and that both confirmed and threatened the survival of the empire. All O'Grady's writings in their immediate occasions respond to the post-Famine land changes, dominated by the depression of 1859–64, which resulted in a switch from tillage to pasture and the emergence of a 'greener' Irish landscape than before, and even more by the greater depression of 1879–82 and the ensuing Land War, the chief result of which was the eventual destruction of landlordism and the financing by the British government of a new system of tenant proprietorship.[68]

The landlords also had their role to play in this dispute about territory and the nature of the various claims to it. But O'Grady needs to supply a defence of the so-called aristocracy in terms that are wider and more hospitable than those of class or creed. He does this by figuring the heroic past of Ireland as one that is older than any other in Europe,[69] more complex and subtle in its stories than any other civilization and that is, above all, an image of permanent truth that must be recovered for use in the present time. In the introduction to his *History of Ireland: The Heroic Period* (1878), he says of the ancient Irish:

It is the same sky that bent over them, which shines or darkens over us. The same human heart beat in their breasts as beats among us today. All the great permanent relations of life are the same. Therefore, I think I am also justified in treating that old heroic history in connection with the enduring facts of nature and humanity. I do not like to contemplate that heroic age as vague, shadowy, and remote, and have not so contemplated it.[70]

This last remark seems odd in a text that is dominated by imageries of sunset and sunrise, mist and vapour, shadows and dim lights. But it has its peculiar rationale, one dependent upon the distinction between history and legend:

A nation's history is made for it by circumstances, and the irresistible progress of events; but their legends, they make for themselves. In that dim twilight region, where day meets night, the intellect of man, tired by contact with the vulgarity of actual things, goes back for rest and recuperation, and there sleeping, projects its dreams against the waning night and before the rising sun.[71]

This is obviously Yeatsian, even to the uncertain grammar of the first sentence and the premonitory indication of the political and cultural uses to which the poet was later to put occult theory and its fetish of dawn, twilight, sleep, dream. It is also a recognizable moment in the long discourse of Protestant Gothic which was, like Catholic nationalism, always seeking for a rhetoric that would both provide an analysis of the political question of the land and its ownership and also an account that would transpose its intractable features into another language.

But O'Grady's Gothic settings are less obliquely political than those of his contemporaries. In *The Crisis in Ireland* (1882), he blames Michael Davitt for dislodging 'the stone' that 'is the landed aristocracy of Ireland'[72] by releasing the forces of 'the Irish democracy' against it. He bemoans the slenderness of the chance of the Irish landed interest 'of making their escape with their pecuniary interests preserved',[73] identifies socialism as the 'more immediate and perhaps more terrible danger'[74] than democracy, attacks the American socialist Henry George as the preacher of the doctrine, shared by the Irish Land League, 'that the land of a people belongs to the whole people',[75] acknowledges that the Irish aristocracy appears to the mass of the people 'as the deadly foe of the Irish nation',[76] and claims that England has 'bit by bit, through the century, transferred the political power here from us to our enemies'[77] and that the Irish landlords have been in Ireland 'England's garrison and right hand',[78] have incurred hatred for that role, and are now to be removed from the 'soil'. This account culminates in his cry for the preservation of the landlords:

The preservation of the Irish landlords as a class . . . I most ardently desire the preservation of that class, noblest and best on Irish soil, to be, and to be felt and known to be, the highest moral element, the light, the ornament, and the conscience of the young barbaric power now ascending in our land, of this fierce, dark, vengeful democracy, soon to be let loose with all its savage instincts uncontrolled—a protection and covering of the new birth forming in Ireland's womb, the caul of the infant Republic . . .[79]

In *Toryism and the Tory Democracy* (1886), O'Grady returns at moments to his Gothic setting, claiming that England is now experiencing the calm before the storm of revolution. To prove this,

Consider but one phenomenon, the dusky flittings of certain birds not of the halcyon kind, and their cries. Karl Marx, Continental revolutionist, settling in London, there joyously maintaining that in the whole world there is not a country in which the conditions of revolution are as amply fulfilled as in England. Henry George, paying us two visits, a third soon to follow, his keen American eyes noting the same fact. Michael Davitt, with eyes no less keen for the signs of the times, labours between England and Ireland. Hyndman and his swart brood, seen and unseen, flit to and fro. Many others, too, of the same stormy petrel race. These are not indications of fair weather, but of foul.[80]

The only recourse for the landlords in such a plight is to throw away the English crutch that has made them into 'the most curious cripple of your kind ever witnessed',[81] abandon the moral weakness of 'neglect of duties and responsibilities, love of pleasure, sport, and ease, lack of union and public spirit, selfishness, stupidity, and poltroonery',[82] recover the force with which they put down the revolution of 1798 and meet 'Revolution number two'[83] with galvanized energy so that they might avoid the operation of the 'law by which corrupt aristocracies fall, crumble, and disappear'.[84] Ireland, in O'Grady's view, had seen three aristocracies come and go—the Celtic, the Hiberno-Norman, and now the Anglo-Irish.[85] They must now form a nucleus of followers tied to them by bonds 'stronger than the feudal feeling between chief and clansmen, stronger than the devotion of soldiers to a brave and popular general.'[86] In this, they will be different and superior to the employers of labour in commercial situations. For in the world of urban capital there are no such bondings and loyalties. The provocation of 'personal loyalty' and 'personal fear',[87] the production of 'discipline, concerted action, men massed, instructed, prompt to obey orders',[88] the discovery of human nature's 'love of orderly, harmonious movement, unity in multiplicity, general harmonious submission to central guiding will', all reinforced by additional aids like music, will be achieved by gentlemen, 'your men in authority'.[89] The mission of this class 'is a world one'[90] and 'this wayward Irish race . . . a tameless people this, none on the earth's surface in such need of whip and rein',[91] will gladly and with relief join in the reinauguration of Ireland, the Heroic Age, in the late nineteenth century. But in his famous pair of essays, entitled 'The Great Enchantment', O'Grady wonders why his programme for renewal has not been effective. 'These ludicrous breaks-down'[92] suffered by the Irish throughout their tragic history he assigns to

a national fault, perhaps a national crime which has checked our progress from century to century, which has brought about the destruction of aristocracy after aristocracy, and which bids fair, as I write, to involve us in one common ruin, and leave this land for the exploitation of tourist touts and commercial syndicates for the promotion of sport in waste countries.[93]

This national fault or crime is the worship of phantoms. Once worshipped, phantoms 'become endowed with a terrible and malignant vitality and activity'.[94] The phantasmal motif recurs here, again in the context of an argument, such as it is, about the retention of tradition, the refusal of modernity, the flaw at the heart of the national character or condition, the preservation of the land, which is also the soil in its more mystificatory renderings, the collusion between history and apocalypse that is Gothicized into the destruction of a class by a vaporous ideology (socialism) that has swept pandemically through a community and transmogrified it into a mob. In O'Grady, as in Yeats, Burke's French Revolution lives on; but Burke's proposed Irish Revolution, involving the political destruction of the Protestant Ascendancy, survives too. One is legend, the other history. O'Grady negotiates with a degree of desperation between the two.

Yet even when he turns on the landlords for their failure O'Grady continues to deploy the terminology of land, soil, earth. The landlords had managed to become 'as earthy and dull as the earth itself'. They had, in his account, lost their ardour and refinement and become brutish foxhunters, people who had come 'to despise your birthright . . . till the very clay of the earth is more intelligent than yours'.[95] The term 'earth' here descends to the lowest rank in the ontological scale. It is purely vegetative, pre-cultural. The landed aristocracy is no longer 'racy of the soil'; it has degenerated into the earth.

So, as these discursive formations proliferate, various alterations in the status of their governing concepts become clear. Recovery of speech and recovery of land are allied projects; but their deepest alliance is with the loss of speech and the loss of land. The nationalist emphasis is, obviously, on recovery; the unionist emphasis is on loss. Neither grouping, however, has mastery over a form of linguistic representation that can embody its condition. For it is not merely a matter of which language—Irish or English—that should be chosen as a medium of representation—even though that is itself important. It is a matter of discovering a regime of representation in which the chosen language can produce the desired meanings. I have been arguing that a civilizational composite formation, national character, was central to any such regime. But as its connections with the projects of recovery and loss altered, it too had to be revised in order to accommodate such changes in the politics of desire. The revisionary model was already in place in Europe; it needed only to be adopted or adapted in and to Ireland. That model exchanged a national for a racial character and, in doing so, made it possible—all too possible perhaps—to link that racial character with a racial destiny that still retained, even exaggerated, its fiercely antimodernist ambition. The Celt as a racial formation was now transposed from its nationalist, antiquarian origins of the eighteenth century into a pan-European *combinatoire* of evolutionary destiny, the preservation of difference, even of anachronism, as a refusal of those adaptations needed to survive into the world of international capital and the nation-state. By remaining a nation and refusing to be a state, by sacralizing not the soil, or the land, but the territory of Ireland as a site of difference, the Celt could pursue his or her destiny against the grain of modernity.

The crisis of the 1840s in Europe and in Ireland, culminating in the 1848 revolutions and in the Famine, was understood by both Mitchel and O'Grady to have a spectral element within it. Both identified it as financial; the emergent world of credit capitalism seemed to both to lack that specificity that the nation, in a renovated form, could preserve and reaffirm.[96] Mitchel made the connection between the new global financial system and the British empire. The destruction of Ireland as a specific civilization and place had been achieved by the incorporation of the country into the phantasmal system of international finance. The revolutions of 1848 were an attempt, on the part of the historic European nations, led by France, to resist this process. Political economy killed Ireland as a distinct civilization in order to possess it as an element within the abstract system of finance. O'Grady was just as hostile as Mitchel to the new forms of capital; but he saw that spectral capital had its companion in spectral socialism. Both of them were transnational, both were devoted to the destruction of traditional pieties. For him the landlords were the only class who could prevent this ruination; for Mitchel, it was the people as such who, had they risen up during the Famine, might have prevented the success of the new system. Mitchel brought the argument home to himself in *Jail Journal*; in the debate between his Ego and Doppelgänger, he confronted the experience of the spectral as an invasion into the recess of the private person and thus made of his personal plight an allegory of the plight of the nation. It was no accident that O'Grady should have invoked the image of Karl Marx in the British Museum as a harbinger of revolution. After all, the spectral element is never absent from Marx's famous analyses of the period, both in *The Eighteenth Brumaire of Louis Napoleon* and in *The Communist Manifesto* (1848) with its famous announcement: 'A spectre is haunting Europe—the spectre of communism.' O'Grady would have agreed. Spectral presences were attempting to take possession of traditional land. The most famous of these was himself a landlord.

LANDLORD AND SOIL: *DRACULA*

Gothic fiction is devoted to the question of ownership, wills, testaments, hauntings of places formerly owned, and, in its most commercially successful manifestation, Bram Stoker's *Dracula* (1897), to the story of an absentee landlord who is dependent in his London residence on the maintenance of a supply of soil in which he might coffin himself before the dawn comes. With him, too, there is a crucial distinction between land, which he buys in England, and his soil, which he brings with him in what is a literal version of the coffin-ship—that resonant image from Famine times—that is wrecked on the Yorkshire coast, at Whitby. This peculiar version of the native soil is an inversion or perversion of the nationalist version propagated by Lalor. For, in this instance, it is the native material that is imported into the 'foreign' legal system of English property relations. In addition, it is a contaminated cargo; Dracula's soil is also his filth, his contaminant. Attached to the soil by day, 'racy of the soil' in a perverse rendering of the epigraph of the *Nation* newspaper, he moves, like an O'Grady version of the Celtic hero, between dusk and dawn. But, landlord that he is, with all his enslaved victims, his Celtic twilight is endangered by the approach of a nationalist dawn, a Home Rule sun rising behind the old Irish Parliament. Dracula's dwindling soil and his vampiric appetites consort well enough with the image of the Irish landlord current in the nineteenth century. Running out of soil, this peculiar version of the absentee landlord in London will flee the light of day and be consigned to the only territory left to him, that of legend. Like O'Grady's and Yeats's Anglo-Irish, he will be expelled from history to enter the never-never land of myth, demonized more effectively but also more clandestinely than by a Lalor, Mitchel, or Davitt.[97] O'Grady's later sponsorship of a policy of internal immigration, from Dublin to the Midlands, from sedentary trades to the physical labour of the soil, is an extension of his lament for the loss of landlordism and an attempt to replace it with a mystical version of nationalist pastoral that has itself a history stretching from AE (George Russell) through Darrell Figgis to de Valera.[98]

However, the political–sexual implications of the Dracula story have been thoroughly investigated in recent years.[99] It is scarcely necessary to note that, in this novel, even more than in the works of Sheridan Le Fanu or in the poetry, plays, fiction, and essays of Yeats, the dominant condition of the protagonists is that of sleeping, dreaming, stupefaction, exhaustion, enervation—all the varieties of supine vulnerability that both produce and are produced by the monstrous images that attend upon such seduced and seductive victims.[100] Such languor, especially dangerous with the Count in the vicinity, has to be contested by an answering energy, supplied with an alarmingly boyish enthusiam, by the Anglo-American cohort of men. The novel's oppositions are multiple and glaring: West against

East, technology against superstition, good money against bad money, men against women, traditional woman against New Woman, madness against sanity, blood against spirit, lasciviousness against chastity, mobility against immobility, health against degeneration, the Living against the Undead. It also has a series of obsessive nightmare images—the claustrophobia of bedrooms, cells, houses, vaults, coffins, all of them locked or otherwise barred to keep danger in or to keep it out; sinister, protean animals such as bats, rats, and wolves; spectral legions of the damned invading the bodies of the city crowd; historical chronology, and time itself, dissolved into legendary timelessness, the physical body dematerializing into a contagion. In short, the full apparatus of Gothic fiction is imported to create the impression of a rich, Western–Christian civilization under threat from a demonic force which is foreign and Eastern, yet also deeply embedded within, banished but not extinguished by the bright light of technological modernity.

Yet it is in the representation of speech that the novel creates effects akin to those that are to be found in *Castle Rackrent*, *The Collegians*, and a whole series of Irish nineteenth-century novels. *Dracula* is a mosaic of reports, a complicated timetable of recorded conversations in journals, diaries, letters, newspaper clippings, shipping logs, memoranda, telegrams—even a phonographic diary. It is entirely fitting that such a painstaking assemblage should be offered as evidence of the truth and yet, in the final 'Note' by Jonathan Harker, dismissed. This is a true story, yet an incredible one; Dracula existed and yet it is difficult even for the tellers of the story to believe he did so, a mere seven years later:

It was almost impossible to believe that the things which we had seen with our own eyes and heard with our own ears were living truths. Every trace of all that had been was blotted out . . . I took the papers from the safe where they had been ever since our return so long ago. We were struck with the fact, that in all the mass of material of which the record is composed, there is hardly one authentic document, nothing but a mass of typewriting, except the later note-books of Mina and Seward and myself, and Van Helsing's memorandum. We could hardly ask anyone, even did we wish to, to accept these proofs of so wild a story.[101]

Of course, the final Note itself is part of the typewritten mass which is the novel. But even the implicit distinction here, between the typewritten and the handwritten, the inauthentic and the authentic, repeats the novel's incessant, anxious defence of the various borders that demarcate its multiple and versatile oppositions and that, for all their apparent fixity, are nevertheless constantly invaded, violated, and dissolved. The text's final distinction between kinds of writing and the truths they carry is dissolved by the very fact that it is produced as print, a mode in which handwritten material is reduced to the inauthenticity of type forms.[102] Nor can the obvious fact that the characters in the novel are all 'types' be ignored either. All of the specific individuals belong to a 'type', even Dracula himself. For type is infinitely reproducible; and the battle in this novel is a battle for reproduction—of the Undead against the living. The Undead are reproduced by a form of illicit and orgasmic sex; the living are reproduced by marriage. It is, once more, the family against the mob; traditional piety against a revolutionary threat that produces, by perversion of the 'normal'—even to the contamination of blood[103]—the ghastly, miasmic crowd.

Just as writing has its hierarchy, so too has speech. We learn as early as chapter II that Dracula is anxious to master the English language so that his strangeness of speech will not call attention to him when he is in London; the madman Renfield switches from foul-mouthed berating to silence, from asocial meanderings to the formal 'gentlemanly' speech of his plea to Godalming, Quincy Morris, Van Helsing, and Seward in chapter XVIII; there is a whole cast of minor characters from the back streets of London whose demotic speech is laboriously rendered, as is the Whitby speech and accent of old Mr Swales; Quincy Morris's speech is stereotypically Texan and laconic; dominating all of these non-standard versions of English is, of course, Van Helsing's eccentric speech and accent, made the more unfamiliar by his abstruse learning and vocabulary. It is, at one level, the jargon of the expert; at another, it is an anachronistic speech because it is expert in the lore of the past, the marginal, which is also, simultaneously, the lore of the present, since it is immemorial. But it is in the speech of the central women, Mina Harker and Lucy Westenra, that the novel's ideology is most blatantly exposed. Both are in command of standard English, but Lucy's English is differentiated from Mina's from the outset by virtue of its initially implicit sexual content, evident in her eager anticipation of her forthcoming marriage, and ultimately explicit in her enslavement to Dracula and her frank sexual invitation to Arthur to kiss her as she is dying (chapter XII). It is only after her orgasmic second death by Arthur's hand that he is permitted by Van Helsing to kiss her. Mina, on the other hand, speaks the language of love and chastity, not of sex and promiscuity. She is the one whom Van Helsing constantly praises as the true heroine:

She is one of God's women, fashioned by His own hand to show us men and other women that there is a heaven where we can enter, and that its light can be here on earth. So sweet, so true, so noble, so little an egoist— and that, let me tell you, is much in this age, so sceptical and selfish.[104]

In the end, Godalming, Seward, Jonathan are happily married; Mina is the mother of Quincy, the child named after the heroic American who must, nevertheless, be banished from this Victorian British ending. It is the speech of Mina, of marriage, that prevails; Van Helsing's final words—no longer disfigured by foreignness, but specifically a literary English,[105]—canonize her. This is the Gothic equivalent of the national marriage of the early century. Deformation of speech has been righted, the land has been cleansed of its demonic landlord, sexual degeneration has been prevented by chaste heroics, the family has asserted its values against those of the mob. Politically, the family is—as it had been for so long since the French Revolution—the embodiment of the nation and the national values, and it speaks the nation without flaw. Mina and Jonathan are national types, and it is in type—the type of Mina the typist—that deformation is overcome.[106]

Ultimately, the question of the land and its relation to the soil lost its political force as landlordism faded and tenant proprietorship became common. But it left a cultural deficit that had to be met. The territory of Ireland, with all its Gothic and all its nationalist graves, with all its estates and farms, its Land Acts and its history of confiscations, was in need of redefinition by the early years of the nineteenth century. Land, soil, and speech remained imbricated with one another in a sequence of relationships that was not in itself obscure but that needed to make a fetish of obscurity for its articulation. Hence Gothic and Celtic twilights, hence the blurring of history into legend, hence the introduction of folklore and occultism, hence the reintroduction of the Irish language and of its ancient literature as a repository of a native eloquence that had almost been lost in the mists of time but still survived in the emaciated economic circumstances of peasant life—all of these were necessary in order to identify the relationship between land, soil, and speech as radically mysterious. The identification of the mysterious, unreal, or phantasmal element in the Irish situation was itself the product of an analysis of that situation. It was a way of specifying colonial otherness, a nationalist attempt to claim for Ireland an exceptional status and, at the same time, to assert that this exceptionalism lay precisely in Ireland's retention of traditional, even immemorial, feeling, no matter how deformed it might appear to be or to have become in the prevailing conditions of a fundamentally British commercial and technological modernity.

NATIONAL CHARACTER, NATIONAL IDENTITY: JOYCE

But there was another position available for cultural analysis. It was one that could retain the notion that there was a tense and problematic relationship between attachment to the native territory and the capacity to speak a language in which that attachment could be articulated. Moreover, it would also retain the notion that the tension between these could be represented as a fierce battle between inertia and energy and that the site of this battle would always be a place that was in some sense undefined. It would be a crepuscular setting. That was the position of exile, the high cultural form of emigration. It was a form of dispossession that retained—imaginatively—the claim to possession. It was a condition in which modernity, associated with the new country in which the exile was borne, could be played off against inherited (and stifling) tradition, associated with Ireland, the place that had been left. It was, in effect, a position occupied by writers of the town population—Dubliners

like Shaw, Wilde, O'Casey, Beckett, and the implacably cosmopolitan Mayo man, George Moore. Joyce, of course, is the most famous
of Irish exiles in this regard. For the Dublin, the Ireland, he wrote of
was, in an important sense, a nowhere, a territory not yet represented, a place caught between geography and history, between
eloquence and aphasia, crippling inertia and a new-found energy.
Dubliners is the classic text for this condition, one in which exile is
internalized and speech gagged, in which the relation between eloquence and aphasia is brilliantly revised by the production of a style
which eloquently represents aphasia.

Dublin, in these stories, is not only a site of paralysis. It is a place
where speech is confined within cliché, where repression excites its
victims to cling to phantoms of liberation while steadfastly remaining within banal routines. Only once, in 'The Dead', does an actual
space for liberation open, in the west of Miss Ivors and Michael
Furey, different although these are from one another. But they have
in common a link with the 'tradition' that the west had come to
represent—the tradition of the old language, the tradition of an old
song. Both the language and the song bespeak the dead; yet they
also bespeak the unexpected revival among the living of an alternative to their conventional gentility of culture.[107] The Ireland that
suddenly opens beyond the hitherto enclosed city of Dublin is certainly a phantasmal place, inhabited by the swirling souls of the
dead. But it *is* a place, a geographical reality as well as a symbolic
'region', the territory of the Famine dead and of the revival of the
culture of which they were the supposed possessors. This is the
world of the Joycean Undead, a Transylvania that has unmasked
itself as lying beyond the Shannon, a traditional boundary in Irish
history and legend. Dublin is, indeed, a world of the Undead too;
but these Dubliners are the Undead of modernity; the rest of the
country contains the Undead of tradition, the phantoms that, in the
writings of Yeats or Pearse, threaten to undergo a revival that is as
attached to blood and violence as the vampires of Stoker. But they
are also attached to articulation, to the rediscovery of speech,
the revitalization of the anaemic English language that so many
Irish writers—Yeats again, Synge, Lady Gregory—advocated so
earnestly. It was important to be earnest about this issue. The

renovation of language and the reconstruction of the national territory were intimate aims. De-Anglicizing Ireland involved the de-Anglicization of the English language.

In *A Portrait of the Artist as a Young Man*, Stephen experiences this tension between geographic space and historical time and, ultimately, between speechlessness and mastery of speech, as he approaches 86 St Stephen's Green, the site of University College. The house once belonged to an anti-Catholic Anglo-Irishman, Buck Whaley. Now it belongs to the Jesuits. But Stephen's experience, which immediately precedes the famous language episode with the Dean of Studies, is of a place that recedes away from the Ireland of history, a place that is in between two dispensations, an interstitial absence:

> The corridor was dark and silent but not unwatchful. Why did he feel that it was not unwatchful? Was it because he had heard that in Buck Whaley's time there was a secret staircase there? Or was the jesuit house extraterritorial and was he walking among aliens? The Ireland of Tone and of Parnell seemed to have receded in space.[108]

This, along with the subsequent conversation with the Dean, is a critical moment in Stephen's obverse vision of Ireland. Previous to this his walk through the city, from north to south, had been an exercise in the rhetoric of familiarity; now this is replaced by the rhetoric of estrangement. Neither cancels the other. They subsist together. A territory is possessed and then the possessor of it is dispossessed. Exile is most profound when it is experienced at home.

It was at such moments in his fiction that Joyce rewrote the idea of national character and replaced it by the idea of a character in search of a nation to which he (Joyce–Stephen) could belong. The convergence of the geography of Dublin and the history of Ireland produces the extraterritorial condition in which the possibility of a collective, national character begins to disappear. Its banality is replaced by the 'originality' of a character, like the Stephen Dedalus of both *Portrait* and, even more, *Ulysses*, who seeks to create himself by refusing all those forces—Mother Ireland, Mother England, Mother Church, the mythic First Mother Eve, and his own mother—that threaten to make him nothing more than an inheritor, with a language or discourse that is theirs, not his. This inevitably leads Joyce to that curious mapping of sexual and national identity that reaches such ambiguous culminating moments as the Molly Bloom soliloquy that ends *Ulysses* or the Anna Livia Plurabelle soliloquy that ends *Finnegans Wake*. Is this the language of emancipation or merely its phantom? Is it the language of the emancipated or is that merely its pretension?[109] The point at issue here is that the escape from national character into a version of identity, or the escape into a newly constituted version of national character, is consistently mediated through a recourse to the phantasmal. The phantasmal subject and the phantasmal territory do not become substitutes for something actual. Their virtuality is the consequence of the analysis of the actual; the real subject and the real country are, in Irish conditions, representable only as the unreal—the unreally real.

No matter how the initial Burkean distinction is made, it returns the maker to the initial crux. If there is a distinction between 'traditional culture' and 'modernity' and if that distinction is understood to be effective only when the first of these is national or native (to Britain, Ireland, 'human nature') and the second foreign and coercive to the first, then 'culture' must be derived from the concept of the 'national', even though the syncopated logic of Burke and so many others since wishes to claim that culture is identical with the national. In such an identity claim lies the justification for the stereotyping of communities. Equally, the claim to modernity, especially when it parades itself as cultural pluralism, suffers the same fate. It may be a benign thing to say that cultures should not be oppressed, that every culture has its right to exist. But that is to concede to the notion of a Celtic or Anglo-Saxon culture or any mutation of these or any of the other myriad categories into which cultural communities are penned (if that is the word). As Walter Benn Michaels puts it:

For insofar as our culture remains nothing more than what we do and believe, it is impotently descriptive. The fact, in other words, that something belongs to our culture, cannot count as a motive for our doing it since, if it *does* belong to our culture we *already* do it and if we don't do it . . . it doesn't belong to our culture . . . It is only if we think that our culture is not whatever beliefs and practices we actually happen to have but is instead the beliefs and practices that should properly go with the sort of people we happen to be that the fact of our belonging to our culture can count as a reason for doing it. But to think this is to appeal to something that must be beyond culture and that cannot be derived from culture precisely because our sense of which culture is ours must be derived from it. This has been the function of race.[110]

National character and the character of nations are both rooted in a concept of culture which they are perfectly willing to expose and develop. But the state that is formed out of such notions and that pretends to go beyond them needs an idea of the collective identity that can be assigned to culture *tout court*, not to something else from which culture derives. For the racial idea, so widely propagated and given the status of a scientific truth in the nineteenth century, has only been able to survive within the transposed, benign discourse of cultural pluralism. As Burke clearly saw, any radical version of individuality that breaks away from the collective wisdom and/or prejudices of the community, is the enemy; it is the barbaric and superstitious energy that would kill patriarchy and affection together.

Once continuity is broken,

No part of life would retain its acquisitions. Barbarism with regard to science and literature, unskilfulness with regard to arts and manufactures, would infallibly succeed to the want of a steady education and settled principle; and thus the commonwealth itself would, in a few generations, crumble away, to be disconnected into the dust and powder of individuality, and at length dispersed to all the winds of heaven.

To avoid, therefore, the evils of inconstancy and versatility, ten thousand times worse than those of obstinacy and the blindest prejudice, we have consecrated the state, that no man should approach to look into its defects or corruptions but with due caution, that he should never dream of beginning its reformation by its subversion, that he should approach to the faults of the state as to the wounds of a father, with pious awe and trembling solicitude. By this wise prejudice we are taught to look with horror on those children of their country who are prompt rashly to hack that aged parent in pieces and put him into the kettle of magicians, in hopes that by their poisonous weeds and wild incantations they may regenerate the paternal constitution and renovate their father's life.[111]

Some of the children of Burke's own country, seeking to conjugate the inherited discourse of nation and state, traditional prejudice and radical originality, racial and national character, paternal solicitude and the dismembering of the father, pursued and were pursued by that image. We have looked at a few of these instances; others, particularly James Clarence Mangan and John Millington Synge, offer themselves as restless inhabitants of a paradigm that was both cultural and racial in an increasingly polarized field of contestation between community and crowd, on the one hand, and individuality as embodiment of or liberation from the national character, on the other.

THREE

Control of Types, Types of Control: The Gothic, the Occult, the Crowd

THE IRISH CHARACTER IN PRINT

I t is conventional to say that Charlotte Brooke's famous volume, *Reliques of Irish Poetry* (1789), which presents the original Irish along with her English translations, was a literary event of signal importance in the development of a specifically national literary tradition that was to claim for itself a bilingual ancestry. The volume has premonitory 'Edgeworthian' features—preface, footnotes, a self-effacing tribute to the 'superior genius of a Father',[1] an anxiety to explain to an English audience the native characteristics of this ancient literature and to hope thereby to make the political relations between Ireland and England less harsh. The example of Macpherson's *Ossian* is clearly present to her mind when she writes of the Irish bards exhibiting a

glow of cultivated genius,—a spirit of elevated heroism,—sentiments of pure honor,—instances of disinterested patriotism,—and manners of a degree of refinement, totally astonishing, at a period when the rest of Europe was nearly sunk in barbarism: And is not all this very honorable to our countrymen? Will they not be benefited,—will they not be gratified, at the lustre reflected on them by ancestors so very different from what modern prejudice has been studious to represent them?[2]

The standard dispute between barbarism and civility is deftly re-hearsed by Brooke to enforce her plea for greater intimacy between the 'British muse' and her Irish 'elder sister'; these 'sweet am-bassadresses of cordial union' might win for the Irish the esteem and finally the affection of the British. So, Brooke's 'firsts' are three: the first extended translation of 'polite literature' from Irish into English; the first presentation of Irish and English enjoying 'parity of esteem' in a literary work; the first outspoken claim for literature to effect a conciliation that would prefigure and lead to political recon-ciliation. But Brooke has another, less noticed, claim to priority. Her book was 'the first purely literary work containing printing in the Irish character which was ever published in Dublin'.[3] The typeface itself has been known variously as the Brooke, sometimes the Bonham (after the printer), and now more correctly the Parker typeface (after Stephen Parker who cut it in his foundry).[4]

Another author of a seminal work of translation who had a typeface named after him was James Hardiman, whose *Irish Minstrelsy, or Bardic Remains of Ireland with English Poetical Transla-tions* (1831) inaugurated a cultural debate on the respective claims of Irish Protestants and Irish Catholics to nationhood, variously advo-cated for the next 150 years as a Celtic–Gaelic, an Anglo-Gaelic, or an Anglo-Irish possession, condition or vocation. The debate was initially dominated by Sir Samuel Ferguson, in his famous review of Hardiman in the *Dublin University Magazine*, published between April and November 1834.[5] But Ferguson's powerful and partisan critique failed to recognize that the presentation of the Irish lan-guage in an Irish typeface was itself, for Hardiman and for many others, before and since, an integral part of that cultural debate. Although the typeface of *Irish Minstrelsy* is sometimes called the Hardiman type, it is more accurately the Figgins type, from the foundry of that name. It had been prepared for the second volume of the great *Rerum Hibernicarum Scriptores Veteres*, by the eighteenth-century antiquarian Charles O'Conor. It was published in 1825.[6]

This work and Hardiman's are the only two works ever published in this type.[7] In his introduction to his work, Hardiman remarks in a footnote that he sent the first Irish type to find its way into Munster to a friend of his in Cork, in 1819.[8] This particular typeface (not the Hardiman type) was cut by James Christie in 1815 in Dublin and was used in the following year for the second edition of Charlotte Brooke's *Reliques*. It was used also in the important anthology by Edward Walsh and John O'Daly, *Reliques of Irish Jacobite Poetry* (1844). In his introduction to *The Irish Language Miscellany* (1876), John O'Daly informs us that

at the urgent request of many friends to Irish literature, we have used Roman instead of the old Irish types, which has entailed upon us much additional labour; and which, most probably, if not generally approved of in the present instance, shall not be used by us again.[9]

In the second edition of Edward Walsh's *Irish Popular Songs* (1883), a letter from Walsh to John O'Daly, dated 10 January 1844, contains the plea:

'*I earnestly beg of you*, unless you wish to ruin *the Irish character of the work*, not to print your *Irish* in either the Roman or Italian character.

   The old Irish type is the type of their nationality; alter that, and *you destroy it* . . .[10]

The links between O'Conor, Brooke, Hardiman, Walsh, and O'Daly in relation to typefaces, the Irish language, translation, and national revival are significant. Irish needed a national typeface in which it could be printed; further, it needed one that was cut in Ireland, not in England; and it needed one that could effectively negotiate the counterclaims of Roman and Celtic typefaces and the economic issues that these raised. For Roman type was commercially much the more sensible to use; culturally, it could be argued, it involved a mutilation of the language, comparable to the Roman representation of Greek or the later Roman representation of German. It is a dispute that is clearly reproduced in the various attempts (most of them to be found in novels, folklore collections, and travel writings), to represent even the English speech of the Irish by various and usually unsightly strategies in Roman type—italicization, phonetic spellings, agglomerations of aitches to indicate aspirants, various forms of contraction. This was also true of popular texts in Irish. Deformity, even monstrousness of appearance, contrasted with upright and disciplined form, is both a typographical as well as a social–political feature in Irish discourse. It is a story of a national character in search of a national character—one that is dominated by the names of foundries (Moxon, Watts, Christie), cities (Louvain, Rome, Paris), learned societies (Irish Archaeological Society, Keating Society), authors (Brooke, Hardiman), presses (Dun Emer, Cuala, the Three Candles, Dolmen), and designers (George Petrie, Colm O Lochlainn, Liam Miller). Yet even the technical discussions of typefaces were governed by the paradigm of Celt and Roman, indiscipline and discipline, authenticity and inauthenticity.[11] Racial or cultural difference—apparently distinct but in truth identical with one another—demanded the production of racial types in the physiognomies of print as much as in the physiognomies of people.

However, there was an additional sectarian element to this history. From 1571 to 1721, almost every book in the Irish language, published in Ireland, England, or Europe, was a work of religious propaganda. Catholic works had to be published abroad, since they were banned in Ireland; they were printed in the Irish typeface, at Louvain and Rome. Proselytizing works on behalf of the Protestant religion were published in Roman type, although none appeared in the Irish language for almost seventy years between the mid-1720s and the mid-1790s. Since war and coercion made the creation of national fonts and a printing industry impossible, Roman type was used for a number of books in the Irish language by Catholics. The Moxon Irish type was manufactured for the printing of Bishop Bedell's translation of the Old Testament into Irish—*Leabhuir na Seintiomna* (1685)—and remained the standard type for books in Irish for over a century. During the Celtic Revival of the late eighteenth century other typefaces, like the Brooke, appeared. In the first quarter of the nineteenth century, five new Irish typefaces were produced—those by Barlow, Christie, Watts, Fry, and Figgins.[12] The importance of Brooke and Hardiman is further heightened when it is realized that their aesthetically pleasing but commercially

expensive typefaces were essentially cultural weapons in a war of
religious and political propaganda. In giving priority to the cultural
element, they were not ignoring the religious and political; rather,
they were, as already mentioned, promoting cultural accord as a
means to the resolution of strife in these other areas.

The evangelical movement of early nineteenth-century England
had its Irish extensions in the efforts of the Hibernian Bible Society
and the British and Foreign Bible Society which, among other publications, produced *An Tiomna Nuadh* (The New Testament) in 1818
in Watts's face and *The First Two Books of the Pentateuch* in 1819 in
Fry's type, the type that became standard for the next fifty years.
The resistance to the Protestant evangelical campaign took many
forms, chief among them the highly charged debate concerning the
prophecies of Pastorini, which identified 1825 as the year of the
extinction of Protestantism,[13] and the official Catholic–papal policy,
which decried the translation of the Bible into the Irish vernacular as
a threat to the faith.[14]

Between the 'high' cultural works of Brooke and Hardiman and
these evangelical texts, there was a mass of other popular works—
catechisms, religious tracts, ballads—in which the perennially vexed
question of the reading audience was addressed with equal degrees
of versatility and confusion. What Niall O Cíosáin has called 'a
transitional phase of literacy', in which the readership was understood to be 'one which spoke Irish but which had learned to read in
English', confronted publishers with the dilemma of which orthographic system to use in Roman—the Irish orthographic system or
phonetic spelling in the English language system?[15] Hardiman's
work was, both in its typography and in its themes, a rebuke to the
English influence that had so mangled the native tradition. It is not
only a specifically pro-Catholic work; it champions the Catholic
cause by offering—as Bunting and Moore in their different ways had
done before him—the cultural heritage of the Irish as one in which
poetry and music were inextricably and uniquely entwined. Taking
up the claim that had been popularized since Sir Charles Vallancey's
Collectanea de Rebus Hibernicis (1786–1804), that the Irish had an
'Eastern' or 'Phoenician' origin,[16] he claims that music in Ireland has
been proved 'to have existed as far back as the annals extend, its

origin, like that of our round towers, must be sought for in the East.'[17] He then goes on to contrast the fortunes of Irish music and Irish poetry:

The music of Ireland is better known to the world, at the present day, than its poetry. In the sweetest strains of natural feeling, the former found its readyway to every heart, and became endenizened in every clime, while the latter, wrapped in an ancient and expressive but proscribed and insulated language, has been generally neglected, particularly since the spread of the English tongue amongst us, and the downfall of the Milesians.[18]

Hardiman's Irish bards 'were, invariably, Catholics, patriots, and jacobites',[19] who refused to Anglicize their names and were on that account considered rude and unlearned. With the destruction of the Courts of Poetry in the wars of the sixteenth century, the Irish language lost its aristocratic prestige:

Thenceforth it was banished from the castle of the chieftain, to the cottage of his vassal, and, from having been the cherished and cultivated medium of intercourse between the nobles and the gentry of the land, it became gradually limited to the use of the uneducated poor. No wonder, then, that it should have been considered harsh and unpolished when thus spoken, but it was as unjust to estimate our language by such a standard, as it would be to judge of the English by the jargon of Yorkshire . . . In the last century, the inquisitors of the Irish parliament denounced it as the dialect of that phantom of their political frenzy, popery. According to a favourite mode of native reasoning, it was resolved to reduce the poor Catholics to a state of mental darkness, in order to convert them into enlightened protestants. A thick cloud of ignorance soon overspread the land; and the language of millions ceased to be a medium of written communication.[20]

Hardiman's account of the fall of the aristocratic Catholic Jacobite civilization and the consequent fall of the Irish language from social grace was influential in its main substance, particularly in its emphasis on the breakdown and dilapidation of an aristocratic system that then became, in its dispersal, the possession of the common people. Here is *in nuce* the account of the Munster poets that John O'Daly and ultimately Daniel Corkery were to construct between 1850 and 1925. But this history is accompanied by a subtext in Hardiman's footnotes that deserves our attention here. In these notes, he not only claims for Irish music and the Irish language an 'eastern' origin; he also claims that Irish, unlike Scots Gaelic, was not Romanized into print. The bards were the chief scribes; they retained the purity of Irish orthography and grammatical structure. Irish, therefore, had more claim to purity and originality than its Scottish counterpart.[21] Here Hardiman is joining with Theophilus O'Flanagan and a host of others in combating the prestige and claims to 'originality' made by James Macpherson on behalf of the Scots.[22] But he, more than they, claims that Irish purity was preserved because there were so few Irish print fonts. Ireland escaped Roman type and remained Celtic by remaining scribal.[23] It is indeed the case that the Irish scribal tradition survived from the insular script of the seventh century to the middle of the twentieth century.[24] It was generally considered that the best Irish typefaces were those that retained the character-istics of the native script. Hardiman's and Brooke's were notable efforts in that direction, although the types designed by George Petrie between 1835 and 1856 were perhaps the finest reconciliation of Irish script with roman type. Appropriately, John O'Donovan's great translation of the *Annals of the Kingdom of Ireland* (1851) was printed in the early Petrie A type.[25]

The web of relationships between speech, script, typeface, national character, religious and political oppression, and national retrieval is complex indeed. I want to trace just one strand or filiation that has been given prominence in the discussion of Hardiman and Brooke. It consists in a sequence that has authenticity as its root and inauthenticity as its terminus. But the larger sequence is reproduced *in parvo* at each individual stage. The speech of the Irish, for instance, is taken to be wholly authentic, whether it be in the Irish or the English language. But every claim to authenticity is shadowed by an answering inauthenticity. For that speech is also a mutilated speech, since it is often in a mixture of the two languages, and that macaronic mix involves a deformation of both. Yet even that produces its opposite since such a mix, whether it be called Hiberno-English, Anglo-Irish, a dialect, or a patois, is equally capa-ble of claiming for itself the authenticity which, through its lack of purity, it had lost, and now, through its impurity, regains. Further, speech combined with music into song can claim an almost ethereal

authenticity; yet, as Tom Moore had demonstrated, both the music
and the words could be altered into forms that were the less authentic for being the more commercial. The cult of Carolan, the efforts
of Bunting, Hardiman, O'Daly, Petrie, and many others were, in
some measure, an antidote to the success of Moore. Yet that success
had been an act of retrieval and had thereby signalled that any
comparable or competing act would, if successful, bring with it the
charge of corruption. What was really authentic could not be retrieved and still retain its original condition. It would bear within
it—either in footnotes, headnotes, introductions, translations, glos-
saries—the marks of its historical transmission. Speech, to be transmitted, had to be what was already said; it was always after,
although it was an afterness that could still attempt to claim for itself
the presence of anteriority. It was the more able to do so when it
acted in the name of a community, when it claimed to record not
what an individual said but what was characteristic of the speech
habits of that individual's community.

Script is secondary to speech but prior to print. The archive of
Irish manuscripts, a millennium thick, was, like the scribes themselves and like the generality of the people, dispersed abroad, fragmented, unknown, disfigured in selective excerpts that lacked the
whole context to which they belonged. The great Gaelic scholars—
the Franciscans at Louvain, Charles O'Conor and Keating in the
eighteenth century, Hardiman, Petrie, John O'Donovan, Eugene
O'Curry, and Osborn Bergin in the nineteenth—had to undertake
the task of collecting, editing, and translating this archive. Of course,
once again, translation was a problem; with it, authenticity disappeared in its purest form. But, in addition, such work had to effect a
translation into print also. Hence the search for the Irish typeface
that would, as closely as possible, reproduce the characteristics of
the native script. Even then, such a script, although it had classic
characteristics, was of its nature more individual and various than
any print tradition could be. So the translation to print necessarily
involved the introduction of a uniformity or discipline that was not
'native'; it *stereotyped* diversity. The further translation of script into
Roman type completed the process of translation and betrayal. It
was an abstract and formal system that robbed the native Irish

materials of their essential and demonic force. Roman typeface was read—*literally*—as a colonial and imperial intrusion to be resisted by a cultural insurgency that, at times unwittingly, questioned its own foundational concept of authenticity as much as it did the British system's inauthenticity. Typography helped to produce and was also produced by the double-sided concept of a national character.

Yet the Irish–English relation in this field, as in others, was mediated through Scotland. As Hardiman and Theophilus O'Flanagan and a host of others had combatively asserted, Ireland could claim priority over Scotland as the 'original' Gaelic culture precisely because the Scots had not kept their Gaelic tradition intact in any comparable way. Scotland had yielded itself to print much earlier than Ireland; it had, therefore, a less enduring manuscript tradition; it was therefore less 'pure', less authentic. Ireland, Scotland, and England were thereby formed into a descending echelon of cultural purity. This was, of course, a political argument, the force of which in Hardiman had been almost entirely missed by Sir Samuel Ferguson. Ferguson regarded Scotland as a model on which Ireland and its relation to England could be based. But the whole political force of the Ossian controversy in Ireland was that Scotland could not have it both ways—claim to be an authentic Gaelic culture and remain in union with Great Britain.[26] It was the Union that had robbed it of its claim to authenticity; it was the Union of Great Britain and Ireland that had to be resisted if Ireland's Gaelic authenticity were to be retained and retrieved. The Scots, as represented by their writers, especially Macpherson, Burns, and Scott (not to mention the *Edinburgh Review*), had duplicated the achievement of their intellectual Enlightenment cohort; they had found a way to reconcile culture and the market, they had blended the discourses of feeling and calculation. Although Moore's *Melodies* and Ferguson's translations and cultural criticism could be described as notable efforts in that direction too, the main thrust of the Irish debate, accelerated in its force by the experience of the Famine and its political and economic implications and consequences, was to refuse that convergence. Political economy was the deadly enemy of Irish culture and the constitutional apparatus that gave the dismal science its priority was the Union. The Ossian controversy was, at root, a dispute between unionism and nationalism as well as a typographical debate. Hardiman's *Irish Minstrelsy* is a key text in setting the terms on which the issues involved would be contested. It seems appropriate in retrospect that Yeats was a cultural nationalist who could not spell English or speak Irish and who was among the first of the modernist writers to recognize the importance of setting his poems in an Irish type font, precisely to emphasise their modernism and their nationality by that archaicizing device,[27] and that Joyce's rewriting of English in his late novels produces a whole series of typographical innovations and textual archaeologies that consistently draw our attention to the materiality of the medium of language and of print.[28] One of the visible marks of modernism, to use Jerome McGann's phrase, was its typographical distinctness. The world of the Yellow Book and of the Yellow Press was divided by many forces, an effect of which was to oppose the field of cultural production to that of commercial production. This led to an intensification of the cultural claim to autonomy, the autonomy of the cultural from the economic field and, within that, the autonomy of the artists's work from other systems of production. Typography, although laden with economic and political implications, nevertheless contributed to the autonomization of high art. In Ireland, it was George Moore, Yeats, and, in a more ambiguous manner, Joyce, who made the autonomy of cultural production and the autonomy of the artist into a fetish that was thereafter interpreted as a truism.[29]

OCCULTISM AND FOLKLORE

The roles of Renan and Arnold in the construction of the Celt are well known; it is also acknowledged, although not quite so readily, that the idea of the Celt as a racial totality also undergoes a mutation into a more complex, more hospitably inflected, category—into the idea of the Gael—in the writings of W. P. Ryan, Thomas MacDonogh, George Sigerson, Lady Gregory, Douglas Hyde, Eleanor Hull, T. W. Rolleston, Pearse, and others.[30] Neither process is my concern here. I want to suggest ways of pursuing the Celt as one of those historically produced ideas that claims for itself freedom from history through two positions that were famously adopted by Irish writers at the turn of the century—occultism and exile. These positions are intimate with one another; more than that, they are positions that attempt to create what I have been saying had not until then been within the horizon of Irish writing as a possibility—the position of distance, the standard precondition for a version of the aesthetic that could, in its withdrawal from the actual, find some means by which the actual could be totalized into a narrative patterned to make typicality consistently prevail over the miscellaneous. What national character could never as a *point d'appui* achieve, racial character might.

Occultism, theosophy, Gothic fiction, the twilight of the Celtic gods, are all recognizable antidotes to the despiritualized Fabianism that Yeats always recognized as the domain of Bernard Shaw. Equally, all of this dimness can easily be understood as a displaced religion, a compensatory attempt to reintroduce by the back door of the unconscious what had been thrown out the front door of instrumental reason. In addition, it seems to many that it is characteristic of nationalism especially to parade these agencies of dimness as saving forms of irrationalism. Yet conceding all of this does not necessarily mean that these modes of thought are merely scandalous, that they have no function other than that of glamorizing regression. It is possible to think of them otherwise.

In Irish conditions, for instance, it is possible to see—in Yeats and George Russell (AE) most clearly, but in many others as well—that occultism is not a solitary discourse that has meaning only in and of itself. Within a series of other discourses, it generates other forms of signification that help us to recognize its functions in a less condemnatory or derisive spirit. As one instance, we might initially observe that occultism is in Yeats especially closely intertwined with the rediscovery of an Ireland that, to a large extent, spoke a different language, the Irish he could never master. Occultism is perhaps the only foreign language Yeats ever learned with any degree of fluency. Like Irish, it was an old language in which much that had belonged to the world before the onset of print culture had been preserved; in not being printed but in remaining predominantly oral, it had conserved its special knowledge, as arcane in its substance as in its mode of transmission. Further, it had been almost erased by the modern world, but still retained a vestigial existence, uninfected by Progress but not unaffected by it. Many of its meanings had been fragmented because the culture in which these had been produced had been broken up and important elements lost. Only a few could speak this arcane language, even fewer could speak with authority of it; but when they did, they spoke of a world that was haunted by permanence as much as was the modern world by transience and fashion.

Folk-art is, indeed, the oldest of the aristocracies of thought, and because it refuses what is passing and trivial, the merely clever and pretty, as certainly as the vulgar and insincere, and because it has gathered into itself the simplest and most unforgettable thoughts of the generations, it is the soil where all great art is rooted.[31]

Seventy years separate this statement from the much more characteristic view of folklore and the purpose of collecting it that was expressed by Thomas Crofton Croker in the heyday of the project of modernizing Ireland by consuming its difference. 'When rational education shall be diffused among the misguided peasantry of Ireland, the belief in such supernatural beings (the Shefro, the banshee) must disappear in that country, as it has done in England, and these "shadowy tribes" will live only in books.'[32]

Any world that was lost had occultism as its friend—whether that of the Irish peasantry, of the old Gaelic, or of the recent Anglo-Irish civilization. Yeats adapted O'Grady, as is well known, to his more sophisticated, less monadic, purposes, took him at his word that the Anglo-Irish landowners had a world mission, and transformed that into a pursuit of lost unity of being through the labyrinth of the occult. Like O'Grady too, Yeats claimed that the land of Ireland was a special territory, with its own achronicity—especially his Sligo, the territory of the west. It was a territory in which there was a leisure class for which the most conspicuous (and only remaining) form of consumption became the amassing of the stories and beliefs of the peasantry, trophies of the hunt for the Irish equivalent of those 'unexplored regions' where the old mapmakers wrote 'Here are lions' and where 'we can write but one line that is certain, "Here are ghosts".'[33] These collections are both trophies and atrophies. Chloroformed within them is another life that Yeats wishes to revive by administering to them the stimulus of his art—a stimulus that is as mysterious in its workings as are they in their meanings. By a species of sympathetic magic, his fairy stories pass into the mimetic forms of his poems, liberated there into a set of meanings that nevertheless still glide dimly behind the opaque material out of which they have been fashioned—even if rather coyly so at times. What Adorno said of Benjamin has its application here: 'He is driven not merely to awaken congealed life in petrified objects—as in allegory—but also to scrutinize living things so that they present themselves as being ancient, "ur-historical" and abruptly release their significance.'[34] The Anglo-Irish, having lost their land, rediscovered their territory—the territory of an art that had its roots in the soil of the peasantry. Nor did it matter that the peasantry had for the most part become tenant farmers or landless labourers. These people were still, in the most honorific sense Yeats could manage, peasants, atavars of a religion the whole world had lost and which they, because of their long history of exclusion from that world, had in fragmentary fashion preserved. Although Yeats was, of course, to rediscover in the various occult societies to which he belonged or with which he had contact a more organized and esoteric system of belief that had its ancestry in Asia, it was still in the West that he first discovered the East. Occultism as a set of doctrines that circulated in the urban worlds of London and Dublin was the ascendancy of folklore, the system of beliefs that circulated among the peasantry without any doctrinal formulation; occultism was the theory of which folklore was the embodied praxis. But it was also a theory that had found a territory, the territory of Yeats's childhood, of his nationality, and of his class. His fascination in *Mythologies* with stories of the stealing of humans by the fairies, integrated in these tales into the Irish population, is part of his desire to belong to a community in which there is no to and fro of loyalty or conviction, where love and hate are separate and perfect in themselves, where a mortal may know 'an even more than faery abundance of feeling'. It is those who 'have never wearied themselves with 'yes' or 'no', or entangled their feet with the sorry net of 'maybe' and 'perhaps' who have not grown old.[35] Yeats has no intention of seeing the shefro and the banshee disappear into books. He wants to reintroduce them into Ireland (as well as into his own books), making them as far as possible the source of a new demographic surge in the pattern of the Irish population, more marked in the west than elsewhere but still fairly evenly distributed over the whole island—with the possible exception of the north. No version of modern Irish history would be complete without having within it the story of an emergent or of a disappearing class or community coming to claim its rights or to surrender its titles.

The fairies, like any class that wishes to survive, must recruit from those below them—preferably, in their strange economy, to recruit not the most energetic but the most beautiful. But beauty is indeed a form of energy in their world as it is in Yeats's. Out of beauty spring history, art, tragedy. Moreover, it is in the form of beauty that permanence is most memorably achieved, precisely because it is in its decay that transience is most painfully experienced. Beauty is, for him, the mimesis of spiritual energy and its preservation an emblem of the spirit's triumph, its fading an emblem of a correspondent failure. Therefore it is in the body—his own or that of his beloved—that the combat between the permanent and the transient is inscribed. It became one of the paradigms in Yeats's poetry that he should steal from the living world beautiful women so that they might dance into eternity in his poems. But it was also a paradigm of the theft that he was to commit upon himself—taking Willie Yeats into the land of faery where he became WBY. It is a serious enterprise. In the vast repertoire of Irish exilic positions, this is one of the most effective. The stolen child or man or woman remains within Ireland as part of its true and permanent history and yet in exile from all that in Ireland is part of its transient and yet actual existence. The two realms are interconnected by memory and forgetfulness, both of which are necessary for the maintenance of their coexistence as, simultaneously, distinct and related zones.

The wonder of these tales is, like the eloquence with which they are told, inversely related to the condition of the country people who tell them. In 'Dreams that have No Moral', Yeats recounts 'one of those old rambling moralless tales, which are the delight of the poor and hard-driven, wherever life is left in its natural simplicity . . . We too, if we were so weak and poor that everything threatened us with misfortune, might remember every old dream that has been strong enough to fling the weight of the world from its shoulders.'[36] The dream is strong, the people weak. Their condition is wretched, their language opulent. These contrasts are the basis for the analogous refusal to accept the linearity of time, to supplant it with a sense of the neighbourliness of history and legend.

History passes over into legend and becomes the more history. This was a common assertion, especially in literature. It was for instance a standard conviction among translators from the Irish that in Irish literature—now being presented belatedly to an admiring world—the erosion of this distinction was characteristic. Eleanor Hull, a key figure in the history of Irish scholarship, says in her introduction to the important anthology, *The Poem-Book of the Gael*:

Two difficulties face the modern reader in coming for the first time upon genuine Irish literature, whether poetry or prose. The first is the curious feeling that we are hung between two worlds, the seen and the unseen; that we are not quite among actualities, or rather that we do not know where the actual begins or where it ends. Even in dealing with history we may suddenly find ourselves wafted away into some illusory spirit-world with which the historian seems to deal with the same sober exactness as in detailing any fact of ordinary life. The faculty of discerning between the actual and the imaginary is absent, as it is absent in imaginative children; often, indeed, the illusory quite overpowers the real, as it does in the life of the Irish peasant today.

There is, in most literatures, a meeting-place where the Mythological and the Historic stand in close conjunction, the one dying out as the other takes its place. Only in Ireland we never seem to reach this point; we can never anywhere say, 'Here ends legend, here begins history'. In all Irish writing we find poetry and fact, dreams and realities, exact detail and wild imagination, linked closely hand in hand. This is the Gael as revealed in his literature.[37]

This belief is also a strategy. Literature in Irish, especially translations from it in the nineteenth and early twentieth centuries, likes to offer itself as a body of writing that, throughout the many and disastrous changes the society that produced it has undergone, nevertheless continues to represent the unchanging and unchangeable spirit of the Gael. This is not an extraordinary position at all—most European vernacular literatures make the same claim. But in Ireland, that claim, which is taken to be central to a nationalist version of the canon of Irish writing, is a politically more exposed position than in other cultures, precisely because it depends upon the exclusion from literary history of the dynamics of historical change and particularly, the actuality of historical atrocity. For what does it matter what the atrocity was, what do 'breaks-down' matter if, in spite of or because of them, the national spirit continues to be represented over and over?

Literary history is the cure for other forms of historical investigation. It produces, more successfully than they, sameness out of difference, triumph out of disaster, the success of representation out of a culture that for a century had been trying to find effective ways of dealing with the conviction that it had not been represented or could not be represented. Translation may have a lot to answer for but that is only because translation answers a lot of questions. For a time at least it answered the question of representation by claiming that what was to be represented was the permanent element within the Irish psyche or racial or national formation and, further, by claiming, as did Eleanor Hull and many others up to Daniel Corkery, that it was in the Irish language that such representation was most continuously and powerfully achieved. Yet that achievement could only be made visible to a wider audience through the act of translation, always unsatisfactory of course, but nevertheless better than nothing. Even the notion that there was such a permanent condition as being Celtic was itself a precondition for the subsequent (consequent?) claim that there was a tradition of writing in Irish or indeed in English, for such a tradition could finally only achieve itself in terms of a continuity that overrode discontinuity, a changelessness that did not only survive change but sublated it into itself. In addition, it was a concept of tradition that could also produce a hierarchy determined by the varying degrees of proximity that writing would have to that notion of perduring permanence—writing in the Irish language, translation from the Irish language, writing in the English language. There were many subdivisions available within that hierachy; it could even be inverted to allow writing in English first-division status, but such writing in English would never be able to free itself from the influence, the presence, the example of writing in Irish. Thus the role of the translator in Irish writing is central to the structuring of that writing as a body of traditional work in which a history is endlessly inscribed, but a history that is powerfully and curiously achronic, a history that is not, in Hull's terms, distinct from legend. An additional advantage, of course, widely remarked, is that in the period of the Revival, as in the late eighteenth century, where these notions had stirred into premonitory life, it was ecumenically useful, especially for Protestant writers, to indicate that there was an Ireland that, in its pre-Christian form, was remarkably identical to the Ireland of sectarian difference that at present existed. Such difference could be elided as a merely transitory intervention in the history of sameness and identity. The Celt served both nationalist and liberal unionist purposes, from the days of Ferguson to those of Yeats—and beyond.

A tradition so imagined and so constructed harbours within itself, both as the operator of its system and as its destroyer, the founding notion that the most authentic and the most representative language is one that has almost died, one that is for the most part, and certainly among the educated classes, unknown or fragmentarily known, even while it is still in possession of the 'folk' or some of the folk. It is, in other words, a tradition that is founded upon the notion, not only of the permanent, but also of the esoteric; not only of the esoteric but of an esoteric that is native to the Irish people and for which some matching esotericism is necessary for the middle or aristocratic classes. Yeats's conception of the folk as a spiritual aristocracy is indebted to this conviction, even though he is of course the writer who gives it its most memorable articulation. But what I edge towards here is the suggestion that we can understand a great deal about the difficulties presented by the English-language texts of

the Revival—and we can understand a good deal about the translation activities of the Gaelic League and later the Irish government—
if we see them as converse operations—one inheriting a so-called
'normal' tradition of writing in English that had to esotericize, the
other an esoteric tradition of writing in Irish that had to be normalized. So while one was, in the hands of a Lady Gregory, an Eleanor
Hull, or a Yeats, emphasizing the wondrous otherness of Irish
writing and exploiting every conceivable means to intensify that
otherness, the other and later activity confines itself to normalizing
the Irish language by translating Jane Austen and Sir Walter Scott
into Irish, the better to normalize relations between the two
languages and the two traditions.[38] It is out of this fission of languages that the tradition explodes; but equally the tradition is
exploded by the same fission. With the collapse comes to an end
the anti-modernist project, an end that, in its shrapnelled ruin and
in its archaizing totalization, is perfectly registered in Joyce's
late fiction.

THE CROWD: 6 OCTOBER 1789 AGAIN

This can be thought of in other, although related, terms. Let us
again assume, as a given of the discussion, the Renan–Arnold conception of the nation as a community that produces, in manifold
ways, various actions and achievements that typify its genius. In
addition, from the same sources, although heavily buttressed by
other nineteenth-century discourses, let us assume the prevalence
of the conviction that a community could at least be negatively
defined as the opposite of a mob or a crowd. This contrast derives
much of its initial political force from the Burkean version of the
French Revolution, progressively heightened, especially in France
throughout the nineteenth century, as a phenomenon that had to be
understood in the light of its aftermath—the emergence of the mass
urban populations and all the associated ideologies—Marxism,
socialism, syndicalism—as the attempt to overturn a traditional
political–cultural community by the rule of the barbarous crowd
or mob.

Taine's *Origins of Contemporary France* is perhaps the classic formulation of this thesis, owing a good deal to Burke, even to his account of the events of 6 October 1789—although it had a considerable number of forerunners among English and French historians and in various popular accounts.[39] The admixture of pseudo-scientific analysis of mob formation and behaviour, with its identification of the overthrow of traditional political authority with the collapse of gender hierarchies, is characteristic both of Taine and of counter-revolutionary discourse throughout the century. The positioning of women within the community and the mob or crowd is central to the political distinction between the two constellations; in Irish writing it is in the poetry of Yeats that this receives its reactionary embodiment in the presentation of Maud Gonne and Constance Markievicz in particular. But no reading of nineteenth-century Irish writing can avoid the recognition that this variation between contrasting images of traditional community and barbarous mob is a continuous feature, frequently imaged as a variation between constitutional politics and revolutionary violence, although even there, in the contrast between O'Connell's and Parnell's political careers, the same operative contrast between crowd and community emerges—O'Connell as the figure who introduces the mass population into Irish politics with all the associated plebification, and Parnell as the solitary hero who is eventually brought down by the mob that he had almost managed to convert into a people. The rise in the Irish population, its immiseration, and its exodus in starving hordes during and after the Famine gave a further impetus to this system of representation. Whatever the sequence of events, this was a paradigm that could consistently organize them into a ready-made schema. This was true of other countries too, although perhaps more so in France than in any other European country, no doubt because France had had the revolution and because it underwent a series of other revolutionary moments in the nineteenth century, culminating in the Commune of 1870. Thus Ireland was a place whose history could be exemplified in this fashion—its folklore recruited towards the notion of community, its politics recruited towards the image of the crowd.

As we have seen, one of the early ways in which the problem of the mass civilization could be read was in terms of a national Irish character that might, by various reforms, persuasions, or coercions, be sufficiently sobered up to allow its wild nature to be converted to an agreeable civility.[40] But this discourse did not survive the shock of the Famine. In post-Famine writing, particularly that of Mitchel and O'Grady, although visible also in Lecky and Froude, Ireland was no longer an issue that could effectively be represented in these terms. The terms had to be altered to allow a wider scope, one provided by the switch from the idiom of nation to the idiom of race, even though these idioms never left one another's company, but instead formed a new relationship. Most particularly, the policy of control remained common to both, even though it was now altered to refer to the control of crowds, of mobs, and indeed of population itself, rather than simply or more narrowly to the control of a composite character that had to Anglicize itself into a state of receptivity to British civilization. More openly and more emphatically than before, the controls had to be exercised in order to preserve traditional community values in the threatening era of modernity.

Perhaps, then, we can begin to see that the Irish Revival's valorization of the community is, in transposed form, the literary equivalent of crowd control. This would be in line with the theoreticians of crowd theory in the nineteenth century. Gabriel Tarde, in *La Philosophie pénale* (1890) saw the crowd and the family as two distinct germs of society: 'But the family spirit, found largely in an agricultural or rural society, venerates tradition, stability and serenity. The mob spirit, which predominates in towns, urges rapid change and social and political levelling.'[41] It is also an integral feature of Catholic ideology in the Free State. The refusal of Ireland to enter modernity, the increasing identification of that modernity as a peculiarly British phenomenon characterized by various forms of social anomie, delinquency, and newspaper-reading, is indeed part of the history of nationalism but it is also part of the history of anti-nationalism, of the defence of a newly constituted élite against the mediocrity of the life of the modern state. This version of the élite belongs both to the Anglo-Irish Protestant and to the Roman

Catholic Gael. They obviously differ in their attitude to population control, but that itself is perfectly explicable in relation to the dwindling numbers of the Anglo-Irish and of their cultural allies, the Irish-speaking peasantry on the one hand and in relation to the Catholic Church's anxiety to see a growth in a population that was increasingly being siphoned off into the metropolitan world by emigration. One could make a virtue of dwindling, the other a virtue of expansion. But both proposed an ideology in which the population, either in its decrease or its increase, could be heroically envisaged as an organic community bonded by a history of hostility to faithless, state-driven modernism.

Still, even in this light, it is interesting to see the Burkean watermark becoming visible throughout the pages of so many apparently distant texts. The population problem in Ireland has always had curious sectarian inflections within it that themselves correspond to class distinctions, even though in complicated ways; but in the nineteenth century there was, especially in France, a population problem that had a class and national resonance too. I want very briefly to sketch the relation this has to the Irish literary situation.

I return to 6 October 1789. The most influential restatement of Burke's description of what happened on that date, is Taine's, although Taine's accompanying descriptions of the preceding Reveillon riots and the storming of the Bastille extend the Burkean terms of reference into a more prolonged but not necessarily more powerful indictment. Two features of these displays of mob power stand out; one is that the mob had a deal of drink taken, the other is that women played a leading role in the assaults. These indications are present in Burke; but in Taine they assume an even more salient role. For in Taine's description, part of the meaning of the revolution is that its assaults are even more threatening in 1882 than they were in 1789, precisely because part of the theory of revolution had become imbricated with the theory of crowds. The link between drink—or alcoholism, as Magnus Huss had recently christened it—and women was, in a word, infertility or degeneracy. Infertility was a tocsin term in late nineteenth-century France because of the alarming decline in the birth-rate and the dwindling size of France's population in relation to that of Germany. Zola's *L'Assommoir* (1877), which had sold more than 100,000 copies by the year Taine's book was published, had made the problem of alcoholism into a national debate. But if infertility was serious, degeneracy was catastrophic. According to the received wisdom, alcohol had two ill-effects: it led to a decline in the 'generative functions'; it also led to the production of degenerate offspring. There always was and would continue to be a certain contradiction in the opinions about alcohol's capacity to reduce the population at one level and to increase it at another. But this is of no consequence beside the fear of the alcoholic proletariat that became one of the spectres haunting Europe, especially after the Paris Commune. As for women—alcoholism in them was indissolubly allied to shamelessness and prostitution. The scandal of their role was of course the greater precisely because of the opaque status assigned to them in what we may call the Burkean–chivalric tradition, in which chastity, the lack of political involvement, and a whole congeries of restraints were interfused with the counter-revolutionary role assigned to fidelity and staying-at-home. The analogies with Yeats's versions of political women in his poetry are tempting here, but I want to refuse that temptation for a moment so that I might the better succumb to it later.[42]

Crowd theory was not content to diagnose the nature of the threat posed by the proletariat; it also developed control systems for them. Its companion set of theories, the theory of criminal types, itself owing a good deal to race theory, analysed the mob into its constituent parts and provided a so-called scientific basis for their genesis. From Sir Francis Galton's *Hereditary Genius: An Inquiry into its Laws and Consequences* (1869) to Lombroso's *L'Uomo Delinquente* (1876) and its expansion in Sighele's *La Folla Delinquente* (1891), to Tarde's *La Philosophie pénale* and the compendium works of Max Nordau's *Entartung* (1892) and Le Bon's *La Psychologie des foules* (1895) and *La Révolution francaise et la psychologie des révolutions* (1912), crowd, race, and criminal theory come together to form a matrix of reaction that is central to literary modernism's hatred of modernity. For the present, I merely indicate the closeness of the connection between alcoholism, infertility, degeneracy, crime, and the governing of these categories by the concepts of community and mob.

Central to any account of what we may call the nationalist version of Irish literature is the figure and the career of James Clarence Mangan. David Lloyd has given a definitive account of the construction of Mangan as a nationalist literary hero.[43] To supplement that, and to situate Mangan within that tradition in a slightly altered form, I suggest that he might be seen as a participant in the discourse of degeneracy and in the discourse of nationalism. For although it was his editors and friends—John Mitchel, C. P. Meehan, D. J. O'Donoghue, John Dalton, Gavan Duffy among them[44]—who moulded Mangan into his reputation, it was Mangan himself who produced the strange autobiographical fragment that is at the heart of his self-styled degeneracy. Although this reading could be extended right through his work and its complicated publishing history, I am going to confine my attention to one late publication, identified on the dust-jacket as *Songs of the Munster Bards* by J. C. Mangan and on the title-page as *The Poets and Poetry of Munster: A Selection of Irish Songs by the Poets of the Eighteenth Century, with Poetical Translations by JAMES CLARENCE MANGAN*, published in Dublin in 1925. The Irish text is revised by W. M. Hennessy; Mangan's 'Unfinished Autobiography', C. P. Meehan's 'Memoir of the Poet's Life', and Joseph Brenan's notice of the book from the newspaper the *Irishman* of 3 November 1849 are included, along with a new introduction by John P. Dalton. This compendium is in fact the fourth edition of John O'Daly's *Poets and Poetry of Munster*, first published in 1849, with a second edition in 1850 and a third edition—which contained Meehan's memoir, in 1885.[45] O'Daly's name has now entirely vanished from both dust-jacket and title-page, although he is acknowledged in the new introduction and, of course, in Meehan's reprinted memoir. Even in the first two editions, Mangan receives a prefatory biographical note that precedes the biographical

notes concerning the Munster poets themselves—a point of some
significance. I choose this book because it is a compendium volume
in which one segment of Mangan's work is situated very carefully
within a sequence of historical commentary that dates from the
Famine years to the early years of the Irish Free State. It is over
that period that the so-called Mangan myth was nurtured and
established.

The first thing to be said is that Mangan appears here in the
company of several poets whose lives were as vagrant and drink-
sodden as his own. They include accounts of the 'freak-loving propensities'[46] (later 'freakish propensities'[47]) of Donogh Mac Con-Mara
and his restless travels within his own country and across the Atlan-
tic and to Germany, followed by anonymity in death; of Sean O
Tuama's improvidence 'in the vintnery business' put down to the
fact 'that poets are rarely frugal or fortunate in the management of
their temporal concerns' and besides could not anyway avoid 'the
malediction which invariably pursues the man who trades upon the
intemperance of others'.[48] O Tuama's house became a rendezvous
for 'the bards and tourists of Munster' and the ensuing 'bardic
sessions . . . exercised a healthful influence in the country and aided
powerfully towards reviving the national spirit, bowed and almost
broken, as it was, beneath the yoke of penal enactments'.[49] Mrs O
Tuama (O Tuomy) was not impressed, but her 'impassioned remonstrances and expostulations' were vain in the face of his in-
corrigible improvidence.[50] He too became 'an adventurer in the
world'[51] and was reduced to the position of a hen-keeper for a Mrs
Quade of Limerick.

Andrew Magrath's biographical note opens:

Perhaps there is nothing more melancholy and deplorable than the sight,
too often, unfortunately, witnessed in this world of contradictions—the
union of lofty genius with grovelling propensities. To see talent of the
highest order debased by an association with vulgar and low-lived habits—
the understanding pointing one way, while the bodily requirements and
appetites drag their degraded victim in an opposite direction—is indeed a
spectacle calculated to excite thoughtfulness and sorrow in every generous
mind.[52]

O'Daly's account then goes through a series of what were by then routine references to literary victims of drink—Savage, Burns, Poe, and Maginn, himself a notable figure in London journalism and in the alcoholic's guide to Irish writing. Magrath's

habitual indulgence in intoxicating drinks—that foe to all aspiring thoughts and noble impulses—was his peculiar besetting sin; and, as a consequence, a great number of his songs are so replete with licentious images and ideas, as to be totally unfit for publication. Many of these, however, but particularly some others, in which his better muse predominates, are sung to this day by the Munster peasantry, and, doubtless, will remain unforgotten as long as the Irish spirit shall remain unbroken by the tyranny under which it has groaned and struggled through ages of misrule and unparalleled oppression.[53]

Magrath too was 'migratory and wandering',[54] mixed with low company and reigned there as John Philpott Curran was said to have done when he dressed up as a tinker and went slumming in the pubs of the Coombe, and as Moore tells us Byron used to do also. Oddly, Aodagáin O'Rahilly's biographical note does not refer to his wildness or wanderings. But, in all, these are, says O'Daly, 'but a few of the great band of native Irish writers whose genius illumed the political gloom and dreariness of the eighteenth century'.[55]

O'Daly's account of Mangan is different from these sketches of the Munster poets, partly because he knew Mangan well and therefore could not quite so readily recruit him to the discursive formation in which they were cast. But, genteelly and hesitantly, it emerges. Mangan's home life forced him to spend all his energies in supporting his parents and family. 'His spirit at length became broken from over exertion, and he was obliged to have recourse to stimulants, which he occasionally abandoned, but finally they produced the usual fatal results.'[56] The subscription to erect a monument to his memory is 'an act of posthumous generosity which adds another name to the sad catalogue of the many men of exalted genius who asked for bread and received a stone'.[57] Mangan, however, soon becomes the leading figure in this list of national Alcoholics Anonymous. By the third and fourth editions of the anthology, Mangan's life and career have expanded to such a degree that they govern the whole work. Now there is a direct correlation between the gloom of the eighteenth century illumed by the Munster poets and the gloom of the nineteenth century, particularly its Famine decade, illuminated by Mangan's genius. The destruction of the poet by drink, his vagrancy and improvidence, his anonymity in his lifetime and the belated recognition that comes with death are all elements in a biographical–ideological matrix which embraces all the lives of the poets and links them indissolubly with the catastrophic history of their country. There is, in addition, an extended confirmation of the legitimating convention of the *poète maudit*— later to reach its full formulation in Baudelaire—by the listing of the names of poets from other cultures—Burns, Savage, Poe, Byron, and so on. But these poets are treated as special cases, eccentric individuals, whose disturbed lives are in direct relation to their vocations as poets. In the case of the Irish writers, their distress is also related to the distress of their nation. A literary construction assumes a central role in a political ideology. That is, so to speak, the first insertion in the complex formation, more firmly ensconced by 1925 but nevertheless implicit from the outset. John P. Dalton, the author of the introduction to the 1925 edition, begins by emphasizing the patriotism of O'Daly in issuing his book in the Famine years 'when Ireland lay stricken, almost unto death'.[58] He goes on:

To some extent . . . the strains of the Munster warblers served, amid the despair of the years 1849 and 1850, as an anodyne for the nation's sufferings. But they did much more. Like seedlings planted in a congenial— albeit a sadly desolated—soil, they struck root and helped to propagate in the next generation a vigorous regrowth of interest in Gaelic literature.

Gaelic scholarship has now regained much of its olden dignity and prestige. Remarkable, indeed, is the fact that the decade following the Great Famine witnessed the dawn of its era of resurrection, and preluded the restoration of its long-forfeited status in the academic world.[59]

At the end of his extremely lengthy and learned introduction, in effect a sustained monograph on Irish poetry and civilization from the earliest times, Dalton appends a bibliography, the last item in which is Daniel Corkery's famous and defining study of eighteenth-century Munster poets, *The Hidden Ireland*, published the previous year. In that book, Corkery gives the ultimate imprimatur to O'Daly's project—the recovery not only of a hidden Ireland but the recovery of an Ireland that had, in the midst of extreme dilapidation, produced a literature characterized by the true 'Gaelic' note.[60] Corkery's book restores O'Daly's poets to the tradition of the people, disengaging them, to some extent, from the philological tradition that O'Donovan and O'Curry and the German scholars of the nineteenth and twentieth centuries had made so important in the recovery of the old language and civilization. Philology and some of its associated disciplines—etymology and anthropology— also played a curious role in the construction of a nationalist literary tradition.[61]

It is in the transactions between Mangan's famously unreliable 'Fragment of an Unfinished Autobiography' and the biographical accounts given of him in the 1925 *Poets and Poetry of Munster* that the more intricate insertions are achieved. The *Autobiography* is clearly one of the most obvious Gothic fictions of the century in Ireland, although this has generally passed unnoticed, since Irish Gothic is generally considered to be a Protestant phenomenon—as indeed for the most part it is. (As a boy, Mangan is said to have followed 'crazed Maturin' through the streets and told many anecdotes about him.[62]) But Mangan introduces us to a new genre—what we may call Catholic or Catholic–nationalist Gothic. The standard elements are all in place—an overpowering sense of doom, related to criminality; reference to German romances; dream-sequences and ruins; a terrifying father-figure whose shadow falls over and dominates the narrator's life; isolating illness; spiritual hauntings and world-weariness; Promethean ambitions and humiliating rebukes; appeals to a select audience for sympathy and contempt for the mass of humankind; religious longings and the refusal of conventional religious consolations. Even the rhetoric and form of the piece have characteristic Gothic notations. It is itself a fragment, a manuscript that breaks off 'suddenly'—a habitual feature of the 'romantic' or Gothic work, much theorized in the German aesthetics of the fragment. Blanchot, in his discussion of *The Athenaeum*, in which the theory of the fragment was developed, cites Friedrich Schlegel's remark, 'I can con-

ceive for my personality no other pattern than a system of fragments, because I myself am something of this sort; no style is as
natural to me and as easy as that of the fragment.' [63] Mangan's work
is, in that sense, doubly fragmented since it sometimes masquerades
as and sometimes is a translation, with the author thereby adopting
a plurality of languages and personalities while remaining bereft of
a name—'the nameless one'.

It is perhaps Mangan's peculiar rhetoric that is most commanding
of our attention, because in it we can observe the operations of his
mode of melodramatic excess. Time and again we are told that his
condition and circumstances are without parallel, incredible, beyond belief; he invokes other writers of autobiography, including
'Goodwin' and Byron among those who did not reveal themselves
thereby, and St Augustine, Rousseau, and Charles Lamb among
those 'who have avowedly laid bare to the eyes of mankind their
own delinquencies without cloak or equivocation.'[64] (Mangan
always wore a cloak, one of the items of his spectacular Gothic
wardrobe.) The rhetoric operates by invoking the impossibility of
similitude or comparison by invoking the possibility of both, only to
dismiss it. This is visible in many local instances in the text. His
house, as he describes it, is 'without . . . a parallel for desolateness';[65]
his arrival in the world is even more unprecedented:

And thus it happened, reader, that I, James Clarence Mangan came into the
world surrounded, if I may so express myself, by an atmosphere of curses
and intemperance, of cruelty, infidelity, and blasphemy, and of both secret
and open hatred towards the moral government of GOD—such as few
infants, on opening their eyes to the first light of day, had ever known
before.[66]

But the general effect of this procedure is formally disturbing at a
deeper level. It gives the fragmentariness, the inaccuracies, the ex-
tremities of the text—its deliberate careening from the sublime to
the ridiculous—a rationale that defends it from the requirements of
realism, partly on the basis that realism as a mode of narration
would be insufficient to deal with realities such as these, partly on
the grounds that realism is predicated on the notion of a coherent
subjectivity belonging to a narrator who is not incriminated within

the shocking and splintering experiences that are being recounted. Such a narrator also has the resource to complete his narrative, to give it a retrospective pattern. The only completion available to Mangan is the non-completion of the fragment, the impossibility of finding a vantage-point from which his life can be viewed as something which forms a whole—which is a 'history'. The dethroned narrator instead re-enthrones himself by appealing to his own special and élite audience. He plays with the notion of establishing a narrative and then disestablishes it, gives accounts, themselves quite confusing at times, of his confused condition and yet assumes the position of control he had a moment before evacuated.

But let me not anticipate my mournful narrative. The few observations that I make in this preliminary chapter I throw out without order or forethought, and they are not intended to appear as the commencement of a history. In hazarding them I perhaps rather seek to unburden my own heart than to enlist the sympathies of my readers. Those few, however, who will throughly understand me, need not be informed why I appear to philosophise before I begin to narrate.[67]

Mangan keeps switching the text's intentionality. It begins as 'a work that may not merely inform but instruct—that may be adapted to all capacities and grades of intellect—and that, while it seeks to develop for the thinking the more hidden springs of human frailty, shall also operate simply in virtue of its statements as a warning to others, particularly to the uneducated votary of Vice.'[68] But the two audiences are at times replaced by Mangan himself —the work is a therapeutic disburdening. The elusiveness of intentionality is reproduced in the elusiveness of the work's direction, towards others, towards himself. This uncertainty is both an organizing and a disorganizing principle, but these functions are as a consequence seen not as opposites, but as implicit in one another.

Thus he can claim, on several occasions, to be telling the absolute truth—'I give my Confessions to the world without disguise or palliation'; 'read the simple and undecorated truth';[69] 'But as I am bound to adhere to strict truth in this autobiography'[70]—even while he manifestly does not, as his editor reminds us. Mangan's description, highly Freudian, of the 'den' in which he lived in Chancery Lane is, we are informed in a footnote, 'purely imaginary; and when I told Mangan that I did not think it a faithful picture, he told me he dreamt it'.[71] He gives the wrong address for the school he attended; he says he was 11 years of age in 1820, but he was born in 1803. The corrections supplied by the editor, not very numerous, nevertheless make a comic commentary on a text which the editor is constantly attempting to bring back within the conventions of realism or at least biography.

What is 'Catholic' in Mangan, as opposed to a Maturin or a Le Fanu, is precisely the autobiographical internalization of the whole Gothic apparatus, the incorporation into the history of an individual of a series of protocols that belong to the historical sequences that characterize the plots of Gothic novels. Mangan's 'explanation' of his misfortunes is that they are the punishments imposed upon him by a just God to rebuke his pride and 'lift me out of the hell of my own nature'.[72] His God, a name that he capitalizes throughout, is a stern father indeed, remarkably similar to Mangan's own.

If anyone can imagine such an idea as a human boa-constrictor, without his alimentive propensities, he will be able to form some notion of the character of my father. May GOD assoil his great and mistaken soul, and grant him eternal peace and forgiveness! But I have an inward feeling that to him I owe all my misfortunes.[73]

In his boyhood, he 'was haunted by an indescribable feeling of something terrible',[74] a formless danger that 'rose on my imagination like one of those dreadful ideas which are said by some German writers of romance to infest the soul of a man apparently foredoomed to the commission of murder.'[75] Yet he declares he does not believe in predestination, but cannot reconcile his 'feelings of impending calamity'[76] with the rational recognition that 'nothing can irreparably destroy a man except his proper criminality' and that the 'verdict of Conscience' should provide a contentment 'beyond the power of Accident to affect'.[77] Mangan is stating here the discrepancy between a Gothic experience of intense formlessness and a Catholic account of the shape a life should have. At the close, the situation is replicated. Mangan, reclining on a grassy knoll at

Rathfarnham, with a copy of Pascal's *Pensées* in his hand, is approached by a stranger who tells him that the *Pensées* are 'a very unhealthy work', to which Mangan characteristically replies that 'Everything in this world is unhealthy'.[78] The stranger identifies himself as a 'Catholic Christian'; Mangan's double argument against this man's sanguine view of life is, one, that his own experiences and sufferings testify to the truth of his conviction of the unhealthiness of the world and, two, that Catholicism itself, in its Pascal–Massillon Jansensist form, teaches that 'the majority of mankind will be irrevocably consigned to eternal misery'.[79] So if the work does merit the title of Catholic Gothic, it is only Catholic in as Protestant form of Catholicism as possible.

Of all the inaccuracies in the *Autobiography*, the most glaring is Mangan's omission of his addiction to alcohol. It is the more glaring of course because it figures so prominently in the memoir and biographies. Mangan is reported by Meehan to have attended a Father Mathew meeting in Dublin 'but could not be tempted to take the pledge, 'simply because he doubted his ability to keep it'.[80] This was after 'he had fallen into the society of grovelling companions who flouted the temperate cup, and made him ever afterwards an irresolute victim to alcohol'.[81] Mangan's struggle to give up the drink and the friendship shown him in this respect, particularly by Gavan Duffy and John O'Daly, is politicized, not only by reference to Father Mathew's crusade, but also by the imaging of Mangan himself struggling to achieve not only sobriety but patriotism—one being a function of the other. Meehan's memoir includes a letter from Mangan to Duffy which is full of the Manganese of despair, 'absolute desolation of spirit', 'abandoned by Heaven and man', 'hardly able to hold the pen . . . dare not take any stimulants to enable me to do so. Too long and fatally have I been playing that game with my shattered nerves.' This is immediately followed by the pledge that Mangan did take, to Duffy, not Father Mathew: 'I promise . . . to live soberly, abstemiously, and regularly in all respects. I promise . . . that I will constantly advocate the cause of Temperance—the interests of knowledge—and the duties of Patriotism—and finally that I will do all these things irrespective of any concern personal to myself.'[82] The subsumption of self into sobriety,

knowledge, and patriotism, a Young Ireland triad, is something that
Mangan only occasionally managed; but of course the point is that
this figure, composed into occasional patriotic sobriety and more
often dispersed into drunken depression and vagrancy, is indeed, as
David Lloyd has shown, a figure for Ireland itself, trying to emerge
from its history and from the clasp of the degraded national character, into a Young Ireland light in which fame will be exchanged for
anonymity and in which that fame will be in great part constituted
by Mangan's own rescuing from drunkenness and anonymity the
Munster poets by an act of translation in which their Irish (of which
he was wholly ignorant) will be restored to the world and to Ireland
in his English. So Mangan is seen to enact for those poets what his
biographers enact for him—a duplicated transfiguration of the Gael
into the Irishman. Emergence from the penal laws and emergence
from the Famine are analogous to one another, although the tragic
element is sustained by the remembrance of the Munster poets'
eighteenth-century victimage and Mangan himself as a Famine
victim.

It was cholera, not alcohol, that killed Mangan. This allows us to
dwell on another discrepancy between autobiography and biography. In the *Autobiography*, Mangan claims that he was infected by
leprosy by a young boy with whom he was forced to share a hospital
bed. This disfiguring disease was scarcely noticed by his family, but
even when it disappeared 'its moral effects remain incorporated
with my mental constitution to this hour',[83] leaving him perma-
nently subject to what he calls 'an incurable hypochondriasis'.[84] The
disease is clearly a figure of his isolation. But in the biographical
account of Mangan's contraction of cholera we are told that Mangan
did not believe there was such a thing as contagion and that therefore all precautions advised on the outbreak of cholera in Dublin in
April 1849 were useless. So Mangan tells us he contracted leprosy,
Meehan that Mangan did not believe in the theory of contagion
when it came to cholera. Despite Mangan's monologues on the
subject, Meehan has 'no difficulty in stating that he [Mangan] had a
presentiment that he was doomed to fall a victim to the terrible
epidemic'.[85] No doubt. Mangan had a presentiment that he would
fall victim to anything and everything. He was vulnerable to all

afflictions; such vulnerability was the defining feature of his self-conception. Cholera may not in his view have been contagious, but woe certainly was and cholera, like leprosy, was only one of the forms in which woe transmitted itself to his tragically receptive spiritual and physical constitution. Thus what turns this apparently nonce discrepancy on the topic of contagion into a designed strategy on the construction of Mangan's reputation is revealed in Joseph Brenan's notice of O'Daly's book in The *Irishman*. For there, in his angry account of the way in which Mangan had been ignored in his lifetime, it is Mangan himself who is now transformed into a disease from which others fled. He was treated as though he were contagious by those who feasted on his poetry and derided him as a drunkard and drug addict. The review begins as an address to Mangan himself:

Six months ago you were a homeless, houseless wanderer, through the streets of this city, shunned by the opulent who could have relieved you with crumbs from their table, and utterly unknown, save in your deathless song, to those epicures of taste who banqueted on the rich repast your genius provided them with in newspapers and periodicals! You were dubbed 'drunkard' by one, and 'opium-eater' by another. The Pharisee whom you asked for alms gave you a homily—the Nice Scented Gentleman who admired your 'soul mated with song,' fled all contact with your person, as though you were a pollution; and need we wonder if that soul of thine, sickened and disgusted at the unrealities of life—at this eternal cant about Christian charity, and commiseration for human errors and frailties—longed and pined for that shelter which God alone can give?[86]

The references to the New Testament—the parables of Dives and Lazarus and of the Pharisee and the Publican (although the latter is not mentioned since his name might strike a discordant note in the alcoholic's martyrology)—are of a piece with the Catholicization of Mangan, itself part of his patriotic status. The rich ignored him, but the nuns and priests of the hospitals looked after him; so too did O'Daly, the Good Samaritan, 'who never shunned or fled you, even when you lay bleeding, wounded, and robbed of right reason by those most accursed of all freebooters, whisky and despair'[87] but gave what he could 'as well becomes the true Celt's generous nature'.[88] Lazarus/Mangan, we learn three paragraphs later, 'was allowed to dree his last moments of agony in a lazar-house'.[89] This imagery and these references to eating and disease, to the fattening rich and the nurturing religious, were potent in that late year of the Famine. Mangan starved, while others ate the produce of his labour—a widespread accusation that Mitchel had most forcibly made about the starving people of Ireland. Similarly, in their distress, the people were looked after more effectively by the Catholic clergy than by any other group. The alliance between people and priests against the (largely Protestant) landed and rich, is thus symbolically forged in the account of Mangan's last illnesses.

There is still, within this politicizing discourse surrounding Mangan, another internal and pathological discourse produced by Mangan himself that supports and disturbs the former. It too centres on the act of eating and of being eaten, drinking and being drunk, and, by extension, of being provider for others and being provided for by others. The boa-constrictor father who crushes his victim son can very easily be imagined with his 'alimentive propensities' because Mangan tells us that he was compelled to work in a scrivener's office in order to support his parents. In thus being forced to surrender his spiritual vocation, he was driven almost insane; or rather, his mind was, for the narrator–subject in this piece is rarely stable enough to sustain the alliance between the mind and the first-person pronoun.

But my exasperated mind (made half mad through long disease) would frequently inquire, though I scarcely acknowledge the inquiry to myself, how or why it was that I should be called on to sacrifice the Immortal for the Mortal; to give away irrevocably the Promethean fire within me for the cooking of a beefsteak; to destroy and damn my own soul that I might preserve for a few miserable months or years the bodies of others.[90]

While he worked to feed others, he was a scrivener; when he had to give that up because of his exhausted condition, he turned to literature and became a writer—it was then he began to feed on himself and to consume and be consumed by the spirit that was always the companion of and the other name for his soul. It is possible to believe from the biographical materials that Mangan was addicted to opium as well as whiskey, partly because of the reputation he had for long periods of indolence punctuated by paroxysms of work (a condition recognizable in the literature of addiction famously described by De Quincey and Coleridge),[91] perhaps subliminally indicated too by Mangan's fantasy of the 'den' he lived in in Chancery Lane to which the only means of access was by a perpendicular ladder down which he frequently fell. So, between the crushing and consuming snake of the father and the ladder of access and exit to the (opium) den and the frequent fall, Mangan finds a way of elaborating the separation of body and soul, assigning to himself the food of the spirit, boasting of his disgust for animal food, and assigning that grosser nutriment to his family. His addiction to things of the spirit (Promethean fire, whiskey, opium), and his father's addiction to things of the world (money, business, improvidence, food), defines the exchange between them—a perverted one, since the father, failing to nurture the son, ends by being nurtured by him. Consumption becomes a fetish; production becomes an unremitting labour. The connections between this plight and Marx's analysis of commodity fetishism are intensified by the problems facing Mangan in the literary marketplace, where he not only received low pay for his endeavours but also had difficulty in selling his literary wares. In fact, he sold himself, and his success depended upon marketing that self in the most exotic packaging he could find. Since his market was the restricted one of the Irish nationalist press, that press found ways of making the commodity suitable for the market by Hibernicizing the 'oriental' alterity of Mangan's persona, by first accepting—as in O'Daly's case—that he had a wide knowledge of foreign languages and by later announcing , as in Meehan's case, that he 'never learnt Gaelic, Persian, Hindostani, Romaic, and Coptic, and that his affected translations from these idioms are the outcome of his own all but oriental imagination'.[92] There was no difficulty in Mangan's knowing German, since German was readily associated with a cloudy romanticism that contained within it strong elements of 'romance' and a Western appropriation of some 'Eastern' Gothic elements. As for Irish, that was even less of a problem. Mangan's ignorance of the native language was both an index of his country's dispossession and, since he 'mated' so instinctively with the works of the Munster (and other Irish) poets, an indication that his Irishness was unaffected by the loss of the language, surviving perfectly within the English that he could convert to Hibernian rhythms and cadences.

Mangan's work is thus both interrupted by the drudgery of family responsibilities and, either because of that or as a corollary to it, fragmentary, achieved so to say in parenthesis between his bouts of addiction, torpor, and frantic bursts of energy. He tells an odd story in his autobiography of his first day at school when, not having read the assigned grammar, he was nevertheless the only one who was able to define the word 'parenthesis'—'I should suppose a parenthesis to be something included in a sentence, but which might be omitted from the sentence without injury to the meaning of the sentence.'[93] He was sent to the top of the class, from his obscure seat at the back, but insisted on surrendering his place to a boy who had struggled to define the word on the grounds that the boy had, nevertheless, done the work. It is a characteristic Mangan parable of fame and obscurity, of the flash of genius against the drudgery of work, of moral integrity and contempt for worldly acclaim. But it is also a parable of his own life and work, of the man who disappeared for long periods and then turned up again for short and sober intervals, of a man under a sentence of woe in which his work was no more than a parenthesis. We might even permit the pun that it was also a parable of the parent-thesis which governed his whole life and led to its interrupted and fragmentary achievements.

The constant theme of the Irish writer publishing in Ireland—especially with the collapse of the nineteenth-century publishing industry after the Union—takes two forms.[94] One concerns fame—the impossibility of attaining it with a wide audience, given Irish conditions. The other concerns money—the impossibility of achieving sufficient economic security to survive as a writer. This theme is extended backwards in time to the Irish poetry of the past, unknown, unread, its practitioners forever economically dislocated and impoverished since the collapse of the old Gaelic patronage system. Therefore, the re-publication and translation of such writers was regarded as a national duty and as an attempt to bring cultural and economic revivals together. But the poet who contradicted the

Irish rule of economic failure and lack of reputation was Thomas
Moore. It was, therefore, essential to the career of Mangan that he
should be seen to replace Moore, that Moore—despite his own
peculiar blendings of Irishness and Orientalism—should be seen as a
false Mangan, one lacking in the authenticity for Irish nationalism
that Mangan came to represent.[95] Mangan himself fired the opening
shot in the campaign in his autobiography. Chapter II opens: 'I
share, with an illustrious townsman of my own, the honour, or the
disreputability, as it may be considered, of having been born the son
of a grocer. My father, however, unlike his, never exhibited any of
the qualities of guardian towards his children.'[96] So Moore has a
head start. Nurtured and cared for, he is as fortunate as Mangan is
unfortunate. In addition, Moore is scandalously successful. But the
press notice of O'Daly's book in the *Irishman* puts that in its proper
place. As against the Munster poets and Mangan's translations,
Moore lacks the real thing. Even though the opening sentence of
the following quotation reads like a gloss on Moore's *Melodies*,
he is nevertheless effectively dismissed from the Irish pantheon:
despite their fondness for drinking-songs and love poems, we
are told, 'undying attachment to the land of their birth and the
religion of their fathers, is the grand and leading idea' of their
compositions.

When we remember that this idea . . . has been cherished and dwelt upon
by thousands long ago gone to the 'lampless land', must we not do honour to the men, who, despite degradation and bondage, fostered the
remembrances of old, and kept the faint heart, though drooping, still
hoping for a day of retribution, which, alas, seems retiring farther and
farther from us, into the dim distance? Moore's songs were made for the
ballroom, and for gentle maidens, who sit down to a piano, manufactured
by some London house—they are, beyond a doubt, matchless in their
caste—but, before Moore sung, our grandmothers at the spinning-wheel,
and our great-grandfathers, whether delving in the fields, or shouldering a
musket in the brigades, sang these time-consecrated verses, to keep alive
the memory of Ireland, her lost glories and cherished aspirations. Before
Moore was, those bards *were*, and it is but fair to give their memory the
honour which some would bestow exclusively on the author of 'The Irish
Melodies'. How few out of the whole mass of our peasantry ever heard a
single song out of the 'Melodies'?[97]

Moore's paternity, in the literal and symbolic sense, must be differentiated from that of Mangan and the Munster bards. They are fathers who have sons of the true Irish kind, whereas Moore's audience is that of gentle maidens and their London-made pianos. The father–son Oedipal obsession remains prominent in Irish discourses about ancestry and language for a long time afterwards, perhaps achieving its fullest formulation in James Joyce's *Ulysses*. But even here Joyce, one of the creators of the Mangan myth, reminds us, in one of his portmanteau words, of Mangan's recreating of that Oedipal anxiety in the idiom of translation from fatherly Irish to son-English, a conversion which is also a perversion. In the Proteus episode, Stephen, thinking of heresies about the relationship between the Father and the Son in the doctrine of the Trinity, produces the implicitly obscene 'word', 'contramagnificanjewbantiality'. This is taken indirectly from a footnote in Meehan's memoir in which Mangan, writing to Gavan Duffy, promises that he will be publishing in the Irish Penny Journal of 1840 'a *transmagificanbandancial* elegy of mine (a perversion from the Irish), on the O'Neills and O'Donnels of Ulster . . .'.[98] (This is the poem 'Lamentation for the Earls of Tyrone and Tyrconnell' with the famous opening line 'O, Woman of the Piercing Wail'.) Yet Joyce found a way to incorporate Moore's *Melodies* within his hospitable embrace, even though he too, like Mangan, was someone who had his own struggles with the marketplace, with alcohol, with a looming father, with a reputation for mastery of foreign languages and ignorance of his own, and with the posthumous experience of becoming an institution—of modernism, not of nationalism, even though the dispute between these appropriations continues.[99]

Still, Mangan's addiction needed political attention in order to confirm his posthumous status. Meehan tells us, 'As for opium, I never knew him to use it—the poppy of the West satisfied his craving.'[100] Mangan's orientalism was perfectly recuperable for an Irish nationalism that still adhered to the antiquarian notions of the Eastern ('Scythian') origins of the Irish race, an ancestry that kept its difference safe from any Romano-British myth of origin. It was, thus, an important part of the Mangan myth that he be an alcoholic, addicted to Irish whiskey rather than a drug addict, addicted to opium—especially as opium was more than ever associated with the British imperial venture that had provoked the opium war with China in 1840.

But so too, within the 1925 volume, as well as its predecessors, is the other contrast which Brennan labours at some length—that between the kind of fame the rich would have bestowed on Mangan had he been rich—newspaper verbiage and a pyramid or mausoleum 'with a verbose epitaph, very gorgeous, and very mendacious, for stone don't blush'[101] and the truer fame of Mangan's poetry, which is his epitaph, some of which appeared in a non-establishment newspaper, some of which remains unpublished, and much of which in this volume itself stands as an epitaph to the Munster poets and to Mangan himself. His monument is his poetry; this particular volume is part of it. And of course, as noticed earlier, almost all the poets later mentioned have no monument, no epitaph either. They, like Mangan, have only their poems. So Mangan, the contagion who was fled from in his life, will now spread in his works—Irish, Catholic, outcast, material for a Christian parable, emblem of the starving Irish, the soul who mated with songs that 'are an integral portion of the history of this hapless land; to know the latter, as we would wish you to know it, you must be familiar with the former'.[102] The final item in the contagion series is Fame. The fame of the name of Mangan is spread by publication, and the role of newspapers, journals, and books in establishing it, or in denying it, is insisted on time and again. Dalton's 1925 introduction cites John O'Donovan and Standish Hayes O'Grady on the bard and schoolmaster of the eighteenth century: 'They discharged the functions and wielded the influence of the modern newspaper and periodical press.'[103] The construction of Mangan in the nationalist periodicals and newspapers is modelled on that earlier role of the poet. So too is the whole notion of re-establishing literature—and particularly poetry—as a central agency in the nationalist recovery, because the version of the old civilization is one in which poetry is a central institution. Again, Dalton's introduction confirms this: 'The title-deeds of the poetic faculty of Ireland to rank among the most primitive and exalted of Gaelic institutions are writ large in the legendary and annalistic history of the country.'[104] Although by 1925

Mangan's role in that institution was beginning to fade and be taken over by the poets whom he had translated, nevertheless we can see in this imbrication of the different discourses within this volume that Mangan himself was for a period of eighty years or so an institution. Having spent so much time in institutions, it was only proper that he finally became one.

Finally, Mangan's contempt for the mass of people, 'worldlings', is matched in the biographical material by the writers' contempt for the low company which Mangan kept when indulging his addiction. It is standard fare that the self-consciously Romantic poet should assume this posture of disdain; but it is slightly less conventional that a nationalist ideology should reassume it, since it makes such a fuss about the people, the folk, the peasantry, the Irish masses. However, as is well known, the people are construed in highly specific ways. They are subjected to a a series of moral testings that reveal them to be strong, virile, chaste, loyal, religious, essentially rural and familial. Their natural opposite, worryingly numerous as well as noisome, is generally to be found among the 'denizens' of the city, a low class of people who are indeed given to addictions— alcohol and opium, to irreligion and to vice, ill-health and pandemic disease. In addition, detached from the people at the other end of the scale, are those who are wealthy, genteel, given to fashion and Anglicization—West Britons and Protestant Ascendancy types. In effect, the peasantry is the class in the middle, but not the middle class, between the crowd and the decadents. Mangan's life hovers between these constellations—a story of degeneracy and delin- quency, indulged with the mob; a story of rejection by the rich and those whose gentility led them to prefer Moore's confections to his more wholesome work; and a story of redemption, chiefly achieved through the translations from the Irish which made him into a national poet and rescued him from becoming wholly involved to his destruction with either of the enemy classes. This is a paradigm of nationalist sociology that was to be variously reproduced in the Revival and beyond—in Yeats, in Synge, and in Corkery. The inflec- tion given crowd theory and race theory in Ireland produces a powerful political aesthetic that is central to any conception of Irish modernism—and of other modernisms as well.

SYNGE: THE MOB, THE COMMUNITY, THE HERO

In relation to Irish literary modernism, I want to look at a famous moment in the history of the Irish Revival, the riots that surrounded the Abbey's production in 1907 of Synge's *Playboy of the Western World* and to attach to that a reading of the play that owes something to the French (and European) background I have just described—noting that the France I have been speaking of was known to Synge. In his opening speech on the debate on the riots on 4 February 1907, Yeats stated:

The National movement 'was democratised' seven or eight years before and passed from the hands of a few leaders into those of large numbers of young men organised in clubs and societies. These young men made the mistake of the newly enfranchised everywhere: they fought for causes worthy in themselves with the unworthy instruments of tyranny and violence . . . It needs eloquence to persuade and knowledge to expound; but the coarser means come ready to every man's hand, as ready as a stone or a stick, and when these coarse means are all, there is nothing but mob, and the commonest idea most prospers and is most sought for.[105]

This is clearly an interpretation of the play. Yeats is conscious, more than most, of the reconstruction of the public sphere, in Habermas's words, that had been achieved in late nineteenth-century Ireland and most especially in the decade of the 1890s.[106] But he is not unaware of the irony that this play, so generally considered, then and now, to be concerned in some nurturing way with the idea of a folk and national community, should have been interrupted so often in its playing by an unruly mob. In place of the mob weapons of the stick and violence, he counterposes the play's weapon of eloquence. In doing so, he alerts us to some of the play's, as well as his own, inherited discourses and tensions. For what we face in *The Playboy* is, after all, the spectacle of a dying community, reinvigorated by the arrival of an ostensibly criminal outsider, that reverts in the end to a mob and thereby indicates its historical doom while the outsider moves off into a legendary world of heroic identity, a place that is not a place but a condition, the condition of having become legendary.

He is also conscious that Synge's work derived much of its power
by negotiating between two languages—the language of organic
vitality and the language of analytic pallor, which he, like Synge
would identify with writers such as Ibsen and Zola. But one of these
languages is associated with decadence—not just the decadence of
the decadents, like Huysmans, but with the general European decadence of which Huysmans and Zola were merely alternate representations. In his negotiation, Synge had obviously gone to the Irish
language and the English spoken by former Irish speakers as a
source for his peculiar species of vitalism. But he had also gone to
the community version of the criminal classes, radically different of
course from their mob-like counterparts.[107]

At the beginning, the villagers, faced with the spectacle of
Christy, indulge in a series of guesses about the crime he might have
committed—larceny, sexual offence, killing of bailiffs, agents, landlords, counterfeiting money, fighting for the Boers (a man in a
neighbouring townland had been hanged drawn and quartered for
this act of 'sedition'). The Land War and the Boer War are conflated
within this list as two forms of rebellion against colonial rule. Still,
this is a criminal community by the definition of the colonial law,
one supported by the Catholic Church. It has all the characteristics
of the crowd—alcoholism, inbreeding, madness, Oedipal nationalism, and the degeneracy exemplified by Shawn Keogh himself and
promised by any offspring that he might have. Synge in one sense
celebrates the community's brief rebellion against patriarchal
fathers, priests, bishops, cardinals, peelers, the 'khakhi cut-throats'
of the British army, bailiffs, agents, landlords, Pope, saints, God. In
another sense, he condemns its inability to see that there is a connection more important than 'a great gap between a gallous story and
a dirty deed'. This is a community that has learned to make the
distinction between history and legend and has therefore disabled
itself as a traditional community; when faced with the necessity of
refusing the distinction, it turns into a mob. As with the represented
community on stage, so with the audience in the stalls. They could
not see that Christy becomes what they once were—not an individual but an embodiment of the People, the man who translated
his past rebellion into an answering and eloquent speech.

For Synge's play—in many ways a rehearsal for Yeats's achieve-ment in poetry—inaugurates in a specific literary form the aesthetic of vigour, of a linguistic as well as a physical strength that is sharply differentiated from the physical as well as the linguistic weakness of the city and its metropolitan decadence. Christy is an athlete as well as a talker; the two vocations are interfused. He outstrips the villag-ers in both areas.

Synge was sufficiently ill and sufficiently a writer of the French decadence to envisage physical health and west Irish unsophisti-cation as countering realities. Nevertheless, he turns these realities into an aesthetic which prides itself on its vigour and immediacy, on its refusal to create a distance between the body and discourse. He writes a discourse of the body which Yeats recognized, but in so doing found a means to incorporate the energy of violence into the energy of speech, to make the Irish accent and the Irish reputation for eloquence integral symptoms of revival rather than sinister indi-cations of a proximity to the barbaric or the revolutionary. This was, in epitome, the great act of translation. Christy does not just leave the Mayo village behind him when he leaves. More than that, he walks out of the nineteenth century, leaving his Ireland in it, bewail-ing her loss of the Playboy of the Western World. In the Yeatsian version, he is of course the Playboy of the Eastern World who has stepped beyond both the Pale and the pallor of the Dublin mob's philistine version of Ireland.

Boucicault's *The Colleen Bawn* and *The Lily of Killarney* are both imprinted on the *Playboy*; all three works make much of a killing that is not a killing, of the liberating consequences of the discovery that a murder has not been committed after all. In Boucicault, the conse-quences are marriage and permission to the Colleen to speak in her own accent, although everyone, even including Ann Chute, is per-mitted a certain thickening of brogue by the end. In Synge, the crime itself is a liberation; it is the discovery that an actual murder has not been committed that leads to the imprisonment of the community and the final release of Christy into mastery ('master of all fights from now on'). The earlier works are, of course, much more obedient to stage conventions, especially the convention of pleasing the audience by transforming the whole Irish element in

the play to a version of local colour that adds variety to the bourgeois ending. Synge's play enraged the audience because it introduced it to the symbolic realm, where the Law of the Father has
been broken and then reinaugurated. It refuses to end in a marriage
that has been for long prepared and promised. But more than that—
the *Playboy* is a work in which the political and the social are surrendered for the 'lonely impulse of delight' that will thereafter define
many of Yeats's heroic figures. He is an exemplar of that turn from
the political to the cultural which Yeats claimed was a feature of the
life of the younger generation after the downfall of Parnell. The
Father is dead, the sons can play. The aesthetic takes over from the
political and the social. The modernist hero of Irish letters—already
prefigured in Stephen Dedalus—is born. National character has
become national identity; blarney has become eloquence; history,
legend. It is as complete a translation as one could wish. Yet, facing
this phenomenon, there is still the mob.

Missing from this account is Pegeen Mike and with her the whole
zone of the sexual, overborne by the virile father–son conclusion,
reduced to a cry of loneliness for her loss of Christy and her presumed fate of marriage to the distinctly unvirile Shawn Keogh.
Keogh is the conventional servile figure in Irish writing, frightened
of the state and of the church, an apology of a man in the most
comprehensive sense, forever enslaved. Pegeen, on the other hand,
is a strong woman, the fright of seven townlands for her sharp
tongue, yet finally no more than a catalyst for Christy's liberation.
As in the case of Stephen Dedalus, male freedom is not accompanied
by freedom for women. Rather it is through freedom from women.
The Widow Quin is, after all, a murderer; Pegeen is, ultimately, a
mob-leader. These women need companionship in order to be fulfilled; they have no capacity to be in and of themselves. The rather
stale punning of the Pegeen (Pagan)–Christy (Christian) names defines her status as that of somone who is ultimately replaced, who
becomes historically anachronistic with the arrival of the new
redeemer figure. Between the Widow Quin, the once-married
woman whose crime achieves only notoriety, not fame, and Pegeen, unmarried, who is equally notorious for her abrasiveness,
women are exiled from glory. Christy temporarily softens Pegeen's

speech; the heart's a wonder indeed, but this is not a play about love. It celebrates the language of heroic solitude over that of unheroic companionship. Women can at best speak only the latter. By their language shall ye know them. Like the Colleen Bawn, they are allowed to spake, not speak. It is no longer a matter of accent; it is now a matter of gendered speech. Men command the speech of sublime self-possession; women the language of those whose selves need to be possessed. They exemplify a national character but they cannot exemplify national identity. The feminization that was always integral to the concept of national character—its combination of wildness, irrationality, imbecility, lack of the pragmatic virtues, childishness—has now yielded to a concept of national identity that has physical virility, both athletic and sexual, as its indicative characteristic. The process of regeneration also involved a process of re-gendering.[108]

FOUR

Boredom and Apocalypse
A National Paradigm

A NATIONAL PARADIGM

I want to readdress here the issue with which, in a reading of Burke, I began—the reconciliation of the cultural with the economic spheres of a culture that is taken to be counter-revolutionary and anti-theoretical in its traditional but threatened form. This is integral to the project of the Union; later, given the obvious and disastrous failure of that project—harrowingly exemplified in the Famine—it becomes integral to the competing project of nationalism. The pursuit of such a reconciliation, I suggest, provides a paradigm for Irish writing in the nineteenth century; one of the discursive formations that paradigm produces is a renovated version of a national character that must, by a variety of procedures, political and cultural, be disciplined into such sobriety of behaviour as would be in accord with the requirements of economic progress and development. Further, I have suggested that in the complex history of that process, there developed from Burke a set of narrative procedures that dealt with the history of Ireland in a series of stories that had in common, not only a rhythm of phases and periodizings, but also—especially in nationalist writings—a totalizing ambition. That ambition was quite simply to provide a narrative predicated on the notion of recovery and redemption from ruin and oppression. It was consistently frustrated by the impossibility of finding an *ab extra* vantage-point from which the story could be told, precisely because the nature of historical experience was too disturbed and disturbing to allow for the establishment of a secure subjectivity, the disengaged individual narrator. When a history is so fragmented that it cannot provide a climactic moment from which a 'Whig interpretation' can be derived, there is no normalizing narrative procedure available. Or, there is none apparently available. In Irish discourse, the compensatory stratagem for this is the generation of a narrative of strangeness, the story or stories of a country that is in a condition that cannot be represented at all or that still has to be represented. This is, indeed, an explicit position adopted by English writers on Ireland, most especially after the Union. Nationalist discourse adopted the English attitude that Ireland was exceptional and recalcitrant and took it in a reverse direction, making a virtue rather than a fault of this, consolidating it into an argument for independence and separation rather than into an argument for dependence and assimilation.

Thus the Irish community is consistently portrayed as one that it is impossible to recruit into the nineteenth-century normalizing narrative of progress and economic development. Linguistically, it is incoherent; its Irish or English, converted or perverted into one another, its dialects and esoteric vocabularies, indicate as much. Alcoholism, political violence, and economic backwardness are additional marks of the community's improvidence and fecklessness. It is a community that is always *in extremis*, either racked by crisis or constantly manufacturing crisis. Worst of all, even when parts of the Irish community were recruited into existing institutions, like the army or the police, they were often castigated as aliens, traitors in their own country. A resident magistrate, writing in 1882 during the Irish Land War, described what happened when native Irish were recruited into the paramilitary police force, the Royal Irish Constabulary:

The transformation that takes place, apparently in every characteristic, is very remarkable, and, I may add, very wonderful, showing, on the one hand, the natural weakness of the Irish character, and on the other, the facility with which it can be moulded and turned to good account. The recruit joins the depot a wild Irishman; he leaves it a steady, loyal, respectable, thoughtful, and disciplined member of society, forming one of a body of men unequalled among nations in character and physique, of which the people of the United Kingdom might well feel proud. It is left to those who designate themselves 'leaders of the people', to apply to their brethren in the Royal Irish Constabulary such terms as 'liveried scoundrels' and 'curs' of low degree.[1]

The situation is in some ways exacerbated by yet one more defining contrast that also emerges in Burke's writings and that is thereafter developed, in many European countries, both as part of the history of European colonialism and part of the history of internal class divisions and their accommodation within the nation-state—that is the contrast between the national community as a formation that is grounded in history, precedent, stability, religion (with its readily available racial extensions) and the inchoate crowd or mob that, because it is ignorant, numerous, violent, degraded and degrading, demands a whole new technology of control, from criminal theory to crowd theory to race theory. It is the threat that such a grouping was presumed to offer to political and economic stability—enforced by a remarkably static reading of the French Revolution, most especially the October days of 1789—that ignited the various apocalyptic terrors that, especially in France, mark much European writing in various fields in the latter half of the nineteenth century and the opening decades of the twentieth.

In Ireland where, time and again, readings of the past depended upon the recounting of a serial apocalypse that had overcome a number of civilizations, and for which the Famine and the death of landlordism were unavoidable contemporary instances, such narratives—whether in history or in literature or in economics—were irresistible. Yet apocalypse, even if it was always now, was, in such narratives, also the prelude to a final regeneration in which the national character and the national history would ultimately be redeemed and the experience of oppression and colonial subjection overcome.

Of course, one of the most obvious and most often tried ways of reconciling a conception of a so-called abnormal but energetic cultural formation, known as national character, with economic development, has been to sell it—to market it as an exotic product that, in its benign 'humorous' form, could be popularized as a consumer good. The target audience for such a product was clearly England and, to a lesser degree at first, America. This has been an inexhaustible resource for many Irish and other writers, not all of them literary, for over two centuries. The Irish landscape, whether in the form of the savage sublime, the picturesque, or the straightforwardly scenic from which the traces of a disastrous history had been removed or aggregated into theme-parks, also helped to situate this endearing abnormality as something that could be visited and consumed as a tonic for metropolitan weariness. Tourism is one of the economic achievements of a state—first British, later Irish—that has discovered a profitable means of converting culture into economics, although it requires the cultural stereotype of the community to remain fixed within prescribed limits, and adhere to a particular 'character'. Of course that was not what Burke meant at all nor is it the only possible means of achieving that conciliation. All I do here is to remark upon the fact that for two centuries tourism and the marketing of Ireland as an object of consumerism has been implicit in much of its literature and history. Both these forms of writing are, indeed, the most influential agencies in the sponsorship of Ireland as an entity that is instantly recognizable and marketable. The internal divisions that mark such writing, as in the variation between a so-called 'romantic' and a disenchanted version of Ireland, between fantasy and realism, are not radical; they do not disturb the security of the entity 'Ireland'; they merely enrich it. Even the division of the island since 1922 is represented in analogous terms, with the British north being caricatured as 'hard-headed' and 'realist', and the Irish south as 'romantic' and impractical, one as modern, the other as archaic, one industrialized, the other underdeveloped, one First, the other Third world. Political propaganda, just like tourism, feeds off such divisions; sometimes they are exploited in order to confirm political and economic power, sometimes to conceal the operation of such power under the guise of a shared, if disputatious, even endearingly attractive because strongly felt, communal loyalty that confirms the shared unity of Irishness by the fissiparous nature of its competing loyalties. For what could be more Irish than the tendency to split into factions? Factions, sectarian and political, confirm the unity they appear to deny.

Thus, as a country for tourists—internal and external—Ireland is in many respects unreal, really unreal, in the sense that the construction of its 'real' status and that of its consumer fantasy are inseparable activities. Yet the system of representation that is so generated can never be at ease because it is never complete. Like any system, it depends on exclusion as well as inclusion. As in political, so in literary forms—there is a system of representation which is not ever identical with a representative system. Even when there is a serious effort to represent minorities, as in the electoral form of proportional representation that is favoured in the Irish Republic, there is always going to be some residue, some peripherality that cannot be centred. But the peripherality need not merely be a matter of numbers—it may be a matter of interpretation. The translation of what Chatterjee calls 'fuzzy communities' to 'enumerable communities' inevitably involves an interpretative act whereby the community so enumerated may claim that it is not satisfactorily defined by number, indeed that to represent it as merely an enumerate minority may refuse it representation as a complex and even central culture.[2] This would, for instance, be true of Northern Ireland where both the Protestant and the Catholic communities, in their different ways, would respectively refuse their enumerative status within the bounds of the northern statelet or within the bounds of the island as a whole, partly but not entirely because they then would be transferred from minority to majority and vice versa. To paraphrase Coleridge, communities ought to be weighed, not counted. Similarly, in the Republic, it is often said that the status of the Irish-speaking community is one that cannot be estimated numerically only, and that the forms of state aid, a kind of economic proportional representation, that are designed to support its historically central role is in fact no more than a mode of peripheralizing it, rendering it archaic, quaint, a residue. Further, that same community would claim, with some justice, that Irish—as a language and as a literature—has been so severely misrepresented in English-language discourse for so long, that it has effectively been produced as an object of tourism—that it is no more than a romantic residue that can only survive in the world of global capital as a species of sentiment, official and thin piety. It is obvious that the ease or difficulty encountered by a community in verbally representing itself has an effect on the ease or difficulty it has in being politically represented. That is clearly a problem that Irish works of fiction engaged with throughout the nineteenth century; it is part of the explanation for 'strangeness' and the aspiration to overcome it so that it might be appropriately represented as it is, in its own normality, rather than misrepresented as an oddity for which there is no available language.[3] Dialect, or any form of vernacular language that is derided as inappropriate, uneducated, has either no linguistic status or a very frail one. Those who speak are correspondingly marginalized or excluded politically.[4]

RENOVATING THE PARADIGM: CORKERY

In Chapter 3 I tried to show how James Clarence Mangan's *Autobiography* operated as an instance of what we may call a self-consuming artefact; and how, for all its dispersion, it was—along with the other items in the fourth edition of *Poets and Poetry of Munster*—also an exemplary instance of the manner in which a position of melodramatized incoherence could nevertheless be made to cohere within a particular consolidating ideology—the ideology of nationalism. Equally, in the case of Synge, whose *Playboy* I read as an attempt to narrate the emergence of a national subject who is simultaneously a late embodiment of a community that has begun to degenerate into a mob, I suggested that, where Mangan had been made malleable to that ideology's project, Synge had not. The riots that marked the first production of his play, despite the Yeatsian gloss on them, were the first refusal. The second came in the renovated ideology of nationalism that, again centring on the Munster poets of the eighteenth century, was articulated in Daniel Corkery's *Hidden Ireland* (1924) and in his *Synge and Anglo-Irish Irish Literature* (1931). I want now to take a closer look at this critique, since it is in its way a founding act of literary and political criticism for the newly emergent Free State.

Corkery, as is well known, wants to distinguish between a colonial writer and a native writer. The writers of the 'Ascendancy' are, by virtue of their maltreatment of and contempt for the Irish people and indeed for the whole concept of Irish nationality, mortally flawed. Two themes, he suggests, are central to nineteenth-century Irish experience: 'The future conquest of the soil was part of Irish consciousness: if it were not, the thing could not have come to pass.' Indeed this had long been 'one of the deepest things' in that consciousness, visible to those who read Irish poetry. The second theme, is or was 'the disintegration of the Ascendancy in Ireland'.[5] Neither of these was treated by or available to the Ascendancy humorists like Maginn, Prout, and others because—in an echo of the objections to Thomas Moore—they wrote 'for London drawing-rooms' and thereby 'failed to speak the secret things in the nation's soul'. Thus they produced tourist, quaint Ireland, a place of 'fox-hunting and rioting or as spell-bound by fairies that troop nightly from our prehistoric ruins, moping out an existence not wholly in this world or quite beyond it'.[6] He then goes on to explain why Ireland had not produced a novel, in the European sense of that form. The novel depends upon intimacy with the society it represents. The Ascendancy lacked this, indeed refused it. Such writers became 'expatriates' and, in consequence, 'the more utterly expatriate the writer the more brilliantly his pages shine'.[7] Thus, instancing Sheridan, Prout, Maginn, Wilde, and Shaw, Corkery claims that the brilliance associated with them derives from the separation in them of intellect and emotion, and this he construes as the opposite of Irishness.[8] In the end, such writers merely become jesters for an English audience. Their finest achievement is Maria Edgeworth's *Castle Rackrent*: 'This Colonial Literature was written to explain the quaintness of the humankind of this land, especially the native humankind, to another humankind that was not quaint, that was standard, normal. All over the world is not that the note of Colonial

Literature?'⁹ Griffin (in *The Collegians*) and Somerville and Ross (in *The Big House of Inver*) are similarly chastised as attempting to represent 'this strange country'¹⁰ in a literary form not native to the Irish experience. This is all the more important now, in the first decade of the state's existence, because, although the 'national consciousness may be described, in a native phrase, as a quaking sod',¹¹ the Irish peasant has finally taken possession of the soil of Ireland and also now 'fills the highest offices in the country, in Church, in State, in Learning—everywhere'.¹² What distinguishes the Irish from the English 'national being' are the well-known three elements—the religious consciousness of the people, Irish nationalism and the land.¹³ This is a consciousness that has never been properly represented even though it is possessed by that famous crowd of 30,000 at the hurling match in Thurles when Corkery 'first became conscious that as a nation we were without self-expression in literary form'.¹⁴

In *The Hidden Ireland*, Corkery, in Yeatsian vein, provides a long perspective on the proposed Irish re-revival, by claiming that Irish eighteenth-century poetry is a pre-Renaissance art. 'The Renaissance . . . whitened every well-known national culture in Europe to something of a common tone'.¹⁵ The poets of Munster are, in a favourite phrase, 'the residuary legatees'¹⁶ of that great medieval tradition, now renewed in Romanticism for 'every Romantic movement is a national effort to discover for present needs forms other than the Classical forms'.¹⁷ This is a position not unlike Synge's own version of the 'dissociation of sensibility theory' as expressed in the preface to the *Playboy*. Medieval Europe, Elizabethan England—it matters little which era is chosen so long as there is a correspondent argument in favour of a once cherished vigour now faded and in need of revival. The place of revival is Ireland; but such a place is also a time. The often remarked discrepancy between development and underdevelopment that allows different peoples inhabiting the same historical moment to inhabit different chronologies is adapted in colonial and modernist discourses to argue that the time of the nation is a sacral time, one that has been broken by history and now must be repaired by aesthetics. Wlad Godzich's critique of Hegel's conception of history is pertinent here:

Hegel's well-known distinction of the various stages of development of the spirit constitutes the privileged chronology against which all human achievements are measured, and their application serves to redistribute contemporaries and predecessors alike according to the logic of that chronology, with the paradoxical effect that people who live at the same time are no longer thought of as true contemporaries.[18]

Benedict Anderson and Homi Bhabha's complex commentary on Anderson elaborate further on the relationships between nationality and temporality.[19] For immediate purposes, we may say that, for Corkery and Yeats, to be backward, archaic, is to possess that fullness that a secular temporality has abandoned. Yet the paradox is that such a sacral time must be provided with a history that is organized, at one level, as a series of discrete moments characterized by fullness and vigour. At another level, it has to argue that such moments are indicators of a timelessness, a human plenitude, that is now understood to be accessible only to or via those suppressed or colonial cultures that have been displaced by a metropolitan one that has suppressed in itself all that those once silenced cultures are now beginning to enunciate. Such enunciation is, of course, a process that, in rehearsing the problematic relationship between discrepant chronologies, has to claim that every so often it is fully exemplified in the work of a writer—such as Mangan or Synge—and is thereby altered. The telling feature of such writing is its capacity to negotiate between the sacred and the secular, to carry from the former the energies lacking in the latter—in the local Irish terms, to translate from Irish into English all those intensities that modern English lacks and to restore all those energies in Irish that have been suppressed. In such a negotiation, it is a matter of some importance to determine the degree of the writer's access to the Irish language—that is to its native vigour. Synge knew Irish much better than did Mangan—if indeed Mangan could be said to have known it at all. But Mangan had, according to the legend, a more intuitive relationship to the spirit of that language; Synge's relationship to it was more mediated, because of his class (and denominational) status.

The position of Synge is, therefore, interstitial. An Ascendancy writer who gains some degree of access to the life of the people and produces one play, *Riders to the Sea*, that is 'a portent in Anglo-Irish literature',[20] Synge achieves emblematic status: 'What we are to understand by nationalism in his case is cultural nationalism—a holding by that inner core of custom of which political nationalism is the shield and the defence.'[21] At the close of his study, Corkery claims that Ireland needs 'a succession of nationalistic movements, rising and falling, each dissolving into a period of reaction, of provincialism, yet each for all that leaving the nation a little more sturdy, a little more normal, a little less provincial than before.'[22] One might indeed 'shrink from the prospect of such a series of movements, each and every one of them using up a large amount of energy in mere propaganda'; but that only underlines the necessity of Ireland's 'having a national language of its own, not only as an indigenous medium of expression, but as a wall of defence'.[23]

Clearly, Corkery is treating Synge as a significant figure because he occupies an important transitional role in the still implicit history of a literary tradition that is being formulated in stages. It begins in a sophisticated Irish-language native tradition, degenerates into an unsophisticated English-language body of writings that overlaps with the expatriate English-language tradition, directed towards a foreign audience. This expatriate writing is brilliant but unfeeling at its best; at its worst, it exploits a politically inspired national stereotype. Then it gives way, in Synge, to a new English-language writing, partly intimate with the Irish language and experience, that in turn is to yield to a still unrealized future of a literature in the Irish language that would have the range and intimacy of other European national vernacular literatures. The chronologies involved here are governed throughout by the notion of a community that has evolved out of dispossession of language and soil into repossession and has equally emerged from nationhood into statehood. The role of cultural nationalism now is to provide representation for all that has been erased or caricatured. Synge is the writer in whom Ascendancy expatriatism begins to fade into communion with the previously Hidden Ireland.

Yeats's famous reformulation of the Irish literary tradition belongs to the same decade as Corkery's. It too may be called a nationalist reading, although it has very different implications. In brief rehearsal, Yeats conjoins Anglo-Ireland with peasant Ireland as two communities that have been distinguished throughout their history by the anti-modern spirit. Further, in opposing modernism, they have refused the Lockean contractarian version of society and its accompanying spirit of abstraction, preferring instead to preserve the intimacies of mystical community and the specific experiences of what is actual, concrete. The main point of difference, however, is that Yeats produces, as a celebratory and simultaneously a tragic gesture, the theory of the occult and its apocalyptic apparatus as a means of providing for his thought a transnational resonance, his reply to the internationalized theories of cosmopolitanism and of progress that seemed to him to be depriving the world of its imaginative aura. In doing so, he brings to a more intense pitch the division between universal reason, understood as such in relation to an Enlightenment model of science and of a progressive humanity, and a national literature, indeed a national ideology, which he deliberately counterposed as the antithesis of that notion. The various geometries he took from occultism, in order to find some replacement for the unilinear conceptions of history that he found so repellent, are figures of cyclic repression and liberation, timed in their motions to contract or expand in relation to the moving hands of the millenial Year that describe the quarterings of a great aesthetic clock, a steady pattern that survives but also accompanies great historical change. It is characteristic of Yeats, as it was of Burke, that the sense of cataclysm should enrich his perception of the past— although that is probably true of any historical narrative written in the light of momentous events such as the French Revolution, or the First World War and the Russian Revolution, world events that were mirrored for Yeats in the 1916–22 period in Ireland. At any rate, the capacity to theorize a whole sequence of events into a national narrative enabled both Corkery and Yeats to distinguish between Ascendancy and native, to assign to each a different tradition, to claim that there was in the 1920s a visible accommodation between the two and that, in the light of such accommodation, the matrix of a national literature had been formed. The characteristic spirit, the distinctively Irish feature, that prevailed in each of these conceptions of the national was its abiding anti-modernism, its adherence to a version of the *ancien régime* that was now rewritten as a deeper history than that which preceded revolutionary France.

Any reading or representation of Irish experience that depends on discursive formations of the kind I have been describing is not only open to the charge of essentialism—it is also, more seriously, open to the charge of monotony. For whatever one may say about the dispersed subject in Irish writing, or about its endless research in pursuit of the definition of Irish difference or exceptionalism, or of the political resonance of such exercises, inescapable in a colonial culture, there is still potency in the complaint that such writing, while not at all being boring, is nevertheless deeply involved with the experience of boredom. As Corkery said, it may be that, from the position of the cultural nationalist, one can only look forward to a series of regenerations and recessions, booms and busts, all of which are directed towards the same end—the emergence of Ireland as its own subject, rather than the repeated re-emergence of Ireland as an object of the scrutiny of others. These others need not be foreigners. They are often the Irish themselves, endlessly engaged with the problematic of Ireland-as-such; endlessly entrapped between representing it as a quaint other to imperial normality, or as a radical otherness for which no canonical system of representation is sufficient. Todorov's description of Columbus' plight might be applied to Ireland:

Columbus's failure to recognise the diversity of languages permits him, when he confronts a foreign tongue, only two possible, and complementary, forms of behaviour: to acknowledge it as a language but to refuse to believe it as different; or to acknowledge its difference but to refuse it as a language.[24]

That is, of course, a description that would fit with English attitudes towards Ireland, the more so if we substitute the word 'nation' for 'language'. But it also fits with many Irish attitudes towards Ireland and the Irish language—and with earlier Irish attitudes towards the English language, although one may wonder at the mind-set that can translate into English Irish poems that claim it is a hated language, dreary and unmelodious, not to be used. But the central point is that difference can be acknowledged in the most repressive spirit, more pronounced when difference itself has historically been both repressed and asserted for various purposes. Essentialism is coercive because it always insists on the necessity of reconciling difference with sameness, discontinuity with continuity, arguing, for instance, that the same Irish spirit prevailed time and again, despite the refusal by its oppressors to acknowledge its legitimate claims. This is not an impossible position but it is a repetitive one. It is productive of monotony, because it orders miscellaneous materials into repetitive, typifying narratives. What I suggest here is that monotony or, to put it otherwise, the repeated manipulation of the same paradigm in Irish writing, leads to an alteration in the aesthetic which had itself been part of that paradigm. That aesthetic was, in effect, a national one; that is to say, it was an aesthetic that identified the success or failure of a work in relation to its capacity to capture the essential national spirit and/or to recapitulate in itself a phase of that spirit's development. But the spirit, so conceived, always had its social counterpart in the national character; and the national character, even when understood as a distillation in exemplary form of that spirit, was always prone to petrifaction. Once the spirit was embodied within it, it ceased to be spirit. The contradiction the paradigm thus produced within itself was not soluble; but it could be exaggerated to the point at which the paradigm itself began to break down. That mode of exaggeration was predictable; the exaggeration of petrifaction, of the national spirit and character, to the point where it became typified into a series of ready-made illustrative models. Although such typification occurred frequently in nineteenth-century discourse, it was in the twentieth century, and more specifically during the decades between the 1920s and the 1950s, that such typification became a conscious literary method, even a satiric technique. For comedy needs typification to be effective.

EXHAUSTING THE NATIONAL PARADIGM: FLANN O'BRIEN

In literature, perhaps the work that represents the ever-shifting relation between the central and the peripheral, between the historical and the contemporary, between all that is pseudo-romantic about Irish and all that is harshly actual about the squalor of the modern metropolis, is Flann O'Brien's *At Swim-Two-Birds* (1939), a 'novel' constructed on the principles of proportional representation rather than on the single transferable vote system that is the political equivalent of the representing narrator in realist fiction. O'Brien's novel, in effect, indicates that the best representation can do is to produce an unhappy coalition of interlocking discourses that remain in uneasy alliance with one another, rather than elect a one-party strong government that will be able to represent the whole *mélange* of history, language, community, and narratives that both compose and discompose his fiction into so many dialects, chief of which is the mock dialect of the translation of the Irish language into the fustian English of a government-sponsored cultural nationalism.[25]

Among the most remarkable features of O'Brien's writings is their organization around an internal schism that bears within itself an interpretation of Irish literary history. The schism is between fantasy and realism. It is endemic in O'Brien's writings, powerfully operative in a number of subtle and usually hilarious forms. But it is also the schism that O'Brien uses in his ongoing battle with James Joyce, especially the Joyce who had been created by the interpretative practices of American academia. Further, O'Brien's battle with Joyce duplicates the Free State's battle with the Irish Renaissance. O'Brien's rebuke to Joyce is of a piece with Patrick Kavanagh's rebuke to Yeats and the Revival.[26] In a strange series of reduplications, a great deal of Irish writing, from the nineteenth century to the mid-twentieth, uses the same paradigm of opposition between 'realism' and 'fantasy', both within the work of individual writers and within those critiques that interpret that work as belonging either to the 'fantasy' (Irish Revival) phase or to the 'realist' (Free State) phase. The paradigm governs both a way of writing and a way of reading. Moreover, this opposition also coincides with the old distinction between linguistic extravagance and eloquence on the one hand and linguistic penury and harshness on the other. Various authors exhibit this: George Moore in the movement from *Evelyn Innes* to *Esther Waters*; Joyce from *Dubliners* to *Finnegans Wake*;

James Stephens from *The Charwoman's Daughter* to *The Crock of Gold*; Eimear O'Duffy from *The Wasted Island* to *King Goshawk and the Birds*; Austin Clarke from *The Vengeance of Fionn* to *Later Poems*; O'Casey from the Dublin trilogy to the later plays that begin with *The Silver Tassie*; and Synge and Yeats, where the variation is constantly produced within individual plays and poems, effecting contrasts between a harsh and impoverished version of Ireland and a radiant transfiguration of it into that imaginative fantasy that draws its strength both from the actuality out of which it grows and from which it turns away in disdain.

This schismatic divide is consciously exploited by O'Brien in his fiction and in his journalism. Indeed, even the division between these, often taken to be disabling, enforces his critique of twentieth-century Ireland and its literature(s) and language(s). In his fiction, he parodies the extravagant solipsism and esoteric jargon of the modernist author/hero; in his journalism, he attacks the extraordinary ready-made banalities of the contemporary hack writer. The first he attacks in one of the chosen genres of high modernism—the experimental novel; the other in the inescapable medium of the mass mind, the newspaper. The mark of the first is its fondness for the arcane, its search for uniqueness; of the second, its helpless subservience to the cliché, its thirst for consensus. The only writing that is permitted any claim to freedom from these extremes is writing in the Irish language; that is to say, what was written in that language several centuries ago, when it was free of the grotesque stereotypes that govern its use in the present day. It is not merely the case that these stereotypes are offensive and degrading; what is worse, they have been so effectively internalized by the Irish themselves that they have now come to be the standard means of Irish self-representation—a process cruelly parodied in his novel *An Béal Bocht* (1941).[27] The revival of the language by its translators and by its new race of speakers—the babbling and ferocious *gaeilgeóirí*—has raised a spectral monster that is a grotesque deformation of the actual speech and writing of the past. Of course, the same is true of the English language; it too has been rendered unrecognizable by modernist authors or all too recognizable by contemporary journalists. O'Brien plays ingenious variations on the opposition between the extraordinary and the infraordinary, between fantasy and realism. The most frequent and successful is the adaptation, as conversation, of the language and formulas of the Civil Service, emphasizing thereby the surrealistic element that is embedded in and even released by bureaucratic conventions. Prominent among these is the questionnaire, transmuted by O'Brien into a literary sub-genre. The questionnaire has a montonous decorum and persistence. It appears in the most opaque linguistic disguises—clichés, circumlocutions, periphrases, literalisms—and produces the most extraordinary and often equally opaque answers. O'Brien's art discovers humour in the repetition of stock words and phrases that come to achieve an almost canonical status in his writing. 'Class' is one of those words; 'a member of the author class'; 'a member of the farming class'; 'choosing his boot, the buttoned class'; 'holder of Guinness clerkship, the third class'; 'a member of the clergy, enclosed class'. Almost equalling it in frequency and effect is the word 'party'—'a party by the name of Bagenal'.[28] The comic relation between the individual person or object and the conventional sociopolitical meanings of 'class' and 'party' highlights the discrepancy between the registers of official and colloquial speech; the eccentricity of the single person or object is the more evident through its association with standard formations that have lost their political life and become clichés. And, of course, O'Brien adopts the questionnaire as an integral element in his narrative in *At Swim-Two-Birds*.

And how is our friend? he inquired in the direction of my bed.
    Nature of my reply: Civil, perfunctory, uninformative.[29]

All of O'Brien's work employs such mock-specifications that exploit the elements of impersonal precision and colloquial familiarity that lie dormant in ordinary speech and in bureaucratic routines. His personae, 'the brother', 'yer man', 'Keats and Chapman', 'the Plain People of Ireland', have the same blend of qualities—intimately known and yet entirely anonymous.[30] It is the predictability and the strangeness of their discourse that make it both familiar and alienated. In the pervasive banality that suffuses all, the surreal lurks—'the surrealism of the habitual'.[31] They collude and collide with one another in deft sequence. The compendium of bureaucratic conventions satirized by O'Brien in his Mylesian disguise is additionally potent precisely because it contains within itself an inversion; the written word, the documentary procedure, the obituarist's format, has become the speech of the common populace. In a bureaucratic world, the formatted document is sovereign; speech is no longer prior to such conventions; it is an after-mimicry of them. There is a peculiar kind of local comedy involved in the personae of the newspaper column, for they combine a specious individuality with a complete typicality; in a comparable manner their reported speech combines the inflections of eccentricity with those of a 'bureaucratic fatality'.[32]

It is true that in *At Swim-Two-Birds* O'Brien, in writing a novel about his undergraduate author writing a novel about Dermot Trellis who is himself writing a novel in collaboration with another writer, William Treacy, about characters who finally rebel by writing Trellis into another fiction, is bringing into question the system of illusion upon which fiction and its putative other, 'real life', depends. But in this book, as in *The Third Policeman*, written directly afterwards, although not published until 1967, and in *The Dalkey Archive* (1964), a strange recycling (if that is the word) of its predecessor, O'Brien explores the sinister implications of the systems of representation upon which literature and indeed the whole social system, depends. The conversion of one world into another—of Joyce into 'Joyce', of men into bicycles, of authorship into a series of infinitely receding personae, of the ordinary world into the extraordinary one of the self (*das Selbst*, De Selby)—is effected not only by a switch of discourse but also by virtue of the credence given to such discourses. Such credence is produced by acts of interpretation. Discourse is not something to be interpreted; it is itself an act of interpretation. All discourse is interpretation; all interpretation is discourse. In the epistemological free fall that is called writing, some halt must be called; at some point, discourse must hit bottom. Otherwise, every believer in discourse becomes a monomaniac, someone who is entirely given over to his or her language as a system that is sufficiently autonomous to replace the world. It is in seeking such a ground that O'Brien (like Kavanagh) is an author of the Free State, the little world that succeeded to the extravagant rhetoric of the Revival and the Rising and the War of Independence and the Civil War. It is a world that has lost faith in the heroic consciousness of the heroic individual and has replaced it by the unheroic consciousness of the ordinary, of the Plain People of Ireland. Of course O'Brien is ironic, to say the least, about the PPI. But the attraction of the Free State world, in its ready-made language, cliché, consensus, is that it is a shared world, that it observes, even relishes, limitation. In that regard, it is an antidote to the preceding world and history of the fantasy worlds of Joyce, Yeats, the revolutionary leaders, the rhetoricians of a form of monomania to which they tried to make the actual world conform. In so far as it had forsaken its earlier, apocalyptic history, it had given up a system of representation, whose literary expression was modernism, for a representative system, whose literary expression was anti-modernist bureaucratese. A bureaucratic democracy has no natural relation to heroicized narratives. In Franco Moretti's terms:

democracy is not interested in the production of good novels. If anything, it aims at limiting the domain of the novelistic, at counterbalancing the destabilizing tendencies of modernity. It aims at reducing the rate of 'adventure' in our lives while expanding the jurisdiction—so inert in narrative terms—of 'security'.[33]

The globalism of the Revival had, in these terms, succeeded to the localism of the Free State; whatever the myriad defects and stupidities of the latter, censored and censorious, it was so steeped in cliché that it would never run the modernist risk of becoming a fantasy that prided itself on its escape from the ordinary. Localism moved in the other direction; its movement into fantasy, or nightmare, was predicated on its power to assimilate everything, especially the drama of personal identity, 'into a culture of procedural rationality'.[34] The vocation of 'non serviam' of Stephen Dedalus had been replaced by the obedient functionary's job in the Civil Service. The fake nation, with its inflated rhetoric of origin and authenticity, had given way to the fake state, with its deflated rhetoric of bureaucratic dinginess. In the passage from the fantasy of one to the realism of the other, the entity called Ireland had somehow failed to appear.

In a similar fashion, it could be shown that many of the Big House plays and novels of the twentieth century in Irish writing, most of them deriving from the Yeatsian model, conversely operate by claiming that it is precisely that cultivated Anglo-Irishness these derelict houses and people represent that has not been incorporated within the new state system—that the Anglo-Irish civilization, like the Irish-speaking civilization, is not represented by being treated as something archaic and remaindered, subsidized by the state but not integral to its functions.[35] One of the most enduring characteristics of a postcolonial state is the presence within it of remaindered communities, formations that cannot be incorporated politically and must therefore be sustained culturally by the life-support machine of the aesthetic or the touristic, two intimately related practices. These display both the power and the failure of a system of representation that can only effect its purposes by a process of peripheralization for those elements within the national state system that are presumed to have served their historical purpose and therefore are fossilized within a regime of tourism or writing or film that has to deal with their complex, fuzzy realities by stereotyping them as typically national, 'Irish' in one or other of the senses of that limited, but monotonously fertile, category. Of course, it is also true that these peripheralities conceive of themselves in the very same terms as the pre-state nation conceived itself—as a form of authenticity environed by inauthenticity, as an élite group environed by a mob, as history incarnated in a group that has been cast away as no longer belonging to the present. If this is true in the Republic, it is much more harshly true of the two communities in the north, both of whom wish to speak the same language of economic development while also adhering to different cultural languages. And both experience the same plight—of being told that their communities must surrender the archaic language of difference—because it is irrational, improvident, insusceptible to civilization—and surrender it to a more controlled and controlling language of ecumenism that will permit economic development to proceed and a sad history to be left behind as nothing more than an object of touristic pleasure.

As always, there is a great deal of shadow boxing carried on in these staged displays. There is always the recourse to the notion that the *Lebenswelt*, the life-world, is threatened by the impersonal system, local custom succumbing to rational uniformity, 'oul dacency' giving way to heartless anonymity, aristocratic splendour fading into plebeian and philistine vacuities. It is not sufficient to call this specious combat boring; it is a combat that has boredom at its centre. Boredom is the only interesting issue that is raised by it.

BOREDOM AND THE PARADIGM

Boredom is a territory susceptible to the stress of aesthetic procedures because it has within it, as part of its difficulty and part of its seduction, the absence of seismic events. It is a standard feature of much modernist literature that there is such a distinction between the quotidian, anomic nature of the monadic life of the metropolitan culture and the grand metanarratives—religion, philosophy, even history—that used to make sense of it, render it meaningful, that nothing is felt to be more urgently needed than a restoration of such structuring narratives. What we have been looking at in Corkery and in Yeats are attempts, in Irish conditions, to effect such a restoration through theosophy and the Irish-language literary tradition respectively. The return of these represseds is figured by both of them as the return of ancient, ancestral energies almost extinguished in the modern era by imperialism, by capital, by Christianity. But both of them also stress the necessity of a national literature that can only be so if the previously sundered elements in Irish society—Ascendancy and peasantry—are in some way reconciled one to another. What Yeats and Corkery both require of the national literary tradition is that it mature into a body of writing that will surpass the crude propaganda of Young Ireland (Yeats) and the debased fiction of Griffin or Kickham or the early productions of the Gaelic League (Corkery). Each wants to establish a tradition that is, therefore, characterized by hierarchy. Each wants to claim for the national literature the power to produce works of universal import, achieved through attention to and intimacy with the local. It may be argued that Yeats begins with the 'universal' and then finds that it has its local habitation and name while Corkery reverses the process. More to the point, both of them, in their different ways, recognized that Synge was an emblematic figure in the development of such a tradition.

Mangan and Synge are central figures in the intricate negotiations of cultural nationalism with its version of a discontinuous history.[36] For such discontinuity can only be understood in relation to such exemplars; it could not, of itself, be comprehensible. Others can have the same role assigned to them—Parnell, Edgeworth, Swift, Burke, the Anglo-Irish intellectuals of the eighteenth century. In such figures, discontinuity is rehearsed within the confines of a career or a body of work; but the central interpretative strategy is that they all, after a career of action or writing in which they consolidate some aspect of Irish experience, even to the extent of making it suddenly appear comprehensible, should have a tragic fall. They become victims of the Irish circumstances over which they had for a time exercised control. Thus, they exemplify both the overcoming of discontinuity and the surrender to it. Each one summarizes a phase of national experience but all display the fatality that attends upon all of its phases. No one was more conscious of this condition than Yeats, who made exemplary heroes of so many but of none more effectively than himself. In fact, making others heroic was one of the means by which he made himself so.

In the myth of Yeats and Synge that Yeats created, the initiating moment is Yeats telling Synge in 1898 to leave Paris for Ireland and for the people.[37] To write of and for the people, even if the writing is not done by one of the people is, in Synge's case, to forgo decadence for health, Paris for the Aran Islands, exile for home. Of all the positions that might be occupied by a writer who sought to gain the point of vantage that might permit some detachment in his or her vision of home, exile is surely the most obvious—especially the form of exile that allows for a return home, imaginatively or literally, so that a species of anthropological investigation can take place. Of course, such an investigation gives rise to the usual questions. What is the nature of the relationship between the investigator and the investigated? How can intimacy with 'the people' be reconciled with 'detachment' from them? Can the writer be both an insider and an outsider, and are these very questions symptomatic of a more general condition that the writer will incorporate in his or her work or in which that work will be incorporated? These questions all have a bearing on the canonical figures of the Revival—Moore, Yeats, Joyce, and Synge—although they include many others as well.

Ireland has, of course, a preoccupation with exile in its many forms—political, economic, the exile of enforced or chosen emigration, the exile of banishment, the expatriatism of which Corkery writes. There is also the difference between exile in London and exile in Paris, important in the modern period because in London, the exile of Shaw or Wilde was one demanded by the need for a metropolitan residence, in the financial and commercial capital of the English-speaking world,[38] whereas exile in Paris—for Moore, Joyce, and Synge—was demanded by the need to live in the capital of the nineteenth century, the art capital of the world. Paris was also a city for Fenian exiles who had had their gaol sentences in England commuted to exile abroad; John O'Leary was perhaps the most famous of these. It was also the city of M. Millevoye, Maud Gonne's lover, the supporter of Boulangisme and of a right-wing nationalistic politics that left neither her nor her other lover, Yeats, totally unimpressed.

Still, the position of exile allows us to approach the question of boredom by exposing some of those features by which boredom is constituted and understood. The first of these is immobility. Two forms of immobility in relation to exile are immediately accessible. One is the immobility that is, so to say, imposed on the native culture by the exilic position. It is a widely canvassed accusation that exiles are always, in their conception of the land they left, archaic; they have not participated in and are frequently ill informed about the changes that have taken place in their absence. Further, they are more susceptible to stereotypic representations of their culture, because the stereotype is the most effective and affixing form of memory and delusion. It may be said that the stereotype is more often chastised when it has been successfully exported abroad than it is when produced at home. Produced at home it is often regarded as an effective way of summarizing and encapsulating Irish difference; its delusional qualities are more remarked upon when the kitsch element is exposed in a territory—like Irish America—and used to make of that difference a political issue.

The second kind of immobility is internally generated. In this instance, the exile remains at home but in a state of deep disaffection from it. Such immobility has all the characteristic features of underdevelopment, of being removed from history—poverty, provincialism, submissiveness to authority, a regressive investment in religion and its consolations, fear of the world beyond. All of this is registered by speech- or language-failure—aphasia, inarticulacy, miscomprehension. To complete the circuit, within such immobility there is a longing to escape that is regularly thwarted by the fear of leaving. In the famous Joycean words—hemiplegia, paralysis. The text that specifies most fully the relation between immobility and exile is *Dubliners*. Dublin, in that representation, is the world capital of boredom, presiding over the country of the dead.

Yet, in Joyce's other fictions, the site of immobilism is expanded—to Ireland in *Portrait*, to the colonial system of which Ireland is a part in *Ulysses*, to the global system in *Finnegans Wake*. Ireland has an increasingly privileged, ultimately global, position in the fiction; it begins as a peripheral place that gradually accretes to itself more and more complex significations until it becomes central, Phoenix Park becoming the Garden of Eden, the iconography of Irish oppression and rebellion becoming a signifying system for the operation of all systems, including that of language. Boredom becomes pervasive in the sense that, for all the diversity of its representations, the Joycean text is constantly referring difference, local or personal eccentricities, national or imperial formulations, back to sameness. The same, the elision of difference, the iterative reproduction of the same story or style within a diversity of other stories and styles, is the ultimate site of boredom. The conquest of a space that attempts to define itself as unique, as not normal, as the custom-bound village in the secular developed world of the metropolis, is an act of domination that has sameness as its goal and its consequence. In the end, Dublin is not just the capital of boredom; it is

Capital that presides over the world of boredom. All exceptionalism, all variety, is replaced by sameness. The stereotype and the archetype are fused into a reading of history that announces the end of history.

The treatment of boredom often involves ethical and political questions, especially in the twentieth century.[39] It is a feature of the advanced industrial world, where the monotony of work, the vacuousness of leisure, the atomization of traditional communities and practices are all routine experiences that make the representation of boredom inescapable, whether in poetry or in fiction. Further, boredom is both a symptom and a technique of repression, both in its psychic and political forms. Joyce's Dublin and Dubliners are exemplary instances of this. Paradoxically, the representation of boredom also involves an intensification of the rhetorical strategies which are needed to create a text that is, simultaneously, driven towards completeness and dispersed amidst fragmentary incoherences. As Jean Ricardou remarks, this process leads one to 'realize how the novel ceases to be the writing of a story to become the story of a writing.'[40] It is not entirely surprising, then, that Ireland has produced a number of writers in the twentieth century who are as remarkable for their fascination with boredom as they are for the virtuosity of their narrative techniques, their constant referral of the reader, through a variety of digressions and descriptions that make a virtue of monotony, to the 'story of a writing', to the text itself as an artefact that is caught in the process of its impetus towards story and its impetus towards the denial of story. It is clearly one way in which the drive towards telling one story (say, the nationalist one) can be stalled, partly on the grounds that such a monocular story is productive of monotony and paralysis even as it attempts to produce, as in an adventure tale, a series of catastrophes that are eventually overcome in a triumphant conclusion. Ireland's colonial history was both a history of emancipation from the monotonies of tyranny and, after the emancipatory movement, a restoration of the same monotonies under the name of freedom. It was economically, politically, culturally, half-baked, just like the Anglo-Irish civilization described by John Wilson Croker at the beginning of the nineteenth century. But in this condition it also had (or bore?) a striking resemblance to all those advanced countries in which the relation between tradition and modernity had become, or had been understood to have become, inert.

In Joyce (as in D. H. Lawrence, T. S. Eliot, and many others) the only energies that are not apparently subject to the domination of boredom and convention are the libidinal energies. It is certainly the case that boredom becomes, in Joyce, a much more male experience than it had been in nineteenth-century English and European fiction, where the experience of boredom, of the trivialized life, had been much more readily associated with and undergone by women.[41] In Joyce, the question is still contentious: who suffers more from boredom—men or women? In so far as women are excluded from the public sphere of social life, they are the more prone to that condition. But, equally, in so far as they are correspondingly given a superior role in the sexual life and the life of the affections, they are, libidinally speaking, more favoured. Their ambiguous status is famously represented by the 'female' voices that close *Ulysses* and the *Wake*. These may be the voices of women immured in the purdah of the personal and the domestic; but they may also be read, because of the undifferentiated flow of the language in which they are registered, as emancipatory. They escape from the immobilizing systems of grammar and punctuation into an unboundaried freedom or, alternatively, they are so devoted to the pursuit of a private, bodily pleasure that they thereby merely confirm their separation from the systematic public world. Thus it is only by mystifying the sexual as a paradigm of the overcoming of the isolation of the individual subject, as a merging of river into ocean, as a restoration of wife to husband, that the history of the subject can be rewritten, in terms of pleasure, as a history of its disappearance into timelessness. Boredom has to pay close attention to chronology in order to define its own condition—entrapped by the passage of time it elaborates an escape from that by envisaging the passing away of time. The bored have to find a way of passing the time; in doing so, they arrive at the position where time passes them by. In the night of the unconscious, they day-dream. Those who are not bored, like the Joycean women, escape from time; they have never had the misfortune to be subjects, merely agencies through which the condition of the sexual—i.e. of the interesting—is established.

But it was Beckett who transposed the issue from the specifically cultural–social realm to the ontological. The immobilism and the garrulous or silent anxieties of his people are implacable extensions of the Joycean investigation of boredom, thematized as the consequences of the fragmentation of the self for which an ontological ground must be sought though never found. The marks of boredom in his work—as in Joyce's, O'Brien's (and Kafka's)—are dinginess of physical circumstance and dress, extreme routinization of action and speech, an individual eloquence that derives from consensual banalities, a sense of personal insignificance that is alternately enhanced by the belief that one is an unimportant element in a vast system or that there is no system, that one is in a void in which the illusion of a system, however impersonal it might be conceived to be, is merely a fictive consolation. Aggravated by these conditions into a depressive boredom, the consciousness cannot but rehearse them endlessly, stunned by the tedium that it produces.

It is curious that the investigation of boredom as a systemic condition should be so pronounced in Joyce's fiction, since he was perfectly ready to accept—as his lectures and occasional writings demonstrate—the standard idea that Irish history was a series of betrayals and catastrophes from which it was almost impossible to escape. In other words, there was no lack of seismic events; even in his own youth, the fall of Parnell seemed apocalyptic enough to be figured time and again in his work and in that of Yeats and others as a turning-point in the history of modern Ireland.[42] Among the other writers glanced at here, Mitchel, O'Grady, Edgeworth, Mangan, and Corkery were all energized by the spectacle of a dramatic historic moment that resonated in its effects throughout the culture and sustained it, even in its immiseration, by its pervasive presence. The decline of landlordism, of the eighteenth- or nineteenth-century kind, the penal laws, the French Revolution, the rebellion of 1798, the Union, the Tithe War of the 1830s, the Famine, the O'Connellite campaigns, the Fenians, the Land War—all of these variously appear as moments in which a change appears, in which a civilization's end is threatened or achieved. In Yeats's work—plays and essays, as well as poems—we may feel at times that a little boredom might be something of a relief from the constant appropriation of almost everything that happened in his lifetime to a visionary apocalypse in which all that 'is past, or passing or to come' flashes up in a conflagration that consumes time and exposes eternity. What I want to suggest here is the natural alliance between Joycean boredom and Yeatsian apocalypse in relation to temporality and therefore to history.

It need hardly be argued that Yeats construes nationality as the opposite of rationality. Rationality's claim to universalism and its accompanying hostility to any form of particularism, especially national particularism, that undermined it, was impermissible in the Yeatsian aesthetic—indeed is impermissible in the whole Romantic aesthetic that reacts against this 'bad' form of Enlightenment ideology. His position is characteristic in the attritional debate between the idea of the nation and the idea of the state. But Yeats wants to counterpose an alternative universalism, one that goes beyond the defence of the nation as a historical agent. His form of universalism gives priority to imagination, religion, myth, folklore, custom—a complex of forces that exist in two constellations. One is the constellation of the folk, the people; with them, it takes the non-cognitive form of wonder. The other is the constellation of the 'ruling company of men', who articulate that complex doctrinally into a cognitive cult of mystery, definable perhaps as that of which one has only ever re-cognition, rather than cognition. Those who do not belong to either constellation are those who have become separated from all that is significant in the life of humankind and who have adopted, as their substitute, rationality, rapacity, progress, science, and the whole ideology of the vulgar bourgeoisie. All this is well known. But there is a further point. Yeats's occultism has the strange merit of being able to preside over its own extinction and then to undergo a process of retrieval, rebirth, in which it returns, always by violent irruption. Violence is its foundational moment—therefore a constructive violence—and destructive violence is the terminal moment of modern rationality's history. These are the features of Sorelian syndicalism, the earliest European articulation of fascist ideology that T. E. Hulme transmitted to the English-speaking world through his translation of Sorel's *Réflexions sur la violence* (1906), his sponsorship of Bergson's vitalist philosophy, and his own *Speculations, Essays on Humanism and the Philosophy of Art*, published posthumously in 1924. (Hulme was killed in the war.) Hulme, as is well known, was much admired by T. S. Eliot, Ezra Pound, Wyndham Lewis, and Yeats.[43] Initially or terminally, the sword is mightier than the pen; it is only in the aftermath of maturity that the pen becomes mightier than the sword. At all points, the seismic event is either present or threatening; certainly Yeats conceived of his own life-span as coincident with the moment of migration from ominous threat to actual cataclysm. As a consequence, his work is in love with the crisis of temporality, the transitional moment in which the past is recovered as a prefiguration of the future, when the rough beast slouches towards its Bethlehem, when the burning towers of Troy are engendered in a mythic rape, when a vision that he called up 'a twelve month since' promises to eventuate in the future perfect of a poem that 'I shall have written him'.[44] Clearly, it is not only the tempo of apocalypse that is audible in Yeats's writings; it is the explosion of chronology that accompanies apocalypse.

APOCALYPSE: COMING SECOND

The classic example of historical apocalypse in Yeats's work is his famous poem on revolution and modernity, 'The Second Coming'.[45] It is a poem that clearly responds to and participates in the pan-European militarization of politics that put an end to nine-teenth-century liberalism. The prestige of violence and the disgust for the compromises and careerism of politics were features of this process that were strongly present in Ireland when the poem was published in volume form in 1921.[46] It is concerned with an ending and a beginning, both interfused so that it is scarcely possible to say where the distinction between them can be found. The poem does indicate the moment when they appear to disengage. 'Hardly are those words out | When . . . ' The phrase 'The Second Coming' has just been completed for the second time when the action of that coming commences with the 'vast image'. Indeed the first eleven lines have several repeated words and phrases: 'Turning and turning', 'falcon/falconer', 'loosed', 'surely', 'at hand'. Further, the definite article, used eleven times, is strategically important in the establishment of the pattern of repetition. It insinuates a complicity with the reader, a knowingness. We can specify what the falcon, the tide, the ceremony, the best, the worst are because the surrounding poems of the volume *Michael Robartes and the Dancer* (1921) tell us. In the vicinity of 'The Second Coming', poems like 'The Leaders of the Crowd', 'Towards Break of Day', 'Demon and Beast', 'A Prayer for my Daughter', 'A Meditation in Time of War', 'To be Carved on a Stone at Thoor Ballylee' provide a narrative sequence of which 'The Second Coming' is an integral part. They help us to know what 'the ceremony of innocence', 'the worst', and all other agents and conditions of the poem's action are.

Michael Robartes and the Dancer has a group of poems at its centre about Easter 1916, and 'The Second Coming' is reputedly about the Russian Revolution of 1917. Both of these historical moments are dramatized as part of a larger theatrical dispute that dominates the whole volume. It takes the usual Yeatsian form of a collision between opposites out of which might come unity or, more likely and less heroically, release from the trial of strength between them into a limp, exhausted freedom. It is the sort that he writes of in 'Demon and Beast', when a floating (not a soaring) bird could please him. The 'freedom' he wins from 'hatred and desire' is not gratifying.

> Yet I am certain as can be
> That every natural victory
> Belongs to beast or demon,
> That never yet had freeman
> Right mastery of natural things,
> And that mere growing old, that brings
> Chilled blood, this sweetness brought;

The freeman, a political–social construct, is a poor thing compared to the bestial and/or demonic energies that create the force field in which we live most vitally. This casts some light on the group of poems about the Easter rebellion ('Easter 1916', 'Sixteen Dead Men', 'The Rose Tree', 'On a Political Prisoner' and, less directly, 'The Leaders of the Crowd'). It is not freedom, its legitimacy or otherwise, that concerns Yeats. It is the energies that fought for it, the demonic return to Ireland of what he believed to have been effectively repressed, even though the last two poems in this sequence would seem to indicate that he believed the repression had been renewed in the intervening five years and that the abstract mind had taken over again. But in the poems about 1916 Yeats is wondering if the rebellion had been a Second Coming of the demonic that had then yielded to its malign intimate, the Bestial, represented by the Black-and-Tan atrocities in the War of Independence and by the era of bloodshed that included the First World War and the Russian Revolution. The ambiguity is not wholly centred on the Easter rebellion as such. It arises from the distinction that this book struggles to make between Demon and Beast, between a violence that is renovatory and one that is destructive. These impulses are so intertwined that they can scarcely be separated. But it is in such a struggle that humankind achieves its greatness. Freedom is what is left after the struggle is over, 'mere growing old'.

'The Second Coming' poses a question in the form of a prophecy; equally, it proposes a prophecy in the form of a question. The prophetic element, the vision of the stirring to life of the Rough Beast from its two-thousand-year-long sleep, almost overrides the question, since it implies catastrophe in so unmistakable a fashion that there is no room left to doubt that this is a demonic energy that has, through repression, become bestial. The echoing of the Book of Revelation (in specific words and phrases like 'loosed' and 'at hand' as well as in the title, repeated twice in the poem, and in the biblical geography) confirms the impression of terror. But the Beast is not imitating Christ's Second Coming at all. It is imitating his first coming, by going to Bethlehem to be born. The second coming is a rerun of the first, not an analogue for the biblical Second Coming. It is, in a very specific sense, like the Beast of Revelation, an Antichrist, a reverse image of the first coming but not a prelude to the second.

It is here that the element of questioning begins to reassert itself against the element of prophecy. This 'Egyptian' beast is going out of bondage over to Palestine to be born. The double biblical reference here—the liberation of the Jews from Egypt and the Flight into Egypt of the Holy Family—collaborates with the tropes of secondness and of reversal of direction that dominate the poem. The manner of the Beast's going ('slouches') is important. But it has already come to life; in what sense then will it be born—or born again? Will it be reborn as the thing it is, or will it be reborn as something different? It would seem that this nightmarish vision can only be known for what it is when it is interpreted, when the Rough Beast of the dream is born again as something which represents what was 'vex'd to nightmare' by the 'rocking cradle'. The manger, mutated into a rocking cradle, a domestic and familial object, emblematic of nursery peace and comfort, is, in this guise, an oppressive emblem. Christianity oppressed, suppressed, or repressed demonic energies that have now gone bad. In their release they bring destruction with them. But it *is* a release. This peculiar version of the Second Coming may, after all, have its redemptive component within it because the therapeutic moment has arrived. The unconscious has finally spoken. The phrase that, in Christian belief, signalled the end of human history, has precipitated the beginning of another phase, one dominated by those very energies that had been hitherto occluded. It is a very potent question, after all, what this Rough Beast is or what it will become when it reaches its Bethlehem, its symbolic place, to be born again in the human imagination. Yeats spent so much of his life in the pursuit of those deep energies of the occult, almost cancelled in the modern world, that he could scarce forbear to cheer their sudden rearrival, however apocalyptic the form it took.

The Second Coming is bestial but it is also vague. It is 'a vast image', 'a shape'—the first nouns in the poem preceded by the indefinite article. Just as the definite article worked its effect by insinuating a complicity with what is known, so the indefinite article conversely achieves its contrasting effect by enhancing the sense of something unknown, the more sinister for being indefinite. It is also the more sinister for being a private, personal symbol. Yeats's own presence comes into the poem at the strategic moment when the first eight lines of what could have been a sonnet like 'Leda and the Swan' are resumed, not into a sestet, but into a full sonnet. We not only have a sonnet and a half, we have an aborted sonnet that is then reborn as a full one, as the poem itself comes for the second time, brought to its full formal strength by the sudden intervention of the poet who now reveals himself to be the speaker.

'The Second Coming! Hardly are those words out.' The words are spoken and suddenly, in a flash, the vision comes. It comes in that second after speech and belongs to sight. The poem began with the falcon that 'cannot hear'; it breaks at a critical point into speech and then continues as sight, vision. But the vision is, paradoxically, the more indelible for its vagueness. It is a personal vision but it is also public, since it is both a shape that is emerging from 'somewhere' in the desert, and it is also recognizably the Egyptian Sphinx. At least, it is Sphinx-like, traditionally mysterious and yet known. But it is also a repetition. This creature too, like the apocalypse that has seized Europe, is announced by the wheeling birds, whose punning action ('Reel shadows') reiterates that of the falcon.

Still, this is not only a second coming, it is a coming that is second to a previous one—or, rather, to several previous comings that belong both to this poem and to the volume in which it appeared. In 'Solomon and the Witch', 'An Image from a Past Life', and 'Under Saturn' images return, prophesying something ominous. Later in the volume, in the poem 'Towards Break of Day', the lovers dream, he of a waterfall on Ben Bulben, she of the white stag of Arthurian legend. The question is,

> Was it the double of my dream
> The woman that by me lay
> Dreamed, or did we halve a dream
> Under the first cold gleam of day?

What all these poems have in common is a questioning of the status of the vision. They are enactments of the issues raised in the fictional correspondence between Michael Robartes and Owen Aherne that Yeats cited in his 1921 note to this volume.[47] Yeats goes on to say that he does not think he 'misstated Robartes' thought' in allowing the woman, and not the man of 'An Image from a Past Life' to see the 'Over Shadower or Ideal Form'. Images, he says, 'in moments of excitement pass from one mind to another with extraordinary ease'. Thus, 'The second mind sees what the first has already seen, that is all.'

As a commentary on the love poems of *Michael Robartes and the Dancer*, this is all quite helpful. Robartes and the Dancer, Solomon and the Witch, the 'He' and 'She' of 'An Image from a Past Life' are engaged in a very Yeatsian kind of love talk—post-coital discussion of how to overcome the sense of imperfection and separation that has been exacerbated by a dream, a vision, an allegory:

> In this altar-piece the knight,
> Who grips his long spear so to push
> That dragon through the fading light,
> Loved the lady; and it's plain
> The half-dead dragon was her thought,
> That every morning rose again
> And dug its claws and shrieked and fought.

This is a dragon that has to be killed over and over; Solomon and the Witch must also make love again in the hope that the language of a real, not a false coming (or crowing) may be heard. Repeated love, repeated sexual climax, is part of the process of atonement, the purgation that will perhaps some day make the Beatific Vision available. But Robartes has not completed his system. Aherne has to be shocked into the further realization that

The mind, whether expressed in history or in the individual life, has a precise movement . . . and this movement can be expressed by a mathematical form . . . A supreme religious act of their [the Judwalis'] faith is to fix the attention on the mathematical form of this movement until the whole past and future of humanity, or of an individual man, shall be present to the intellect as if it were accomplished in a single moment. The intensity of the Beatific Vision when it comes depends upon the intensity of this realisation.

This passage leads on to the well-known characterization of the intersecting cones and gyres, outward- and inward-sweeping, with the contemporary world reaching its greatest and fatal expansion, preparing 'not the continuance of itself but the revelation as in a lightning flash, though in a flash that will not strike only in one place, and will for a time be constantly repeated, of the civilization that must slowly take its place.' The historical turn, like lovers, has to come again and again; with each flash of contact, the images appear, slowly emerging out of phantasmagoria to achieve their full form in a mathematically defined system. These images have to keep coming. They are never originary, since they have taken their form, inverted, from what has gone before and is now at the point of exhaustion. They are always coming second, and they come in a second, in a flash, and each sexual–historical lightning-strike produces an image that may or may not be sufficient to represent the end of life and history. The only vision that can represent that is, *per impossibile*, the Beatific Vision which does not represent anything but itself, which simply is.

Nevertheless, the poem 'The Second Coming' is clearly a hellish vision. Just as it has its anticipations within the volume in which it occurs, it also has its anticipations in history, some of which are visible in the early drafts. The Russian Revolution of 1917 had, as its great prefiguration, the French Revolution. The degree to which Yeats drew upon and concealed his sources in Burke, Blake, Shelley, Wordsworth, Nietzsche, and others has been well documented, as has the contribution of his early experiments with MacGregor Mathers in the Order of the Golden Dawn. He envied the women of the circle for their capacity to form vivid mental images. Patrick J. Keane tells us that, in the experiments with Mathers, Yeats reported that, for him, 'sight came slowly, there was not that sudden miracle as if the darkness had been cut with a knife, for that miracle is mostly a woman's privilege.' This simile reappears in the drafts of the clairvoyant section of 'The Second Coming'. Groping for figurative language with which to introduce the mysterious moment just prior to the vision of the vast image rising up 'out of *Spiritus Mundi*', Yeats first wrote: 'Before the dark was cut as with a knife.' The 'woman's privilege' is repeated in the vision of this poem. We know that Yeats was deeply affected by Burke's lament for Marie Antoinette in his *Reflections on the Revolution in France* and that the sexual mutilation of the Princesse de Lamballe's body was one of the horrific moments of the Terror of September 1792 that registered deeply on him. The murder of the Tsar's family in Russia, the monstrous rebirth there of German Marxism, the drafts that speak of the 'second birth' rather than the Second Coming, the reference to Bethlehem and the inevitable association with the virgin birth (later reimagined in the Greek fable of 'Leda and the Swan'), the fact that the phrase 'Rough Beast' is applied by Shakespeare to Tarquin in *The Rape of Lucrece* all give to the second stanza of the poem a more specific inflection of sexual violation threatened by 'A shape with lion body and the head of a man.'[48]

Between the idea of a second 'coming' and that of a second 'birth', the poem reveals its conflict. There is a welcome given to the male coming, to its brute strength, its renewable energy, its destructive power. But there is also a horror at the consequences of its emergence, the suffering of the female figure who is represented only by contextual reference and echo and yet who is the reigning figure over 'the ceremony of innocence' celebrated in the succeeding poem, 'A Prayer for my Daughter'. The second coming of this male force will be a violation that results in a monstrous birth. The hand that rocked the Bethlehem cradle may have, like the Virgin, or Marie Antoinette, or the Tsarina of Russia, ruled the world in some sense. But now the mob–beast has risen in male fury to put an end to all that Christian, family-centred ceremony in a threatening, slouching rapist's walk into the Holy Land that is a dreadful parody of its biblical antecedents.

How differently might we read the poem had Yeats made it, as he made the opening poems of the volume, a dialogue between a 'He' and a 'She'. In this instance, it is the second stanza, the born-again sonnet, that would be spoken by the 'She'. However, the central point is that the vision of history and the vision of love relationships, both of which are part of Yeats's preoccupation in this book of poems, are superimposed one upon the other in 'The Second Coming' and that Yeats's contradictory emotions of horror and welcome are ultimately visible in the poem's inner dialogue between a highly present male voice and an almost wholly concealed female one.

From 1910 onwards, Yeats remained loyal to a double narrative that generated conflict and regenerated energy in his poems. One was the narrative of revival, especially associated with Ireland and the occult; the other was the narrative of degeneration, especially associated with the modern world and science. 'The Second Coming' is a poem that produces both narratives simultaneously. It is about the return of barbarism and about the return of the lost energies of the occult. In some respects, the poem wishes to interfuse these, to make one the function of the other; in other respects, it wishes to distinguish them and, further, to dwell on that moment, that split second, when the distinction becomes clear. The poem (or its final question) is itself lacking in all conviction and full of passionate intensity. The Beast's hour has 'come round at last' and this is a matter for celebration. But it is also a ravening beast that threatens violation and endless monstrosity. Caught between two value-systems, Yeats represents one as male, the other as female, one as triumphant, the other as horrified, imbricating into the form of the poem itself the ironic admission that the best that can be said is second-best. 'Things' could hardly be worse. But the threatened rape, when it does take place in 'Leda and the Swan', answers the final question of 'The Second Coming' with a question of its own. If the knowledge of the occult is to be reintroduced to the world, then that might be compensation for the destruction that it, vengefully and necessarily, has to bring with it. But in the coming of the Swan,

> Did she put on his knowledge with his power
> Before the indifferent beak could let her drop?

If not, the darkness drops again. It all depends on that sexual–historical second in which knowledge comes with power. Otherwise, it will have to wait again for its second coming. And the demonic, when it comes second, comes as the Bestial. Can the Bestial find a Bethlehem in which it can be born again as the demonic? Can the mob be born again as a people, as a nation? That would truly be a second coming. It became known as fascism. In terms of Yeats's infantile geometry, the gyre of the contemporary world is reaching its greatest and fatal expansion, preparing for 'the civilization that must slowly take its place'.[49] The coming of that civilization is always a second coming, a return, and is also always coming, always revealing itself, in a second, in a series of repeated lightning flashes. Any time now it will happen; that is the temporality of Yeats's work; and it will happen now because it has happened before; that is his chronology.

Here is a form of iteration that does not allow for boredom. This is an emergent, not an emerging, literature and politics; that which is emerging indicates something not yet sufficiently developed to become canonical, but having the ambition to become so; an emergent discourse challenges the very idea of the canonical, even in a threatening manner.[50] For the canon that would exclude such discourse is clearly coercive. Yet it contains within it the revolt that defines its canonicity, as harmony is defined by dissonance. So the Yeatsian Anglo-Irish grouping—Burke, Swift, Goldsmith, Berkeley—can lurk within the Lockean–Whig interpretation of history, the fierceness of their rebuke to its ultimate glorification of the British state and modernity the threat to that state's repression of the Irish nation and of the deep psychic energies it exemplifies.

IRISH HISTORY: THE INSTITUTION OF BOREDOM

'We approach the final stage in the condition of historical learning . . . The long conspiracy against the knowledge of the truth has been practically abandoned.'[51] Lord Acton's resonantly optimistic statement of 1896 could be taken as an epigraph for what he then regarded as the necessary professionalization of English history, free from the amateur Whig narratives of Macaulay and his ilk, by diverting it towards a proper study of the archives, exemplified in the achievements of German historicism.

In any institution there is a link between knowledge and power. It is obviously a form of power to redistribute knowledge and reconduct it through new channels. This is even more the case where there is a persistent claim that knowledge has previously been deformed in order to exercise a legitimating power on behalf of the deformers. So nationalist discourse consistently claims to expose the lies, the caricatures, the disguises of imperialism and colonialism in order to replace these with its own regime of truth.

What differentiates the nationalist from the revisionist project is not merely its filiation with apocalypse but its equally important, and acknowledged, alliance with myth. Myth, properly understood, is not a lie or a fantasy; it is not a false origin or an inflationary supplement. The various myths of the gods that are claimed by religious institutions as their foundation are ontologically distinct from the institutions themselves. Once that distinction is made, the institution has really only one function—interpretation. Yet it is an interpretative action that is both endless and superfluous; superfluous since it can never actually lay claim to the truth in itself—for that is radically other—and endless, because it is therefore obliged to produce commentary upon its own commentary. Neverthless, this is an exercise of power. In Burke's case, there is indeed such an ontological divide, between the God-given origin of society and the human interpretation of it. To enquire into the origins of society is, in his view, impious. The consequence is that humans should admit to their ultimate inadequacy and confine themselves to being directed by that instinctive relation to the divine that is possessed in common and manifest in custom, law, and precedent. The remoteness of the divine from the human institutions is asserted and denied simultaneously. God may be mysterious but our human constitution is alert to and moulded by his presence.[52] There is, therefore, a degree of mediation required. That is supplied by a clergy, a clerisy, an aristocratic class, a group of adepts. Such a group mediates between power and the powerless.

That group controls the relation between institutions and interpretations. Interpretations owe their power to the foundational moment in which it is asserted that the social world has of itself a meaning that is not of the social world—that is mysterious, other, originary, whatever. The social world cannot be understood as such unless its meanings are ordered—but they must be ordered in relation to something of which the social world is, or is to be, a realization. Even if the divine or religious dimension of human experience is denied, the situation does not change in its structure, although it does of course dramatically change in its interpretative tone. If, for instance, we recognize that the European Enlightenment was—to a highly self-conscious degree—a vast and complex institution, we must with that recognize too that its project, as Habermas calls it, was one that took a particular direction from its constitution of an otherness—the dream of a fully rational and humane society. The principles of such a society are obscure to most people; education, a reorganization of their sense of the priest-dominated past, must be the task of those who are—as Burke pointed out—the self-appointed interpreters of the human condition. Ultimately, the function of interpreting meaning, of claiming that the anarchic is impermissible, that everything belongs to a system, belongs to the state. Any opposition to the state will be classified—has to be classified—as belonging to an order that is beyond the zone of interpretation and of reason. In the post-Enlightenment era, any system opposed to its regime of rationality, especially any counter-revolutionary system that appealed for its legitimation to forces or agencies that were not susceptible to rational analysis, was dismissed from consideration as a species of myth that was dependent for its survival on irrational procedures.

It is easy now to assert that the myth of the Enlightenment is itself productive of the worst exercises of power and domination.[53] But I prefer instead to look at the myth of nationalism, and especially to look at the manner in which nationalism acknowledges its debt to myth—something the Enlightenment has consistently denied. In the Irish context, it is a well-known and much abused claim that the assertions of Irish difference from Britain are mythically founded in a strange amalgam of confused and confusing claims for which there is no tenable historical ground. It may be a Scythian, Celtic or Gaelic difference; it may be a claim by an O'Grady or a Pearse that the Irish difference demands the forging of a heroic alliance between the distant saga figures of the old Irish cycles and a socio-religious group, Protestant or Catholic, of the contemporary era; it may be the myth of a national character that has had a destiny pre-inscribed within it from the beginning of time. Whatever it may be, it is not 'historical'. Even worse, such mythologizing is productive of a grand narrative that proceeds by a series of uniform strategies to describe Irish experience as one of almost endless oppression, designedly pursued, justifiably resisted, now entering on its final stages—whether that stage be understood as belonging to the period from 1916 to 1922 or to the period since 1968. Within that narrative there are to be found a series of other subsidiary myths—the myth of genocide during the Famine or during the Elizabethan plantations, the myth of the penal laws as an instrument for the oppression of a whole people, the myth of the predatory landlord of the nineteenth century, the myth of 1916—and so on. The coherence of this reading is both its weakness and its strength. Like any institution, nationalism does not allow anything to happen 'accidentally'; it is all recuperable within the capacious system of interpretation that it has produced and that also has produced it.

Destiny and myth are notions that historical discourse produces and dismisses at different conjunctures. The myth of Irish destiny or difference is not, obviously, an exclusively Irish notion; it is also, and even more emphatically, an English one, several centuries old. The myth of a specific destiny for a particular political or racial grouping is shared by many European countries, usually as a rationale for colonial and imperial adventures. All imperialisms are founded on nationalist myths; it is only their global success that permits them to naturalize these. Insurgent nationalisms, on the other hand, even when successful, retain their founding myths as marks of local particularity, even when, as in the case of Ireland, they can find a global extension in a myth of their intimacy with an old-world culture, an *ancien régime* of the mind. Irish nationalism, in one of its versions, especially that version dominated and formulated by the Anglo-Irish literati from O'Grady to Yeats, was in many ways the 'dialectical opposite of imperialism';[54] it constantly strove to assert that the native tradition belonged to a cultural empire that had been overcome by science, democracy, abstract thought—all the marks of the Beast called modernity. But in another version, Irish nationalism wanted to embrace a modernity from which, through British economic oppression, it had been excluded. Would it be possible to retain the cultural capital it had accumulated and achieve economic prosperity, or would that cultural capital, given its 'hostility' to economic development of the modern (British–utilitarian) kind, inhibit the attainment of such prosperity? This was a pressing question both for the new Free State, after 1922, and for the new Northern Ireland state, where unionists had a vision of their own culture as indissolubly allied to economic development, a latter-day version of the Scottish convergence of the economic and the cultural that Adam Smith and others had developed in the late eighteenth century and to which the idea of the Union was, culturally and economically, central.[55] It was not until 1958 that the Republic found it politically and culturally possible to make economic development the central dynamic for cultural preservation; the drive towards 'modernization' in both the Republic and Northern Ireland weakened the cultural bases of both; it became identified with a general if slow liberation from provincial and sectarian beliefs.[56]

The rewriting of modern Irish history is said to have begun, in what is now called its revisionist phase, with the founding by R. Dudley Edwards and T. W. Moody of the journal, *Irish Historical Studies* in 1938. In a sense, their project has been understood—in some ways quite rightly—as the moment of professionalization in historical writing in Ireland. With the journal and all the attendant apparatus of conferences, university departments, and doctoral theses, history in Ireland was institutionalized to an unprecedented degree.

The new history's credo, as formulated by T. W. Moody in his 1977 essay 'Irish History and Irish Mythology', depends upon the standard positivist opposition between myth and science:

But nations derive their consciousness of their past not only—and not mainly—from historians. They also derive it from popular traditions, transmitted orally, in writing, and through institutions. I am using the word myth to signify received views of this kind as contrasted with the knowledge that the historian seeks to extract by the application of scientific methods to his evidence.[57]

The distinction between 'received views' and 'knowledge' is naïve in itself; but it is also self-defeating, since part of the purpose of this essay is to replace the former with the latter. Does 'knowledge' then become a 'received view'? If so, does it then become 'myth'? If this 'knowledge' does not successfully become the 'received view', does that mean the populace is ineducable, too long exposed to 'myth' and therefore, in a traditional Irish stereotype, too given to fiction and too Celtic to accept 'the despotism of fact', as Arnold called it?

Further, is history, especially when so professionalized and 'scientific', not also an institution from which nations 'might derive their consciousness of their past'? Moody does not, of course, address these questions. Instead, he gives a series of examples of myths that appertain to certain dates and movements in Irish history—the Catholic rebellion of 1641, Orangeism, the genocidal myth of the Famine, the republican predestinarian myth, and so on. Given the date of the essay, ten years into the Northern Irish crisis, this last receives particular attention, since it is the myth that is currently deforming the course of Irish history. The conclusion is:

> But if 'history' is used in its proper sense of a continuing, probing, critical search for truth about the past, my argument would be that it is not Irish history but Irish mythology that has been ruinous to us and may prove even more lethal. History is a matter of facing the facts of the Irish past, however painful some of them may be; mythology is a way of refusing to face the historical facts.[58]

It may be salutary to remember at this point that the senior Irish historian of the nineteenth century, W. E. H. Lecky, was so affected by the Land League and the Home Rule movement in the 1880s that he abandoned his former liberalism and turned more and more to Burke's interpretation of the French Revolution, as that had been reconstructed by Matthew Arnold and Lord Acton, to support his increasingly fervent unionism.[59] His pose of magisterial impartiality was not sustainable; can we understand his liberalism or his unionism, then, to have been myths? For the only myth-free position is, it would seem, that of 'scientific' impartiality, in which 'facts' are faced. The discourse of the historian is taken to be a record of the world of objective facts; any elision or distortion of these produces 'myth'. Such a discourse, which claims for itself a fundamental realism through which things as they really are or were could be presented in a narrative, depends upon a narrator who is not implicated. This 'impartial spectator' is, indeed, what has been absent in much of the writing I have been looking at in these lectures. It is a position that has been ousted, time and again, by the rhetoric of strangeness, by the assumption that there is no discursive means of making the Irish reality intelligible because it is so disrupted, broken, violent, exotic, incoherent. In a variation of that rhetorical mode, dominated by nationalists, the intelligibility of the national reality is, so to say, postponed, deferred until that moment when the emergence from colonial misrule is finally complete; in the meantime, it is a matter of indicating the various stages of extreme dilapidation and repair.

The pedagogical nature of Moody's historical project, later confirmed by his editorship of the *New History of Ireland* (1976–   ) and his co-authorship of a standard school textbook, *The Course of Irish History* (1967), is clearly indicated in his essay. Hence its reliance on examples of mythology. Carefully chosen as they are to culminate in the republican mythology of violent insurrection, they serve the purpose of isolating 'history' as a discourse that has only (or largely) existed heretofore in a warped form. There is no question that history has a meaning; it is simply not that meaning or those meanings that mythology produces. 'True' history *presupposes* a meaning which the authoritative historian displays in a factual narrative.[60] Examples of falsification of that 'truth' are produced and analysed in order to show the meaning that has been obscured. Myth says the landlords are predatory. Fact says they are not. Therefore, the true meaning of the Famine has to supplant the false one. Britain was not to blame, the landlords were not to blame; indeed blame itself is not to be attributed—except to those who attribute blame; the Famine was a catastrophe that happened because of a series of conjunctural contingencies. Ultimately, one has to say that reality is a matter of contingencies which it is the task of the historian—somehow—to render intelligible. Of course, it is plain that 'mythology' of the kind Moody describes is itself part of history; but his anxiety is to ensure that his conception of history is not numbered among the mythologies. The claim to impartiality is a necessary one; but it has been made by many historians who are now more renowned for the eccentricity of their opinions than for the respect for the facts to which they nevertheless believed themselves obedient. John D'Alton, a believer in the Phoenician origin of the Irish language and much else besides, closed his prize-winning *Essay on the History, Religion, Learning, Arts, and Government of Ireland, from the Birth of Christ to the English Invasion* of 1830 with the boast that 'I have ever kept myself beyond the electricity of factions, political prejudices, and unholy bigotries.'[61] It is the standard boast of the historian, regularly exploded by the history produced on foot of it.

Still, a mode of historical writing that prides itself on objectivity, scientific procedure, and archival research does indeed appear to be a welcome alternative to the popular histories that have scant respect for any of these. From a rich array of possibilities, I will choose one example of the latter, aware that exemplarity is a rhetorical device that, as in Moody's essay, can demonstrate the intelligibility of a position even when it is lacking in factual support.

The following passage closes Thomas D'Arcy McGee's *A Popular History of Ireland* (1862). The terminus of the account is the granting of Catholic Emancipation in 1829. McGee's interpretation of this event is that it marks the end of the long night of the penal laws against Catholics that had begun the political settlement of the 1690s, for which the siege of Derry in 1689 was a founding event—a siege in which a Protestant garrison, led by one Governor Walker, had resisted the Catholic armies of King James II. The role of Walker in the siege was commemorated by the erection of a column on the walls of Derry, topped with a statue of Walker—a column, incidentally, blown up by the IRA in 1976. McGee declares:

A lofty column on the walls of Derry bore the effigy of Bishop Walker, who fell at the Boyne, armed with a sword, typical of his martial inclinations, rather than of his religious calling. Many long years, by day and night, had his sword, sacred to liberty or ascendancy, according to the eyes with which the spectator regarded it, turned its steadfast point to the broad estuary of the Foyle. Neither winter storms nor summer rains had loosened it in the grasp of the warlike churchman's effigy, until on the 13th day of April, 1829—the day the royal signature was given to the Act of Emancipation—the sword of Walker fell with a prophetic crash upon the ramparts of Derry, and was shattered to pieces. So, we may now say, without bitterness and almost without reproach, so may fall and shiver to pieces, every code, in every land beneath the sun, which impiously attempts to shackle conscience, or endows an exclusive caste with the rights and franchise which belong to an entire People![62]

Factually, this is nonsense. No such event took place; it is a 'popular tradition'. The 'facts' have been invented to provide a symbolic account, the monument endowed with the agency of history, the view over the river Foyle, and the seasonal changes that did not loosen the grip of clerical–military oppression (although Walker was not a bishop) transmuted into a panoptic view of human history. Yet, precisely because the account is so glaringly 'symbolic', it is also intelligible. It is, perhaps, not the 'reality'—that these laws were not so oppressive, more honoured in the breach than the observance, locally enforced in different places at different conjunctures, not at all extraordinarily harsh in the context of eighteenth-century Europe, even unwittingly to the commercial advantage of the Catholics. Mythology, in this instance, meets the science of archival research; even the testimony of eighteenth-century commentators—Edmund Burke or Charles O'Conor—is to be mistrusted or modified. McGee is an amateur purveyor of folklorish superstition for a political end; his account is to be consigned to the lumber-room of history. The 'fact' of the penal laws is dispersed into a sequence of complex contingencies, in their intentionality, purpose, and consequences. This is realism; McGee is fantasy.

Thus, it would seem that no monocular account of the penal laws is 'reality'; it is merely sectarian to accuse the Protestant ruling class of that period of having created an early version of an apartheid state, just as it is so to describe the present state of Northern Ireland in these terms. It may be intelligible, but it is not true to the facts.[63] It is revealing, however, to find that the historian who has contributed most to this reappraisal of the penal laws, Professor Louis Cullen, can forgo all the complexities of contingency and fact when he wishes to describe Irish nationalism and Catholicism. In a 1980 essay entitled 'The Cultural Basis of Modern Irish Nationalism', he claims that 'the intense sense of racial awareness in Irish nationalism' goes back to the Middle Ages, 'predates colonialism', and is alive and well with unbroken continuity in the Crossmaglen (an area in South Armagh dominated by the IRA) of the 1970s.[64] Apart from the ignorance or the ignoring of the history of racial theory in the nineteenth century, and much else, this prattle exceeds any 'grand narrative' of Irish Catholic oppression produced by the most fanatic nationalist. But its ideological desire is clear. It wishes to claim that, whatever catastrophes may have overtaken Ireland in the colonial period, they were already potentially there *in nuce* in the Irish national character. The British were merely catalysts who hastened an already inscribed and desolate destiny. This too is intelligible; but its intelligibility is in part derived from the same historian's revisionist account of the penal laws. He merely moves the charge of racial sectarianism from one group to levy it against another. Perhaps science and mythology are not opposites, after all, but cousins. Behind 'history' lies destiny; behind the doctrineless account of the eighteenth century lies the fervently doctrinal account of the period from the Middle Ages to the 1970s.

One consequence of the valorization of the scientific against the mythological is the denigration of what historians are pleased to call 'rhetoric'. Because nationalism, with all its poets and dreamers, is an ideology that has a pronounced 'literary' element, it is *therefore* much more dependent upon 'rhetoric'—that is to say on the purely imaginary, the folklorish, on all that is unrelated to the deflationary facts of the case.[65] Among those literary elements, is the dramatization of Irish history as an apocalyptic experience out of which a rebirth will emerge. This in turn leads to a naïve but condescending assertion of the autonomy of literature as a discipline that is the more itself the more removed it is from the political; and, conversely, the autonomy of history as a discipline that is the more itself the more it is removed from the literary. Any activity of interpretation that refuses to accept the autonomies so constituted is reified as 'theory', that fancy and fashionable discourse that applies the 'foreign' theories of Marx, or Gramsci, or Derrida to a native history that is insusceptible to their charms because it, unlike them, is free from ideological investments—whether as literature or as history.[66]

Yet revisionism itself, although its practitioners seem not to know it, in its opposition to what it presumes is the new version of nationalist history—postcolonial writing—evinces a suspicion of grand or meta-narratives that is characteristically postmodernist.[67] (The description of each as 'post-' does not necessarily indicate that they have a great deal in common.[68]) Its hostility to 'theory' or 'master

narratives', replicated in literary studies by those who regard literature as untheorizable, as a collection of particular texts, leads to a
corresponding geniality towards micronarratives, monographic
studies, in which 'Ireland' as the object of study gives way to an
analysis of regions, phases, issues.[69] Consistently, there should be no
history of Ireland but a variety of histories of various Irelands; yet
the assumption remains that, in the light of the new research accumulated over time, it will be possible to rewrite the history of
Ireland, but in such a fashion that it will be a history free, not only
of nationalist ideology, but of all ideology as such. This, in turn,
raises again the question—from what subject-position can such a
history be written? Is an impartial spectator or narrator position
available?

According to T. W. Moody, the answer is in the positive; this is
the historian's position, and 'scientific method' is his/her technique.
By adopting such a position, the historian will be free of the
folklorish, the atavistic, the literary, the rhetorical, the reduction of
infinitely complex materials to the simplicities of any -ism. Thus, to
speak of 'colonialism' or 'imperialism' as a system becomes 'ideological'. Instead, historical writing is more legitimately concerned to
examine the complexities of Irish experience, to forgo the British–
Irish axis of nationalist history, to claim that there was nothing
systematic either in the penal laws or in the Famine—to take two
obvious examples—that could properly be called a sustained or a
deliberate campaign for the oppression of the Irish. In fact, to go
further, colonialism really only appeared in order to conspire with
certain features that were internal to Irish life in order to produce
benefits that might not otherwise have been available.

One of the early and classic instances of this claim is Sean
O'Faolain's important book on Daniel O'Connell, *King of the Beggars*
(1938) and his essays in *The Bell*, in one of which, 'The Gaelic Cult',
he continues his repudiation of his old master, Daniel Corkery, and
claims that the Hidden Ireland was a ruined civilization that had
only one option left open to it—the option O'Connell persuaded
them to adopt—that of modernization.[70] Thus colonialism entered
only to redeem an already broken civilization from chaos and myth;
even if it be argued that colonialism actually broke that civilization,

the response is that this only revealed its inner weakness, its inca-
pacity to survive in the modern world of which colonialism was the
harbinger.

The polemic involved in such writing matches the polemic
involved in nationalist writing. The critical category and the central
argument is that of modernity, although modernity is almost always
made identical with modernization. Whatever the deficiencies of
English rule in Ireland may have been—and they were not as melo-
dramatically vicious as nationalists say—the major benefit, of which
the Irish Republic is the fortunate legatee, was a series of structures—political, legal, bureaucratic, and, to a much lesser extent,
economic—that enabled it to join the modern world. Once the state
was founded, it could disembarrass itself of all the nationalist myth
and baggage that had led to its formation in the first place. The state,
so conceived, is an institution that relates to the moment of its
instituting by denial, just as the institution of history does in a
replicatory fashion.

Two points need to be made here. One is that the argument for
difference has now been abandoned except in the most residual
forms. Indeed any claim to difference of a radical kind is subsumed
into the argument against nationalism, as a kind of atavistic hang-
over, or consigned to tourism for exploitation. But such abandon-
ment is, at another level, impossible. Modernization has the production of sameness as one of its goals and even the production of
sameness in relation to a universalist concept of humanity as one of
its preconditions. Yet, to assert the 'arrival' of Ireland with the
triumph of modernization (and to ignore the distinction between
that process and the condition of modernity),[71] and to argue that this
is a goal finally reached after all that nonsense about difference and
apocalypse, is to inhabit the same discursive formation as nationalism itself.[72] For nationalism, the idea of the nation, finds itself
rebuked by the state which was its goal and is now its cancellation at
one level; at another, it finds itself fulfilled in the state, because it has
now reached the stage at which it is no longer merely concerned to
achieve recognition of its uniqueness by itself but also by others. It
can now rejoin the world from which it had been so long excluded.
For the revisionist, then, the state rejects nationalism as an ideology

that constrains it within provincialism and that also—importantly—
refuses to concede to it the monopoly of violence. The nationalist
rejects revisionism because it is an institution that reproduces as
history a form of knowledge that denies the atrocities of colonialism
in order to defend the state as the outgrowth of colonialism rather
than the achievement—however flawed—of nationalism. Revisionism legitimates colonialism, while denying that it ever existed,
because Ireland was never a colony in the accepted(?) sense of
the term; nationalism legitimates rebellion against it, by saying that
it has been *the* formative (or deformative) traumatic experience
from which recovery has to be made. Revisionism legitimates those
Irish cultural formations that wish to adhere to the British system,
even if by violent means; it refuses legitimacy to those who wish to
break from it, especially if their means are violent. Fundamental to
the debate is the link between the cultural formation and the economic system that sustains it. Any ideology that refuses to acknowledge economic reality—by which is meant the economic reality of
global capitalism—is thereby to be understood as irrational—as
belonging to precisely that kind of blind atavism that cannot recognize anything other than the misty shapes of its own imaginings.
The possibility that a community might actually surrender
economic well-being for something less boring, might ignore the
quiet life for the sake of 'freedom', for instance, while it is something
to be lauded in other parts of the world, is not at all to be welcomed
in Ireland.

The rhetoric of revisionism obviously derives from the rhetoric
of colonialism and imperialism. It defines its nationalist opponent
always in terms of an irrationality for which it is the saving alternative. It has to deprive nationalism of agency, of self-consciousness,
envisaging it as a mystification, a mythology, an impulse by which
its adherents are driven; although almost any passage from any
revisionist historian would reveal this charge to be applicable to
itself, revisionism remains happily ensconced not only in ignorance
of its own theory but the more happily so because it regards such
ignorance as the badge of its peculiar notion of professionalism.

Thus, in literature as in history, we see cognate interpretations
surrounding the identification of Ireland as the unreal country, the

country that does and does not belong to the West and modernity, the country that offers an alternative to it or is consigned to a perennial laggard status within it. I have been using the terms boredom and apocalypse as intimate and also oppositional agencies or conditions that permit readings of Joyce, Yeats, Flann O'Brien, and others. As far as revisionist history goes, perhaps we could say that its keynote is boredom with apocalypse, especially or exclusively where Irish nationalism is the subject—as in one form or another it almost always is. The analysis of the rhetorical procedures employed in the critique of nationalism can usefully display the basic revisionist distinction between the belief that myth, or apocalypse, produces violence and that economic development, or boredom, produces peace. In situations where this does not occur, there is obviously a puzzle. A passage at the end of F. S. L. Lyons's first chapter in *Ireland since the Famine* worries this issue: he is writing of the transformation of the Irish situation between 1916 and 1918:

Yet although . . . the British government by its own infirmities and errors of policy contributed much to the transformation, it did not contribute everything. The key to change was to be sought, as always, in Ireland itself. That men were found in sufficient numbers to fight a long war of independence between 1919 and 1921, that the population was prepared to endure stoically, if passively, the reprisals which the war brought in its train, suggests that more than the pursuit of economic well-being, more than the love of a quiet life uncomplicated by any emotion more profound than the itch to add field to field, was involved in the last act of the drama. The impulse to fight, to hold on, to contend with almost insuperable difficulties and almost impossible odds, had its roots in a tradition of insurrection and a spirit of resistance which, however irrational, were too strong and too deeply implicit in the history of the country to be ignored. The embers of Irish identity had been subdued, they had not been extinguished; and out of them, as dedicated and desperate men blew on the glowing coals, rose once more the phoenix of independent nationality.[73]

Here, in one of the more sinuous writers of the revisionist history, we witness the action of a rhetoric that works to conceal what it nevertheless exposes. The resounding clichés of the first two sentences open the way for an ostensible perception. To what incident in Irish history *could* the British government be said to contribute 'everything'? Equally in Irish history, where else but in Ireland would one seek the 'key to change'? There is no need to create the antithesis anyway, since this key is to be sought in Ireland 'as always'. Therefore why make it sound like a perception, why structure it as an insight? For the very good reason that the sequence depends on a series of antitheses that are always already there, in the form of a passive–active variation. The British contribute to, the Irish are the key for, the transformation (or change). The republicans fight, but the people passively endure. Reprisals are brought by the war itself, a consequence of it, rather than by agents (the British forces); that the people's Paudeen-like desire to add 'the halfpence to the pence', the field to the field, in the pursuit of their quiet life (although the desire for such accumulation a few decades earlier indicated no love for the quiet life), does indeed suggest that more than this petty ambition was involved but equally does no more than 'suggest' it. The suggestion is that the Yeatsian contrasts of 'September 1913' and of 'Easter 1916' are still alive; there is the petty-bourgeois world of money-grubbing, of clerks and offices, and there is the heroic world of revolutionary politics. Somehow, the first of these has produced the latter; out of a boring ordinariness has sprung an irrational extraordinariness. 'That men were found', that 'the people were prepared'—the passive voice introduces actualities while denying agency and in denying agency softens the blow, while deepening the sense of mysterious forces at work. For these are clearly people in the grip of something which makes them act; they are not actors in their own right.

Therefore, the key phrase is 'however irrational'; the key problem is the behaviour of the Irish in preferring this irrationality to economic well-being. Economic well-being is, however, in a betraying condescension, identified with an emotion no more profound than an itch to add field unto field. A life uncomplicated by nothing more than an itch for accumulation is surely the consumer society's dream; but instead the Irish people have chosen to participate in the last act of a political drama. To present the events of those years in this stock figure sustains, although in a feeble manner, the insinuation that this was a sequence in which the Irish people were caught up, as though in a fatality, a doom. Passivity, or the lack of agency, has to be emphasized. The 'last act' in the theatrical sense is very different from the 'last action'; an act is scripted in advance, an action has no such security. Simultaneously, the same people sustain 'an impulse to fight, to hold on'; again the wording implies something other than the rationality of a decision, especially since the impulse is drawn from deep recesses (could the British not be said to have had an 'impulse to fight' in Ireland, 'to hold on'?) and is directed against the almost insuperable and impossible.

There follow immediately some traditional nationalist figurings —the 'roots' of a 'tradition' and of a 'spirit' that are, however, not implanted—as roots might normally be expected to be, but 'implicit'. As opposed to 'explicit'? Of course there is a reason for their implicitness. They are *in* a 'tradition' which is itself *in* the 'history of the country'. Is tradition thereby to be understood as an irrational element within a rational discourse? Is it the opponent of history, awaiting its chance to become 'explicit'? These roots are too deep 'to be ignored', although it is plainly a pity that they were not ignored. This is a depth out of which a Rough Beast might arise, since it seems to owe its profundity to the fact that it was 'subdued' but not 'extinguished', like a fire. Indeed, the fire immediately appears in the Fenian emblem of fire and phoenix, the cliché of embers brought to life now by—agency at last!—very active dedicated and desperate men. The miracle bird of independent nationality arises, but like that bird it belongs of course to fable and myth, to 'tradition', yet also uncomfortably belongs now to 'history'. Lyons is confessing to being unable to understand that element *in* history that is not 'history'.

Within this series of sliding prevarications, there is no doubt that the key to all the mythologies is to be found in Ireland while the British, although prone to infirmity and error, are nevertheless safely within the precincts of the rational. This is nothing more than the rhetoric of Yeatsian cultural nationalism, masquerading as analysis in virtue of the claim that it is being written from a subject-position free of that rhetoric's irrational or anti-rational sources. The paradigm prevails; in order to be understood, Ireland must be split between the rational and the national. It is a strange country, resist-ant to the normalization that is offered to it by the historian who has been emancipated from the strangeness that his version of normal-ity constitutes. Monotonously, the choice remains—apocalypse or boredom? Professor Lyons did not live to write Yeats's biography; but Yeats lived on to enable him to write his history. The country remains strange in its failure to be normal; the normal remains strange in its failure to be defined as anything other than the nega-tive of strange. Normality is an economic condition; strangeness a cultural one. Since Burke, there has been a series of strenuous efforts to effect the convergence of the twain, even though the very prem-iss of their separation has been powerful in assuring that the twain will never meet.

Notes

Notes to Chapter One

1. Michael Foucault, 'What Is an Author?', *The Foucault Reader*, ed. P. Rabinow (Harmondsworth: Penguin,1984), 101–20.
2. See Robert Mahony, *Jonathan Swift. The Irish Identity* (New Haven and London: Yale University Press, 1995).
3. On Swift, see, among many, Louis Landa, *Swift and the Church of Ireland* (Oxford: Clarendon Press, 1954); Phillip Harth, *Swift and Anglican Rationalism* (Chicago: University of Chicago Press, 1961); Irvin Ehrenpreis, *Swift: The Man, his Works and the Age*, 3 vols. (Cambridge, Mass.: Harvard University Press, 1962); Carole Fabricant, *Swift's Landscape* (Baltimore: Johns Hopkins University Press, 1982); F. P. Lock, *Swift's Tory Politics* (London: Duckworth, 1983); Edward Said, 'Swift's Tory Anarchy', in *The World, the Text, and the Critic* (London: Faber & Faber, 1984); Warren Montag, *The Unthinkable Swift: The Spontaneous Philosophy of a Church of England Man* (London: Verso, 1994); Ian Higgins, *Swift's Politics: A Study in Disaffection* (Cambridge: Cambridge University Press, 1994).

   On colonial nationalism and Protestant nationalism in Ireland in the eighteenth century, see J. G. Simms, *Colonial Nationalism: 1692–1776* (Cork: Mercier Press, 1976); id., 'Protestant Ascendancy, 1691–1714', in T. W. Moody, F. X. Martin, and F. J. Byrne (eds.), *A New History of Ireland*, vol. iv (Oxford: Clarendon Press, 1986); J. L. McCracken, 'Protestant Ascendancy and the Life of Colonial Nationalism, 1714–60', ibid.; Thomas Bartlett, *The Fall and Rise of the Irish Nation: The Catholic Question 1690–1830* (Dublin: Gill & Macmillan, 1992), 30–44; Roy Foster, *Modern Ireland 1600–1972* (London: Penguin, 1988), 241–58; S. J. Connolly, *Religion, Law and Power: The Making of Protestant Ireland, 1660–1760* (Oxford: Clarendon Press, 1992); Oliver MacDonagh, *States of Mind: A Study of Anglo-Irish Conflict 1780–1980* (London: George Allen & Unwin, 1983); Joep Th.

Leerssen, *Mere Irish and fíor-Gael* (Amsterdam and Philadelphia; John Benjamins, 1988); *Remembrance and Imagination: Patterns in the Historical and Literary Representation of Ireland in the Nineteenth Century* (Cork: Cork University Press/Field Day, 1996), ch. 1.

On Burke and Coleridge, see Alfred Cobban, *Edmund Burke and the Revolt Against the Eighteenth Century: A Study of the Political and Social Thinking of Burke, Wordsworth, Coleridge and Southey* (London: Allen & Unwin, 1929); John Colmer, *Coleridge: Critic of Society* (Oxford: Clarendon Press, 1959); David Calleo, *Coleridge and the Idea of the Modern State* (New Haven: Yale University Press, 1966); John Morrow, *Coleridge's Political Thought* (London: Macmillan, 1990).

4. See Pierre Bourdieu, *The Field of Cultural Production*, ed. and introd. Randal Johnston (New York: Columbia University Press, 1993), 29–73.

5. Daniel Carey, 'Travel Narrative and the Problem of Human Nature in Locke, Shaftesbury, and Hutcheson' (D.Phil. thesis, Oxford University, 1994). On travel writing in the eighteenth century, see Charles Batten, *Pleasurable Instruction: Form and Convention in Eighteenth-Century Travel Literature* (Berkeley: University of California Press, 1978). For more general and theoretical analyses, see Edward W. Said, *Orientalism* (1st pub. 1978; London and Harmondsworth: Penguin, 1985); id., *Culture and Imperialism* (New York: Knopf, 1993); Michel de Certeau, *Heterologies: Discourse on the Other*, trans. Brian Massumi (Minneapolis: University of Minnesota Press, 1986); Mary Louise Pratt, *Imperial Eyes: Travel Writing and Transculturation* (London: Routledge, 1992), 15–37; Tzvetan Todorov, *On Human Diversity: Nationalism, Racism, and Exoticism in French Thought*, trans. Catherine Porter (Cambridge, Mass.: Harvard University Press, 1993), 264–352; Susan Stewart, *Crimes of Writing: Problems in the Containment of Representation* (Durham and London: Duke University Press, 1994), 173–205; Dennis Porter, *Haunted Journeys: Desire and Transgression in European Travel Writing* (Princeton: Princeton University Press, 1991); Sara Mills, *Discourses of Difference: An Analysis of Women's Travel Writing and Colonialism* (London and New York: Routledge, 1991).

6. 'Indulging myself in the freedom of epistolary discourse, I beg leave to throw out my thoughts and express my feelings just as they arise in my mind, with very little attention to formal method.' *Reflections on the Revolution in France*, ed. J. G. A. Pocock (Indianapolis and Cambridge: Hackett Publishing Company, 1987), 9.

7. David Hume, *Political Essays*, ed. Knud Haakonssen (Cambridge: Cambridge University Press, 1994), 49. Cf. J. G. A. Pocock, 'Empire, Revolution and the End of Early Modernity', in id. (ed.), assisted by

G. J. Schochet and L. G. Schwoerer, *The Varieties of British Political Thought, 1500–1800* (Cambridge: Cambridge University Press, 1993), 282–320: '[Burke] constructed in his later writings the image of Jacobinism as an international fanaticism religious in every respect but its atheism, in which the unchained intellect revolted against property and society; an extension of Hume's earlier account of enthusiasm' (304).

8. See Seamus Deane, 'Swift and the Anglo-Irish Intellect', *Eighteenth-Century Ireland*, 1/1 (1987), 9–22; David Bongie, *David Hume, Prophet of Counter-Revolution* (Oxford: Oxford University Press, 1965), 33–4; J. G. A. Pocock, 'Edmund Burke and the Redefinition of Political Enthusiasm: The Context as Counter-Revolution', in F. Furet and M. Ozouf (eds.), *The French Revolution and the Creation of Modern Political Culture*, iii: *The Transformation of Political Culture 1789–1848* (Oxford: Pergamon, 1989), 19–35.

9. Seamus Deane, *The French Enlightenment and Revolution in England 1789–1832* (Cambridge, Mass., and London: Harvard University Press, 1988), 5–6: David Simpson, *Romanticism, Nationalism and the Revolt against Theory* (Chicago and London: University of Chicago Press, 1993), 126–48.

10. Burke, *Reflections*, 70.

11. Cf. C. P. Courtney, *Montesquieu and Burke* (Oxford: Basil Blackwell, 1963).

12. Todorov, *On Human Diversity*, 171–263; Perry Anderson, 'Fernand Braudel and National Identity', in *A Zone of Engagement* (London and New York: Verso, 1992), 251–78.

13. Hume, *Political Essays*, 40.

14. Simpson, *Romanticism*, 133.

15. See Francis Barker's powerful reading of *King Lear* in *The Culture of Violence: Tragedy and History* (Manchester: Manchester University Press, 1993), 3–31. Barker's description of one of the play's 'set of ideological equations' echoes moments in the *Reflections*: 'sexuality is in the nature of monstrous women, sexual women are monstrous; and the play's coding of sexuality is part of its demonisation of the new, and reciprocally associates the new with all that is fearsome in what it constructs as woman and beast, in beast-woman.' (19). Cf. Burke, 'On this scheme of things, a king is but a man, a queen is but a woman; a woman is but an animal, and an animal not of the highest order' (67).

16. Burke, *Reflections*, 66.

17. Burke's apotheosis of Marie Antoinette is also, in part, a response to the accusations of sexual promiscuity made against her in a series of libellous pamphlets published in France in the 1780s. See Chantal

Thomas, *La Reine scélérate: Marie-Antoinette dans les pamphlets* (Paris: Éditions du Seuil, 1989); Lynn Hunt, 'The Many Bodies of Marie Antoinette: Political Pornography and the Problem of the Feminine in the French Revolution', in id. (ed.), *Eroticism and the Body Politic* (Baltimore: Johns Hopkins Press, 1990), 108–30. For accounts of Marie Antoinette's role in the *Reflections*, see Steven Blakemore (ed.), *Burke and the French Revolution: Bicentennial Essays* (Athens and London: University of Georgia Press, 1992); id., *Burke and the Fall of Language: The French Revolution as Linguistic Event* (Hanover and London: University Press of New England, 1988), 70–6; Tom Furniss, *Edmund Burke's Aesthetic Ideology; Language, Gender and Political Economy in Revolution* (Cambridge: Cambridge University Press, 1993), 138–96; Robert Tracy, 'The Mobbed Queen: Marie Antoinette as Victorian Ikon', *LIT*, 4 (1993), 275–90; Terry Eagleton, *The Ideology of the Aesthetic* (Oxford: Basil Blackwell, 1990), 52–62; id., 'Aesthetics and Politics in Edmund Burke', in Michael Kenneally (ed.), *Irish Literature and Culture* (Savage, Md.: Barnes & Noble, 1989), 25–34; Neal Wood, 'The Aesthetic Dimension of Burke's Political Thought', *Journal of British Studies*, 4/1 (1964), 41–64; Linda M. G. Zerilli, 'Text/ Woman as Spectacle: Edmund Burke's 'French Revolution', *The Eighteenth Century: Theory and Interpretation*, 32 (Spring 1992), 47–72; Leah Price, 'Vies privées et scandaleuses: Marie Antoinette and the Public Eye', *The Eighteenth Century: Theory and Interpretation*, 33 (Summer 1992), 176–92; Julie A. Carlson, *In the Theatre of Romanticism: Coleridge, Nationalism, Women* (Cambridge: Cambridge University Press, 1994), 140–4. On Burke's tragic 'emplotment' of these events, as compared to the different interpretations of Michelet, Tocqueville, Marx, and others, see Hayden White, *Tropics of Discourse. Essays in Cultural Criticism* (Baltimore and London: Johns Hopkins University Press, 1978; repr. 1985), 61–2. For a general theoretical account of these issues see Ann Rigney, *The Rhetoric of Historical Representation* (Cambridge: Cambridge University Press, 1991).

18. Burke, *Reflections*, 70–1.

19. The theatrical figure in the *Reflections* resumes the argument put forward by Burke in his treatise on the Sublime, notably in the second edition of 1757. There he takes pains to distinguish between 'real' and staged events. See *A Philosophical Enquiry into the Origin of our Ideas of the Sublime and Beautiful*, ed. J. T. Boulton (London: Routledge & Kegan Paul, 1958), 47: 'But then I imagine we will be much mistaken if we attribute any considerable part of our satisfaction in tragedy to a consideration that tragedy is a deceit, and its representations no realities. The nearer it approaches reality, and the further it removes us from all idea of fiction, the more perfect its power.' See also Peter

de Bolla, *The Discourse of the Sublime: Readings in History, Aesthetics and the Subject* (Oxford: Basil Blackwell, 1989), esp. 281–300.

20. Cf. Elizabeth Heckendorn Cook, 'The Limping Woman and the Public Sphere', in Veronica Kelly and D. von Mücke (eds.), *Body and Text in the Eighteenth Century* (Stanford: Stanford University Press, 1994), 23–44, esp. 34–6.

21. On the relation between the financial and cultural-political considerations in Britain at the end of the eighteenth century, see P. J. Cain and A. G. Hopkins, *British Imperialism: Crisis and Deconstruction 1914–1990* (London and New York: Longman, 1993), 302: 'When the crisis of empire came in the late eighteenth century, financial considerations were at its centre. The American revolution, the first great act of decolonisation, linked taxation to representation. The French Revolution, and the wars that followed, brought the prospect of invasion, which endangered Britain's finance and credit as well as the political status quo, and threatened to close continental Europe to her re-export trade. These fears strengthened the body politic, despite the loss of the American colonies. As the national debt swelled to safeguard the realm, so too did national solidarity. The resurgent conservatism which caused gentlemen of wealth to rally to the defence of property postponed radical reform, encouraged a unifying religious revival, and authorised the suppression of dissidence. It also promoted firmer measures abroad, above all in India, where the extension of British power was part of an emerging global strategy for keeping the world safe from French imperialism and the attendant horrors, fostered by the United States too, of republicanism and democracy. Among Napoleon Bonaparte's various unintended legacies to Europe was the emergence in Britain of a sense of patriotism founded on the principles of godliness, social discipline and loyalty to the crown, which in turn prepared the way for the invention of the nineteenth-century gentleman.'

22. *The Writings and Speeches of Edmund Burke*, gen. ed. Paul Langford, vol. viii: *The French Revolution 1790–4*, ed. L. G. Mitchell (Oxford: Clarendon Press, 1989), 313–19.

23. *Émile, or, On Education* (1761), trans. Allan Bloom (New York: Basic Books, 1979), bk. I, p. 39.

24. Cf. Charles Taylor, *Sources of the Self: The Making of Modern Identity* (Cambridge, Mass.: Harvard University Press, 1989).

25. See C. D. A. Leighton, *Catholicism in a Protestant Kingdom: A Study of the Irish Ancien Régime* (Dublin: Gill & Macmillan, 1994), 141–4, 152–3.

26. See Dáire Keogh, *The French Disease: The Catholic Church and Radicalism in Ireland 1790–1800* (Dublin: Four Courts Press, 1993); Kevin Whelan, 'Catholics, Politicisation and the 1798 Rebellion', in R.

O'Muirí (ed.), *Irish Church History Today* (Armagh: Cumann Seancháis Ard Macha, 1990), 63–84; Jim Smyth, *The Men of No Property: Irish Radicals and Popular Politics in the Late Eighteenth Century* (Basingstoke: Macmillan, 1992).

27. See Luke Gibbons, ' "The Stranger Within": Adam Smith, Edmund Burke and the Colonial Sublime' (forthcoming in id., *The Colonial Sublime: Edmund Burke and the Politics of Irish Culture*). I am grateful to Luke Gibbons for letting me see a draft of this essay.

28. John Barrell, ' "The Dangerous Goddess": Masculinity, Prestige, and the Aesthetic in Early Eighteenth-Century Britain', *Cultural Critique*, 12 (1989), 101–31: 103. See also his remarks on Burke's theory of abstract language and the Sublime in relation to Wordsworth's 'language of the sense' in 'Tintern Abbey', in *Poetry, Language and Politics* (Manchester: Manchester University Press, 1988), 164–6.

29. J. W. Croker, *A Sketch of the Present State of Ireland, Past and Present* (Dublin: M. N. Mahon, 2nd edn. 1808), p. iv.

30. Stewart, *Crimes of Writing*, 66–101.

31. Ibid. 90.

32. Paul Bové, *Mastering Discourse: The Politics of Intellectual Culture* (Durham and London, Duke University Press, 1992), 85.

33. Seamus Deane, 'The Reputation of the French *Philosophes* in the Whig Reviews between 1802 and 1824', *The Modern Language Review*, 70 (Apr. 1978), 271–90.

34. Anthony Grafton, *Defenders of the Text: The Traditions of Scholarship in an Age of Science, 1450–1800* (Cambridge, Mass., and London: Harvard University Press, 1991), 218.

35. Ibid. 216.

36. J. G. Pocock, 'Burke and the Ancient Constitution', in id., *Politics, Language and Time: Essays on Political Thought and History* (New York: Atheneum, 1971), 202–32.

37. A point made by Lord Acton. See Acton MSS, Cambridge University Library, Add. 4967.65, 4967.66, *et seq.* See also Seamus Deane, 'Lord Acton and Edmund Burke', *Journal of the History of Ideas*, 33/2 (Apr.–June, 1972), 325–35.

38. Cf. Georg Lukács, *Goethe and his Age*, trans. Robert Anchor (London: Merlin Press, 1968), 101–35.

39. Among the most widely noticed in the reviews of the period were Madame de Genlis, *Précis de la conduite de Madame de Genlis depuis la révolution* (Hamburg: B. G. Hoffmann, 1796); id., *Les Dîners du Baron d'Holbach* (Paris: C. J. Trouve, 1822); id., *Mémoires inédits de Madame la comtesse de Genlis sur le dix-huitième siècle*, 8 vols. (Paris and London: Colburn, 1825); Marie du Deffand, *The Unpublished Correspondence of Mme. du Deffand*, trans. Mrs Meeke, 2 vols. (London: A. K. Newman, 1810); id., *Letters of the Marquise du Deffand to the Hon. Horace*

Walpole . . . to which are added Letters of Madame du Deffand to Voltaire
from 1759 to 1775, ed. M. Berry, 4 vols. (London: Longman, Hurst,
Lees & Orme, 1810); L. F. P. de la Live d'Épinay, *Mémoires et cor-*
respondance de Madame d'Épinay, 3 vols. (Paris: Didier, 1818).

40. See Martin Thom, *Republics, Nations and Tribes* (London and New
    York: Verso, 1995), 200–11, 272–80.

41. Dena Goodman, *The Republic of Letters: A Cultural History of the French*
    Enlightenment (Ithaca and London: Cornell University Press, 1994), 6.
    See also Norbert Elias, *The History of Manners* (Oxford: Blackwell,
    1978), and id., *The Civilizing Process* trans. Edmund Jephcott (Oxford:
    Blackwell, 1982).

42. Goodman, *Republic of Letters*, 16.

43. On the literature of adventure and imperial romance see Patrick
    Brantlinger, *Rule of Darkness: British Literature and Imperialism 1830–*
    1914 (Ithaca and London: Cornell University Press, 1988); Martin
    Green, *Dreams of Adventure, Deeds of Empire* (New York: Basic Books,
    1979); Fredric Jameson, *The Political Unconscious: Narrative as a Socially*
    Symbolic Act (Ithaca and London: Cornell University Press, 1981);
    John McClure, *Late Imperial Romance* (London: Verso, 1994).

44. See J. M. S. Tompkins, *The Popular Novel in England, 1770–1800* (Lon-
    don: Constable, 1932; repr. Methuen, 1961); Harrison R. Steeves,
    Before Jane Austen: The Shaping of the English Novel in the Eighteenth
    Century (London: Allen & Unwin, 1966); Mary Poovey, *The Proper*
    Lady and the Woman Writer: Ideology as Style in the Works of Mary
    Wollstonecraft, Mary Shelley, and Jane Austen (Chicago: University of
    Chicago Press, 1984).

45. *Waverley*, ch. 1: 'those passions common to all men in all stages of
    society . . . It is from the great book of Nature, the same through a
    thousand editions . . . that I venturously essayed to read a chapter to
    the public.'

46. See *Sale Catalogues of Libraries of Eminent Persons*, ix: *Politicians*, ed.
    Seamus Deane (London: Mansell-Sotheby Parke-Bernet, 1973),
    319–89.

47. See Oliver MacDonagh's comments on O'Connell and Edgeworth
    and on the powerful influence upon him of William Godwin's novel,
    Caleb Williams, in *O'Connell: The Life of Daniel O'Connell 1775–1847*
    (London: Weidenfeld & Nicolson, 1991), 300–1.

48. Stephen D. Cox, *The Stranger Within Thee: Concepts of the Self in Late*
    Eighteenth-Century Literature (Pittsburgh; University of Pittsburgh
    Press, 1980); David Marshall, *The Figure of Theater: Shaftesbury, Defoe,*
    Adam Smith and George Eliot (New York: Columbia University Press,
    1986).

49. See Vivienne Brown, *Adam Smith's Discourse: Canonicity, Commerce*

and Conscience (London: Routledge, 1994); Istvan Hont and Michael Ignatieff (eds.), *Wealth and Virtue: The Shaping of Political Economy in the Scottish Enlightenment* (Cambridge: Cambridge University Press, 1983); John Dwyer, *Virtuous Discourse: Sensibility and Community in Late Eighteenth-Century Scotland* (Edinburgh: John Donald, 1987); Andrew S. Skinner and Thomas Wilson (eds.), *Essays on Adam Smith* (Oxford: Clarendon Press, 1975).

50. See Gibbons, '"The Stranger Within": Adam Smith, Edmund Burke and the Colonial Sublime'.

51. Cf. Phillippe Lacoue-Labarthe and Jean-Luc Nancy, *The Literary Absolute: The Theory of Literature in German Romanticism*, trans. Philip Barnard and Cheryl Lester (Albany: State University of New York Press, 1988), 29: 'although it is not entirely or simply philosophical, romanticism is rigorously comprehensible (or even accessible) only on a philosophical basis . . .'.

52. See Kevin Whelan, 'The Republic in the Village: The United Irishmen, the Enlightenment and Popular Culture', in id., *The Tree of Liberty: Radicalism, Catholicism and the Construction of Irish Identity 1760–1830* (Cork: Cork University Press, in association with Field Day, 1996), 59–98; Luke Gibbons, ' "A Shadowy Narrator": History, Art and Romantic Nationalism in Ireland 1750–1850', in Ciaran Brady (ed.), *Ideology and the Historians* (Dublin: Lilliput Press, 1991), 99–127. 'The problem posed by history painting to the idea of a national art was similar to that presented by republicanism to romantic nationalism: how to convert the universal into the local, and historical abstractions into a living relationship with a fractured past' (122).

53. See the important essay by Kate Trumpener, 'National Character, Nationalist Plots: National Tale and the Historical Novel in the Age of *Waverley*, 1806–30', *English Literary History*, 60/3 (Fall 1993), 685–731.

54. Maria Edgeworth, *Castle Rackrent*, ed. and introd. George Watson (Oxford: Oxford University Press, 1981), 97.

55. Ibid.

56. See, among many commentaries, Marilyn Butler, *Maria Edgeworth: A Literary Biography* (Oxford: Clarendon Press, 1972); Michael Hurst, *Maria Edgeworth and the Public Scene: Intellect, Fine Feeling and Landlordism in the Age of Reform* (London: Macmillan, 1969); Tom Dunne, *Maria Edgeworth and the Colonial Mind* (Cork: Cork University Press, 1984); Thomas Flanagan, *The Irish Novelists 1800–1850* (New York: Columbia University Press, 1959); W. J. McCormack, *Ascendancy and Tradition in Anglo-Irish Literary History from 1789 to 1939* (Oxford: Clarendon Press, 1985); id., 'Maria Edgeworth' in S. Deane, A.

Carpenter, and J. Williams (eds.), *The Field Day Anthology of Irish Writing*, 3 vols. (Derry: Field Day, 1991), i. 1011–52; id., 'French Revolution . . . Anglo-Irish Literature . . . Beginnings? The Case of Maria Edgeworth', in Hugh Gough and David Dickson (eds.), *Ireland and the French Revolution* (Dublin: Irish Academic Press, 1990), 229–43; J. M. Cahalan, *Great Hatred, Little Room: The Irish Historical Novel* (Syracuse: Syracuse University Press; Dublin: Gill & Macmillan, 1984); Barry Sloan, *The Pioneers of Anglo-Irish Fiction, 1800–50* (Gerrards Cross: Colin Smythe; Totowa, NJ, Barnes & Noble, 1986); Terry Eagleton, *Heathcliff and the Great Hunger: Studies in Irish Culture* (London and New York: Verso, 1995), 161–77.

57. Joseph Cooper Walker's 'The Life of Turlough Carolan' appears as an appendix to the *Historical Memoirs of the Irish Bards* (1st edn. 1786; 2nd edn., 2 vols., Dublin: J. Christie, 1818), i. 234–339. On Carolan's 'fondness for spiritous liquors' see 307–10.

58. James Hardiman, *Irish Minstrelsy, or Bardic Remains of Ireland with English Poetical Translations*, 2 vols. (London: Robins, 1831), vol. i, pp. lxvii–lxviii.

59. Ibid., p. lxviii.

60. Ibid., p. lxvi.

61. See notes to pp. viii–x and p. xxiv of Hardiman's Introduction. There is, of course, a specifically English hostility to Macpherson. For recent discussions see Leah Leneman, 'Ossian and the Enlightenment', *Scotia*, 11 (1987), 13–29; Derick Thomson, 'Macpherson's *Ossian*: Ballads to Epics', in Bo Almquist, Seamus Ó Catháin, and Padraig Ó Héaláin (eds.), *The Heroic Process: Form, Function and Fantasy in Folk Epic* (Dun Laoghaire: Glendale Press, 1987), 243–64; Fiona Stafford, *The Sublime Savage* (Edinburgh: Edinburgh University Press, 1988); Fiona Stafford and Howard Gaskill (eds.), *Ossian Revisited* (Edinburgh: Edinburgh University Press, 1991); Murray G. H. Pittock, *Poetry and Jacobite Politics in Eighteenth-Century Britain and Ireland* (Cambridge: Cambridge University Press, 1994), 178–86.

62. Grafton, *Defenders of the Text*, 224.

63. Theophilus O'Flanagan, *Advice to a Prince, by Thaddy Mac Brody or Mac Brodin, Son of Dary; being the inauguration ode of Donach O'Brien, Fourth earl of Thomond, when elected prince of his nation, according to ancient Irish Usage . . .* , from *Transactions of the Gaelic Society of Dublin, established for the investigation and revival of Ancient Irish Literature* (Dublin: J. Barlow, 1808), 7.

64. Hardiman, *Minstrelsy*, i. 137–8.

65. Ibid. 138–9.

66. Ibid. 168.

67. Ibid. 177.

68. George Watson, introduction to *Castle Rackrent*, p. xxv. There were a number of attempts in the 1780s and 1790s to reconcile educational ideas of discipline with Rousseauistic theories of the development of feelings and affections. A representative text would be Henry Home, Lord Kames's *Loose Hints upon education, chiefly concerning the culture of the heart* (Edinburgh: John Bell & John Murray, 1781).

69. Barrington, *Personal Sketches of His Own Times*, 2 vols. (London: Colburn, 1827), i. 4.

70. *Castle Rackrent*, 97.

Notes to Chapter Two

1. See, among modern discussions, Ernest Barker, *National Character and the Factors in its Formation* (London: Methuen, 1927); Simone Weil, *The Need for Roots: Prelude to a Declaration of Duties towards Mankind*, trans. A. F. Wills (London: Routledge & Kegan Paul, 1952); Elias Canetti, *Crowds and Power* (1st pub. 1960; Harmondsworth: Penguin, 1984), 197–234; Hans Kohn, *The Age of Nationalism* (New York: Harper, 1962); Ernest Gellner, *Nations and Nationalism* (Ithaca, NY: Cornell University Press, 1983); id., *Culture, Identity and Politics* (Cambridge: Cambridge University Press, 1987); Anthony D. Smith, *The Ethnic Origins of Nations* (Oxford: Blackwell, 1987); Benedict Anderson, *Imagined Communities: Reflections on the Origin and Spread of Nationalism*, 2nd edn. (London: Verso, 1991); Gerald Newman, *The Rise of English Nationalism: A Cultural History, 1720–1830* (New York: St Martin's Press, 1987); Eric Hobsbawm, *Nations and Nationalism since 1750: Programme, Myth, Reality* (Cambridge: Cambridge University Press, 1990); James Laughlin, 'Some Comparative Aspects of Irish and English Nationalism in the Late Nineteenth Century', in Myrtle Hill and Sarah Barber (eds.), *Aspects of Irish Studies* (Belfast: Institute of Irish Studies, 1990), 9–15; Perry Anderson, *English Questions* (London and New York: Verso, 1992), 48–104, 193–301; id., *A Zone of Engagement* (London and New York: Verso, 1992), 251–78; Tzvetan Todorov, *On Human Diversity: Nationalism, Racism, and Exoticism in French Thought*, trans. Catherine Porter (Cambridge, Mass.: Harvard University Press, 1993); Edward Said, *Culture and Imperialism* (New York: Knopf, 1993); David Simpson, *Romanticism, Nationalism, and the Revolt against Theory* (Chicago: University of Chicago Press, 1993).

2. The most significant inflection of the Burkean argument in England was provided by Coleridge's reordering of the relationship between the nation and the state. This itself owed a good deal to Friedrich Schiller's *On the Aesthetic Education of Man in a Series of Letters* (1801),

ed. Elizabeth M. Wilkinson and L. A. Willoughby (Oxford: Clarendon Press, 1967), fifth, sixth and seventh letters. See also David Lloyd, 'Arnold, Ferguson, Schiller: Aesthetic Culture and the Politics of Aesthetics', *Cultural Critique*, 2 (Winter 1985/6), 139–52.

3. Classic statements of this position can be found in George Petrie, *The Petrie Collection of the Ancient Music of Ireland: Arranged for the Pianoforte* (Dublin: Dublin University Press, 1855–82), vol. i, introduction; James Fintan Lalor, 'A New Nation', *The Nation*, 24 Apr. 1847 in *Collected Writings*, ed. Nathaniel Marlowe (Dublin: Maunsel, 1918), 7–28; Michael Davitt, *The Fall of Feudalism in Ireland* (London: Harper & Brothers, 1904), ch. 5.

4. See Cormac Ó Gráda, *The Great Irish Famine* (Houndmills: Macmillan, 1989), 63–75; id., *Ireland: A New Economic History, 1780–1939* (Oxford: Clarendon Press, 1994), 236–72; Christine Kenealy, *This Great Calamity: The Irish Famine, 1845–52* (Dublin: Gill & Macmillan, 1994), 265–96, 352–9. Among other recent works on the Famine, see Cathal Poirtéir (ed.), *The Great Irish Famine* (Cork: Mercier Press, 1995); Mary E. Daly, *The Famine in Ireland* (Dublin: Dundalgan Press, 1986); Donal E. Kerr, *'A Nation of Beggars'? Priests, People and Politics in Famine Ireland, 1846–1852* (Oxford: Clarendon Press, 1994). See also Kevin Whelan, 'Ireland in the World-System, 1600–1800', in Hans-Jurgen Nitz (ed.), *The Early-Modern World-System in Geographical Perspective* (Stuttgart: Franz Steiner, 1993), 204–18.

5. Cf. Chris Morash, *Writing the Irish Famine* (Oxford: Clarendon Press, 1995), 1–51.

6. Joseph Th. Leerssen, 'On the Edge of Europe: Ireland in Search of Oriental Roots, 1650–1850', *Comparative Criticism*, 8 (1986), 91–112. The form of exceptionalism most often assigned to the Irish was, of course, that of their exceptional degradation, barbarity, criminality. See L. Perry Curtis, *Apes and Angels: The Irishman in Victorian Caricature* (Washington: Smithsonian Institution Press, 1971).

7. For a sustained commentary on the conflict beween modernization and the nationalist project see Partha Chatterjee, *Nationalist Thought and the Colonial World: A Derivative Discourse* (Minneapolis: University of Minnesota Press, 1986), 79–81; id., *The Nation and its Fragments: Colonial and Postcolonial Histories* (Princeton: Princeton University Press, 1993), 200–19; Homi Bhabha, *The Location of Culture* (London: Routledge, 1994), 123–70; Aijaz Ahmad, *In Theory: Classes, Nations, Literatures* (London: Verso, 1992), 10–15.

8. Kevin Whelan, 'Settlement Patterns in the West of Ireland in the Pre-Famine Period', in Timothy Collins (ed.), *Decoding the Landscape* (Galway: Social Sciences Research Centre, 1994), 60–78.

9. See Anderson, 'Fernand Braudel and National Identity', in id., *A Zone of Engagement*, 251–78; Raphael Samuel (ed.), *Patriotisms: The Making and Unmaking of British National Identity*, 3 vols. (London: Routledge, 1989); Said, *Culture and Imperialism*, 62–190; Linda Colley, *Britons: Forging the Nation, 1707–1837* (New Haven and London: Yale University Press, 1992); Tom Dunne, 'Haunted by History: Irish Romantic Writing, 1800–1850', in Roy Porter and M. Teich (eds.), *Romanticism in National Context* (Cambridge: Cambridge University Press, 1988), 68–91; Seamus Deane, 'Irish National Character, 1790–1900', in Tom Dunne (ed.), *The Writer as Witness: Literature as Historical Evidence* (Cork: Cork University Press, 1987), 90–113; id., 'National Character and National Audience: Races, Crowds and Readers', in Michael Allen and Angela Wilcox (eds.), *Critical Approaches to Anglo-Irish Literature* (Gerrards Cross: Colin Smythe, 1989), 40–52.
10. Gerald Griffin, *The Collegians: A Tale of Garryowen*, introd. John Cronin (Dublin: Appletree Press, 1992), p. ix. See also John Cronin, *Gerald Griffin 1803–40: A Critical Biography* (Cambridge: Cambridge University Press, 1978).
11. Peter Brooks, *The Melodramatic Imagination: Balzac, Henry James, Melodrama, and the Mode of Excess* (New Haven: Yale University Press, 1976; repr. 1984), 16–17.
12. *The Collegians*, 36.
13. Ibid. 19.
14. Ibid. 18.
15. Ibid. 19.
16. Ibid. 23.
17. Ibid. 72.
18. Ibid. 3.
19. Ibid. 2.
20. Ibid. 4.
21. Ibid. 21.
22. Ibid. 49.
23. Sir Julius Benedict, *The Lily of Killarney: Opera in Three Acts. The Words by Dion Boucicault and John Oxenford*, ed. J. Pitman (London and New York: Boosey & Co., 1861).
24. Simpson, *Romanticism*, 136–7.
25. Thomas Moore, *Irish Melodies* (London: Longman, 1810), p. iv. In 1811, in response to a rumour that the government was going to prevent the continuation of the *Melodies*, Moore asserted his usual disclaimer in relation to the political impact of the songs: 'But we live in wiser and less musical times; ballads have long lost their revolutionary powers, and we question if even a "lillibullero" would pro-

duce any very *serious* consequences at present.' (*Irish Melodies and Miscellaneous Poems with a Melologue upon National Music* (Dublin: W. Power, 1833), 212.

26. Esp. in Edward Bunting's famous collections: *A General Collection of the Ancient Irish Music* (London: W. Power, 1796); *A General Collection of the Ancient Music of Ireland* (London: Clementi, 1809); *The Ancient Music of Ireland* (Dublin: Hodges & Smith, 1840); also in James Clarence Mangan, *The Poets and Poetry of Munster: A Collection of Irish Songs . . .* (Dublin: John O'Daly, 1849; 2nd edn. 1850; 3rd edn. 1884; 4th edn. James Duffy, 1925); Petrie, *The Petrie Collection*; see also *The Spirit of the Nation* (Dublin: J. Duffy, 1843–4).

27. 'Irish Language Movement: Some Reminiscences', *Manchester Guardian Commercial*, 10 May 1923; see Douglas Hyde, 'An Craoibhin Aoibhinn': Language, Lore and Lyrics. Essays and Lectures, ed. Brendan Ó Conaire (Dublin: Irish Academic Press, 1986).

28. See Nigel Leask, *British Romantic Writers and the East: Anxieties of Empire* (Cambridge: Cambridge University Press, 1992), 110–14.

29. See Thomas Moore, *Memoirs of Captain Rock, the Celebrated Irish Chieftain, with some account of his Ancestors* (London: Longman, 1824), p. iv. The reference to the Sheehy case is on p. 155. On Burke and Sheehy, see Louis Cullen, 'The Blackwater Catholics and County Cork: Society and Politics in the Eighteenth Century', in Patrick O'Flanagan and Cornelius G. Buttimer (eds.), *Cork: History and Society. Interdisciplinary Essays in the History of an Irish County* (Dublin: Geography Publications, 1993), 535–84.

30. Thomas Moore, *The Life and Death of Lord Edward Fitzgerald*, 2 vols. (London: Longman, Rees, Orme, Brown and Green, 1831), i. 196.

31. Isaac Butt, *The Irish People and the Irish Land* (Dublin: Falconer; London: Ridgeway, 1867), 267–8.

32. E. Stokes, *The English Utilitarians and India* (Oxford: Clarendon Press, 1959), 82. See also R. D. Collison Black, 'Economic Policy in Ireland and India in the Time of J. S. Mill', *Economic History Review*, 2nd ser., 21 (1968), 321–36. The most powerful analysis of the imperial exchanges between India and Ireland is S. B. Cook, *Imperial Affinities: Nineteenth Century Analogies and Exchanges between India and Ireland* (New Delhi and Newbury Park, London: Sage Publications, 1993), esp. 81–136.

33. Thomas Davis, *Prose Writings*, ed. T. W. Rolleston (London: W. Scott, 1890), 51. On Davis and the Young Ireland movement, see J. M. Hone, *Thomas Davis* (London: Duckworth, 1934); Malcom Brown, *The Politics of Irish Literature from Thomas Davis to W. B. Yeats* (Seattle: University of Washington, 1972); Richard P. Davis, *The Young Ireland Movement* (Dublin: Gill & Macmillan, 1987); John

Hutchinson, *The Dynamics of Cultural Nationalism: The Gaelic Revival and the Creation of the Irish Nation State* (London: Allen & Unwin, 1987); John N. Molony, *A Soul Came into Ireland: Thomas Davis 1814–1845. A Biography* (Dublin: Geography Publications, 1996).

34. Davis, *Prose Writings*, 53.
35. Ibid. 66–7.
36. Ibid. 58.
37. Ibid. 56.
38. Ibid. 74.
39. Ibid. 88.
40. Ibid. 51.
41. Ibid. 72.
42. 'Art Unions', in D. J. O'Donoghue (ed.), *Literary and Historical Essays* (Dundalk: Dundalgan Press, 1914), 163.
43. Michael Davitt, *Some Suggestions for a Final Settlement of the Land Question* (Dublin: Gill & Son, 1902), 9.
44. Ibid. 11.
45. James Fintan Lalor, *Collected Writings*, ed. Nathaniel Marlowe (Dublin: Maunsel, 1918), 56–7.
46. Ibid. 57.
47. Ibid. 58.
48. See Graham Davis, 'Making History: John Mitchel and the Great Famine', in Paul Hyland and Neil Sammels (eds.), *Irish Writing: Exile and Subversion* (London: Macmillan, 1991), 98–115.
49. John Mitchel, *Jail Journal; or, Five Years in British Prisons* (Dublin: M. H. Gill,1913), p. xxxv.
50. Ibid., p. xxxvi.
51. Ibid.
52. Ibid., p. xxxv.
53. John Mitchel, *History of Ireland, from the Treaty of Limerick to the Present Day*, (Dublin: James Duffy, 2nd edn. 1869), 308.
54. See Karl Marx and Friedrich Engels, *Ireland and the Irish Question*, ed. R. Dixon (London: Lawrence & Wishart, n.d.).
55. Mitchel, *Jail Journal*, p. xlvi.
56. Ibid. 80.
57. Ibid. 81.
58. Ibid. 80.
59. Ibid. 81.
60. Ibid. 82.
61. Ibid. 84.
62. Ibid. 86.
63. Ibid. 87.
64. Ibid. 88.

65. Ibid. 92–3.
66. Ibid., p. xxvii.
67. Ibid.
68. Michael Turner, 'Rural Economies in Post-Famine Ireland, c.1850–1914', in Brian J. Graham and Lindsay J. Proudfoot (eds.), *An Historical Geography of Ireland* (London: Academic Press, 1993), 293–337.
69. Standish O'Grady, *History of Ireland*, ii: *Cuculain and his Contemporaries* (London: Sampson Low, Searle, Marston and Rivington; Dublin: E. Ponsonby, 1880), 34–5, 38–9.
70. Standish O'Grady, *History of Ireland*, i: *The Heroic Period* (London: Sampson Low, Searle, Marston and Rivington; Dublin: E. Ponsonby, 1878), p. xii.
71. Ibid. 22.
72. *The Crisis in Ireland* (Dublin: E. Ponsonby, 1882), 5.
73. Ibid. 7.
74. Ibid. 19.
75. Ibid. 23.
76. Ibid. 30.
77. Ibid. 32.
78. Ibid. 37.
79. Ibid. 49–50.
80. Standish O'Grady, *Toryism and the Tory Democracy* (London: Chapman & Hall, 1886), 104.
81. Ibid. 219.
82. Ibid. 215.
83. Ibid. 225.
84. Ibid. 215.
85. Ibid. 237.
86. Ibid. 256.
87. Ibid. 260.
88. Ibid. 261.
89. Ibid. 270.
90. Ibid. 277.
91. Ibid. 289.
92. Standish O'Grady, *Selected Essays and Passages*, introd. Ernest Boyd (Dublin: Talbot, 1917), 177.
93. Ibid.
94. Ibid. 178.
95. O'Grady, *Toryism and Tory Democracy*, 241.
96. Cf. David Harvey, *The Condition of Postmodernity: An Enquiry into the Origins of Cultural Change* (Oxford and Cambridge, Mass.: Blackwell, 1990; repr. 1994), 260–83.
97. See Terry Eagleton, *Heathcliff and the Great Hunger: Studies in Irish Culture* (London and New York: Verso, 1995), 215–16.

98. For an analysis of O'Grady's essays of 1908–9 in the weekly periodical
the *Irish Peasant*, see Catherine Nash, 'Landscape, Body and Nation:
Cultural Geographies of Irish Identities' (Ph.D. thesis, University of
Nottingham, 1995). See also William J. McCormack, *From Burke to
Beckett: Ascendancy, Tradition and Betrayal in Literary History* (Cork:
Cork University Press, 1994), 233–9, and D. George Boyce '"Trem-
bling Solicitude": Irish Conservatism, Nationality and Public Opin-
ion, 1833–86', in D. G. Boyce, R. Eccleshall, and V. Geoghegan (eds.),
Political Thought in Ireland since the Seventeenth Century (London and
New York: Routledge, 1993), 124–45.

99. See e.g. Franco Moretti, 'Dialectic of Fear', in id., *Signs Taken for
Wonders*, trans. S. Fischer, D. Forgacs, and D. Miller (London:
Verso, rev. edn. 1988), 83–108; Cannon Schmitt, 'Mother Dracula:
Orientalism, Degeneration, and Anglo-Irish National Subjectivity
at the Fin de Siècle', in John S. Richard (ed.), *Irishness and
(Post)Modernism* (Lewisburg: Bucknell University Press; London: As-
sociated University Presses, 1994), 25–43; David Glover, '"Dark
Enough fur Any Man": Bram Stoker's Sexual Ethnology and the
Question of Irish Nationalism', in Roman de la Campa, E. Ann
Kaplan, and Michael Sprinker (eds.), *Late Imperial Culture* (London:
Verso, 1995), 53–71; Marjorie Howes, 'The Mediation of the Femi-
nine: Bisexuality, Homoerotic Desire, and Self-Expression in Bram
Stoker's *Dracula*', *Texas Studies in Literature and Language*, 30/1
(Spring 1988), 104–19; Daniel Pick, '"Terrors of the Night": *Dracula*
and "Degeneration"' in the Late Nineteenth Century', *Critical Quar-
terly*, 30/4 (Winter 1988), 72–87; id., *Faces of Degeneration: A European
Disorder, c.1848–c.1918* (Cambridge: Cambridge University Press,
1989), 167–75; Anne Cranny-Francis, 'Sexual Politics and Political
Repression in Bram Stoker's *Dracula*', in Clive Bloom, Brian
Docherty, Jane Gibb, and Keith Shand (eds.), *Nineteenth-Century Sus-
pense: From Poe to Conan Doyle* (New York: St Martin's Press, 1988),
64–79; Rhys Garnett, '*Dracula* and *The Beetle*: Imperial and Sexual
Guilt and Fear in Late Victorian Fantasy', in Rhys Garnett and R. J.
Ellis (eds.), *Science Fiction Roots and Branches: Contemporary Critical
Approaches* (New York: St Martin's Press, 1988), 30–54; Mark S. Paris,
'From Clinic to Classroom while Uncovering the Evil Dead in
Dracula: A Psychoanalytic Pedagogy', in James M. Cahalan and David
B. Downing (eds.), *Practicing Theory in Introductory College Courses*
(Urbana, Ill.: National Council of Teachers of English, 1991), 47–56;
Carol A. Senf, '"Dracula": Stoker's Response to the New Woman',
Victorian Studies, 26/1 (Autumn 1982), 33-49; Judith Halberstam,
'Technologies of Monstrosity: Bram Stoker's *Dracula*', *Victorian Stud-
ies*, 36 (1993), 333–52, repr. in Sally Ledger and Scott McCracken
(eds.), *Cultural Politics at the Fin De Siècle* (Cambridge: Cambridge

University Press, 1995), 248–66; Alexandra Warwick, 'Vampires and the Empire: Fears and Fictions of the 1890s', ibid. 202–20; Richard Wasson, 'The Politics of *Dracula*', *English Literature in Translation*, 9 (1966), 24–7; Geoffrey Wall, ' "Different from Writing": *Dracula* in 1897', *Literature and History*, 10/1 (Spring 1984), 15–24; Richard Astle, 'Dracula as Totemic Monster: Lacan, Freud, Oedipus and History', *Sub-Stance*, 25 (1980), 98–105; C. F. Bentley, 'The Monster in the Bedroom: Sexual Symbolism in Bram Stoker's *Dracula*', *Literature and Psychology*, 22/1 (1972), 27–34; Kathleen L. Spencer, 'Purity and Danger: *Dracula*, The Urban Gothic, and the Late Victorian Degeneracy Crisis', *English Literary History*, 59 (1992), 197–225; Chris Morash, ' "Ever under some unnatural condition": Bram Stoker and the Colonial Fantastic', in Brian Cosgrove (ed.), *Literature and the Supernatural* (Dublin: Columba Press, 1995), 95–119.

100. On Le Fanu and the Gothic tradition in general, see William J. McCormack, *Sheridan Le Fanu and Victorian Ireland* (Oxford: Clarendon Press, 1980); id., *Dissolute Characters: Irish Literary History through Balzac, Sheridan le Fanu and Bowen* (Manchester: Manchester University Press, 1993); id., 'Irish Gothic and After 1820–1945', in Seamus Deane, Andrew Carpenter, and Jonathan Williams (eds.), *The Field Day Anthology of Irish Writing*, 3 vols. (Derry: Field Day, 1991), ii. 831–949; Neil Cornwell, *The Literary Fantastic; From Gothic to Postmodernism* (Hemel Hempstead: Harvester Wheatsheaf, 1990), 87–94; Julian Moynahan, *Anglo-Irish: The Literary Imagination in a Hyphenated Culture* (Princeton: Princeton University Press, 1995), 109–35.

101. *Dracula* (Dingle: Brandon Books, 1992), 351–2.

102. There is a link between writing and self-preservation throughout; Dracula actually destroys the account that has been compiled to destroy him, but is frustrated by the fact that a copy has been kept. See Jim Collins, *Uncommon Cultures: Popular Cultures and Post-Modernism* (New York and London: Routledge, 1989), 87–8. The links between eating and writing, especially eating of a savage and cannibalistic kind, are explored in various *fin-de-siècle* novels—H. G. Wells's *The Time Machine* (1895), Conrad's *Heart of Darkness* (1899). See Tim Youngs, *Travellers in Africa: British Travelogues, 1850–1900* (Manchester: Manchester University Press, 1994), 54–80.

103. A dubious but interesting etymology derives the name 'Dracula' from the Irish *droch-feola*, meaning 'bad blood'. Further, the common notion of 'bad blood' between feuding families is also pertinent here.

104. *Dracula*, ch. XIV, p. 177.

105. Ibid. 352: 'This boy will some day know what a brave and gallant

woman his mother is. Already he knows her sweetness and loving care; later on he will understand how some men so loved her, that they did dare much for her sake.'

106. On language, family, school, race, and nation, see Etienne Balibar, 'The Nation Form: History and Ideology', in Etienne Balibar and Immanuel Wallerstein, *Race, Nation, Class: Ambiguous Identities* (London: Verso, 1995), 86–106.

107. 'Ivy Day in the Committee Room' is perhaps the most notable of the other stories in which the world of the dead is evoked in verse. But the world of Parnell lies in past time; the ritual of revival and commemoration here is abortive. There is no language for a Parnell revival. Glasnevin is not Rahoon.

108. *A Portrait of the Artist as a Young Man*, ed. Seamus Deane (London: Penguin, 1993): see introduction, pp. xxx–xxxi.

109. See Emer Nolan, *James Joyce and Nationalism* (London and New York: Routledge, 1995), 163–81.

110. Walter Benn Michaels, 'Race into Culture: A Critical Genealogy of Cultural Identity', in Kwame Anthony Appiah and Henry Louis Gates, Jr. (eds.), *Identities* (Chicago: University of Chicago Press, 1995), 32–62: 59–60.

111. Burke, *Reflections*, 84.

Notes to Chapter Three

1. *Charlotte Brooke, Reliques of Irish Poetry* (Dublin: George Bonham, 1789), preface, p. iv. Her father was Henry Brooke (1703–83), novelist (*The Fool of Quality* (1765–70)), playwright, and pamphleteer.

2. Ibid., p. v.

3. Edward W. Lynam, *The Irish Character in Print 1571–1923* (Oxford: Oxford University Press offprint, 1924; Shannon: Irish University Press, 1968), 19–20.

4. The classic work in this field is Dermot McGuinne, *Irish Type Design: A History of Printing Types in the Irish Character* (Dublin: Irish Academic Press, 1992). On Brooke, see pp. 70–4 . The first publication to use the type was the 1788 volume of the *Transactions of the Royal Irish Academy*, in its Antiquities section.

5. Samuel Ferguson 'Hardiman's Irish Minstrelsy', *Dublin University Magazine*, 3 (1834), 465–78; 4 (1834), 152–67, 447–67, 514–30. On Ferguson, see Mary Catharine (Lady) Ferguson, *Sir Samuel Ferguson in the Ireland of his Day*, 2 vols. (Edinburgh: Blackwood, 1896); Malcolm Brown, *Sir Samuel Ferguson* (Lewisburg: Bucknell University Press, 1973); Robert O'Driscoll, *An Ascendancy of the Heart; Ferguson and the Beginnings of Irish Literature in English* (Dublin: Dolmen Press, 1976);

Terence Brown, *Northern Voices: Poets from Ulster* (Dublin: Gill & Macmillan, 1975), 29–41; Terence Brown and Barbara Hayley (eds.), *Samuel Ferguson—A Centenary Tribute* (Dublin: Royal Irish Academy, 1987); Robert Welch, *History of Verse Translation from the Irish 1789–1897* (Gerrards Cross: Colin Smythe, 1987); Shaun Richards and David Cairns, *Writing Ireland: Colonialism, Nationalism and Culture* (Manchester: Manchester University Press, 1988), 25–31; Peter Denman, *Samuel Ferguson: The Literary Achievement* (Gerrards Cross: Colin Smythe, 1990); W. J. McCormack, 'The Intellectual Revival (1830–1850)', in Seamus Deane, Andrew Carpenter, and Jonathan Williams (eds.), *The Field Day Anthology of Irish Writing*, 3 vols. (Derry: Field Day, 1991), ii. 1173–200; Greagóir O Dúill, *Samuel Ferguson: Beatha agus Saothar* (Dublin: Clóchomhar, 1993); Joep Th. Leerssen, *Remembrance and Imagination: Patterns in the Historical and Literary Representation of Ireland in the Nineteenth Century* (Cork: Cork University Press / Field Day, 1996).

6. The first volume was published in 1814: *Rerum Hibernicarum Scriptores Veteres*, 4 vols. (London: T. Payne, 1814–26). This typeface was not used for vols. iii (1824) and iv (1826). The National Library of Ireland copy of vol. i was George Petrie's; it contains MS notes by Petrie and John O'Donovan.

7. See Lynam, *The Irish Character in Print*, 27; McGuinn, *Irish Type Design*, 93–8. McGuinn cites a further use of the type, discovered by Séamus Ó Casaide, in a religious poem, published in Drogheda in 1851.

8. James Hardiman, *Irish Minstrelsy, or Bardic Remains of Ireland with English Poetical Translations*, 2 vols. (London: Robins, 1831), vol. i, introduction, p. xxxiii; McGuinn, *Irish Type Design*, 81.

9. John O'Daly, *Irish Language Miscellany: being a selection of Poems by the Munster Bards of the last Century* (Dublin: John O'Daly, 1876), pp. v–vi.

10. Edward Walsh, *Irish Popular Songs: with English metrical translations, and introductory remarks and notes* (Dublin: McGlashan, 1847; 2nd edn., rev. and corr., Gill, 1883), 36–7, italics in original.

11. See Lynam, *The Irish Character in Print*, on the Queen Elizabeth type of 1571: 'The Roman letters interspersed among the less well-disciplined Celts make a firm and even rank, such as we shall not see among the pure Celts for over two hundred years.' (p. 7). For a summary, see McGuinne, *Irish Type Design*, ch. 11, 'The Roman v. the Irish Character', 163–93.

12. See Lynam, *Irish Character*, and McGuinn, *Irish Type Design*, passim.

13. Charles Walmesley (1722–97), published *The General History of the Christian Church from her birth to her final triumphant state in heaven chiefly deduced from the apocalypse of St. John The Apostle and Evangelist*

in 1771 under the pseudonym 'Signor Pastorini'; there were Dublin editions in 1790, 1800, 1805, 1813; a Cork edition in 1820 and a Belfast edition, also in 1820. The work claimed that the Reformation had two phases, 1525–1675 and 1675–1825. After that, it would disappear from history. Excerpts from the work were published in pamphlets and broadsheets in the 1820s and a small-scale pamphlet war broke out. Among many Protestant responses, that of 'Pastor Fido' may be taken as typical: *Pastorini Proved to be a Bad Prophet and a Worse Divine in an Address to the Roman Catholics of Ireland. Earnestly recommended to their Serious Perusal* (Dublin: M. Goodwin, 1823), 20: 'Though I am far from supposing that the year 1826 will usher in the complete destruction of Antichrist, is it not infinitely more likely, that such an event will take place in that year, than that in the year 1825, the light of the Reformation will be extinguished? Never did that light shine more brightly or more extensively than at this moment—witness the gigantic strides of the British and Foreign Bible Societies all over the world. Never was the dark night of Popery so near its close . . .' It was widely recognized that the Pastorini prophecies helped to inflame the various insurgent agrarian groups like the Rockites. See e.g. Eyre Evans Crowe's tale 'The Carders', from *Today in Ireland* (1825), introd. R. L. Wolff, 3 vols. (New York and London: Garland, 1979), vol. i, ch. vii, p. 110, in which the Anglican curate Mr Crosthwaite barricades himself in his glebe parlour, with whiskey, a blunderbuss, and a symbolic selection of books that includes Pastorini's prophecies, described as privately printed in Ireland and widely disseminated among the lower orders. In this tale, as in many anti-Pastorini pamphlets, the threat of extinction to the Protestants is regularly associated with the Catholic rebellion of 1641 and the United Irish Rebellion of 1798. See e.g. the anonymous *Prophecies of Pastorini Analyzed and Refuted and the powerful tendency of Inflammatory Prediction to excite Insurrection, satisfactorily demonstrated from incontrovertible Historical Records, with a Cursory View of the Dangerous State of Ireland, from an exclusively Popish Conspiracy, Humbly submitted to the Consideration of the Protestants of the British Empire by a Graduate of Trinity College* (Dublin, 1823), 46.

14. See *The Encyclical Letter of Pope Leo XII. Annexed to Pastoral Instructions by the Roman Catholic Archbishops and Bishops* (Dublin: Richard Coyne, 1824), 16–17: 'You are aware, Venerable Brethren, that a certain Society, commonly called the *Bible Society*, strolls with effrontery throughout the world . . . labours with all its might . . . to translate— or rather to pervert—the Holy Bible into the vulgar languages of every nation . . . if the Sacred Scriptures be every where indiscriminately published, more evil than advantage will arise thence.'

The Encyclical goes on to lament the Bible Society's skill in printing its translations and its delight in distributing them. 'Nay, to allure the minds of the simple, at one time it sells them, at another, with an insidious liberality, it bestows them.'

15. Niall Ó Cíosáin, 'Printed Popular Literature in Irish 1750–1850: Presence and Absence', in Mary Daly and David Dickson (eds.), *The Origins of Popular Literacy in Ireland: Language Change and Educational Development 1700–1920* (Dublin: Trinity College and University College, 1990), 45–57.

16. On the eighteenth-century Celtic revival, and the role of Vallancey, Joseph Cooper Walker, Sylvester O'Halloran, and others, see Thomas Davis's essay 'Udalism and Feudalism' (1843), in Davis, *Prose Writings*, ed. T. W. Rolleston (London, 1889), 88: 'To the exertions of Walker, O'Halloran, Vallancey, and a few other Irish academicians in the last century, we owe almost all the Irish knowledge possessed by our upper classes until very lately. It was small, but it was enough to give a dreamy renown to ancient Ireland; and if it did nothing else it smoothed the reception of Bunting's music and identified Moore's poetry with his native country.' For general accounts, see Edward Snyder, *The Celtic Revival in English Literature, 1760–1800* (Cambridge, Mass.: Harvard University Press, 1923); Donal MacCartney, 'The Writing of History in Ireland, 1800–1850', *Irish Historical Studies*, 10/40 (Sept. 1957), 347–62; Norman Vance, 'Celts, Carthaginians and Constitutions: Anglo-Irish Literary Relations, 1780–1820', *Irish Historical Studies*, 22/87 (Mar. 1981), 216–38; Oliver MacDonagh, *States of Mind: A Study of Anglo-Irish Conflict 1780–1980* (London: George Allen & Unwin, 1983); Leerssen, *Remembrance and Imagination*.

17. Hardiman, *Irish Minstrelsy*, introduction, p. viii. The reference to the Round Towers of Ireland anticipates the long dispute about their origin and function that culminated, but did not end, in George Petrie's famous essay, *The Ecclesiastical Architecture of Ireland* (Dublin: Hodges & Smith, 1845). See Leerssen, *Remembrance and Imagination*, for a full account.

18. Hardiman, *Irish Minstrelsy*, pp. ix–x.

19. Ibid., p. xxv. The two most strategically important sections in Hardiman's work are the first, which gives pride of place to Carolan, and the third, 'Jacobite Relics'. Hardiman made the important cultural–political connection between eighteenth-century popular culture's hostility to the penal laws and nineteenth-century popular opposition—led by O'Connell—to the Union.

20. Ibid., pp. xxxi–xxxiii.

21. Ibid., p. xxxiii; see footnote on the scarcity of Irish type fonts in 1819.

22. See Theophilus O'Flanagan, *Advice to a Prince, by Thaddy Mac Brody or*

Mac Brodin, Son of Dary; being the inauguration ode of Donach O'Brien,
Fourth earl of Thomond, when elected prince of his nation, according to
ancient Irish Usage . . . , from *Transactions of the Gaelic Society of Dublin,*
established for the investigation and revival of Ancient Irish Literature
(Dublin: J. Barlow, 1808), where he identifies the 'traditional memory
of the Albanian Scots, the descendants of a colony sent from Ireland'
as the source for Macpherson's 'Oisin', whose 'visionary history' he
considers 'utterly exploded' (pp. 24–5). However, he concedes that
'For the credit of his talents, however perverse their application, we
should not omit observing, that, from scanty and disfigured original
materials, he has compiled and left to posterity a lasting monument
to his genius. Let not this tribute of praise however, encourage the
prejudice of that nation, to palm, on an enlightened age, the detected
forgeries of a modern corrupt dialect, as the admirable effusions of
ancient genius' (pp. 25–6). This is followed by a dismissal—'Away
with the imposition on the learned world as "Tales of Other times"—
the modern fictions of Albano-Scotic fabrication' (p. 26).

In the same volume, in the 'Proeme' to his translation of *Deirdri, or*
The lamentable Fate of the Sons of Usnach, An Ancient Dramatic Irish Tale,
one of the three tragic stories of Erin, O'Flanagan claims that the Deirdre
story is the source of Macpherson's *Darthula;* his indebtedness, inter-
polations, and anachronisms are evident. The connection between
Scotland and Ireland, and the priority of Ireland in that respect, is
expanded upon in a long footnote on pp. 10–12; a sustained attack on
Macpherson's *Darthula* and *Ossian* is launched on pp. 135–44; and the
vacillation between hostility and reconciliation is captured in the
following quotations: 'Let us, both modern Scotch and Irish, pursue
the more honorable end of preserving the valuable remains of our
ancient literature, which was of yore, and may again be our common
property. At no very remote period, we were united on the martial
plain, against a nation whom we then considered as a common
enemy, though happily now in union with us.' (p. 11 n.); 'Many of my
countrymen . . . have attacked this many-headed wily monster of
Scottish generation; but they hurled the weapons of abstract reasoning only, which were eluded by the shield of sophistical deception.
But I come in the simple, defensive armour of comparative fact,
while my offensive weapons are historic truth, a professed acquaint-
ance with my native language; with all that the destructive works of
time and war have left in it for contemplation; and with a critically
accurate knowledge of its most abstruse, difficult, sublime and
elegant poetry' (p. 143).

Further commentary on Macpherson appears on pp. 189–92, 211–
23. On pp. 212–13, Ireland is described as *'The school of the west',*

effectively suppressed before the invention of printing; O'Flanagan
further claims that the 'Donegal Masters' had procured a type font
which they took with them to Louvain, where some of it still survives. Among Flanagan's predecessors in the scholarly assault on
Macpherson, the most noteworthy were Charles O'Conor, *Dissertation on the First Migrations, and Final Settlement of the Scots in North-
Britain; with occasional Observations on the poems of Fingal and Temora*
(Dublin: George Faulkner, 1766), 22–65; see also the National Library
of Ireland copy of Macpherson's *Temora, an ancient epic poem* (Dublin:
Leathly, 1763), which has extensive annotations by O'Conor.
Another early critic was Bishop John O'Brien, who published his
critique in the *Journal des Sçavans*; see Diarmaid Ó Catháin, 'An Irish
Scholar Abroad: Bishop John O'Brien of Cloyne and the Macpherson
Controversy', in Patrick O'Flanagan and Cornelius G. Buttimore
(eds.), *Cork: History and Society. Interdisciplinary Essays on the History of
an Irish County* (Dublin: Geography Publications, 1993), 499–533.

23. Hardiman, *Irish Minstrelsy*, introduction, pp. xxxii–xxiii.
24. See Francis John Byrne, *A Thousand Years of Irish Script: An Exhibition
of Irish Manuscripts in Oxford Libraries'* (Oxford: Bodleian Library,
1979), introduction, 4–5.
25. McGuinne, *Irish Type Design*, 99–117. In a despairing letter of 25 July
1763 to Dr Francis O'Sullivan, Charles O'Conor had suggested that
the Dublin Society might be persuaded to fund the printing of the
Annals; if so, he suggests that 'Malone or Percy should be employed
to cast a handsome Irish type of which I could give a good cut . . .'.
The Letters of Charles O'Conor of Belnagare, ed. Catherine Coogan Ward
and Robert E. Ward, 2 vols. (University Microfilms International,
1980), i. 165–6.
26. See Christopher Harvie, *Scotland and Nationalism: Scottish Society and
Politics 1707–1994* (London and New York: Routledge, 2nd edn. 1994),
22, where he describes the 'fruitful schizophrenia' of Scotland after
1885 that 'enabled the Scots to run with the ethnic hare and hunt with
the imperial hounds'.
27. Jerome McGann, *Black Riders: The Visible Language of Modernism*
(Princeton: Princeton University Press, 1993), 3–41. The first and
most famous production by the Dun Emer, later the Cuala, Press was
Yeats's *In The Seven Woods*. The work of Lolly and Lily Yeats, who,
along with Evelyn Gleeson, created the Cuala Industries, included
embroidery, and craftwork of various kinds. This venture was indebted to the example of William Morris in England. See Joan
Hardwick, *The Yeats Sisters* (London: Pandora, 1996).
28. Jerome McGann, 'Ulysses as a Postmodern Work', in id., *Social Values
and Poetic Acts: The Historical Judgment of Literary Work* (Cambridge,
Mass., and London: Harvard University Press, 1988), 173–96.

29. The classic analysis of this process has been made by Pierre Bourdieu, *The Field of Cultural Production*, ed. and introd. Randal Johnston (New York: Columbia University Press, 1993), esp. ch. 3, 'The Market of Symbolic Goods', pp. 112–41.

30. On Renan, Arnold, and Celticism, see Matthew Arnold, *On the Study of Celtic Literature*, in *The Complete Prose Works of Matthew Arnold*, ed. R. H. Super, vol. iii: *Lectures and Essays in Criticism* (Ann Arbor: University of Michigan Press, 1962); John V. Kelleher, 'Matthew Arnold and the Celtic Revival', in Harry Levin (ed.), *Perspectives of Criticism* (Cambridge, Mass.: Harvard University Press, 1950), 197–221; Rachel Bromwich, *Matthew Arnold and Celtic Literature: A Retrospect* (Oxford: Clarendon Press, 1965); Frederick Faverty, *Matthew Arnold, the Ethnologist* (Evanston: Northwestern University Press, 1951). On Renan, see also the selection of Renan's essays in *'The Poetry of the Celtic Races' and Other Essays*, trans. W. G. Hutchinson (London: W. Scott, 1896), and the less read but more important *Souvenirs d'enfance et de jeunesse* (1883), ET: *Recollections of My Youth*, trans. C. B. Pitman (Boston: Houghton Mifflin, 1929); also Tzvetan Todorov, *On Human Diversity: Nationalism, Racism, and Exoticism in French Thought*, trans. Catherine Porter (Cambridge, Mass.: Harvard University Press, 1993), 50–5, 107–13, 140–6, 219–29; Robert Young, *Colonial Desire: Hybridity in Theory, Culture and Race* (New York: Routledge, 1995). Other key texts in this complicated sequence would include Henri Martin, *Histoire de France depuis les temps les plus reculés jusqu'en 1789*, 17 vols. (Paris: Furne, 4th edn. 1855–60); Johann Kaspar Zeuss, *Grammatica Celtica* (Lipsiae: Weidmannos, 1853); Wilhelm von Humboldt, *Über die Verschiedenheit des menschlichen Sprachbaues* (1st pub. 1836; Bonn: F. Dummler, 1960). On the Celtic–Gaelic variation, see Luke Gibbons, 'Constructing the Canon: Versions of the National Identity', in Seamus Deane, Andrew Carpenter, and Jonathan Williams (eds.), *The Field Day Anthology of Irish Writing*, 3 vols. (Derry: Field Day, 1991), ii. 950–1223; see also Richards and Cairns, *Writing Ireland*.

31. W. B. Yeats, 'By the Roadside', *Mythologies* (London: Macmillan, 1959), 139. For a full account, see Mary Helen Thuente, *W. B. Yeats and Irish Folklore* (Dublin: Gill & Macmillan, 1980).

32. T. Crofton Croker, *Fairy Legends and Traditions of the South of Ireland*, 3 vols. (London: Murray, 1825–8), i. 362.

33. 'Village Ghosts', *Mythologies*, 15.

34. Theodor W. Adorno, 'A Portrait of Walter Benjamin', in *Prisms*, trans. Samuel and Shierry Weber (Cambridge, Mass.: MIT Press, 1994), 233.

35. *Mythologies*, 78 and 79.

36. Ibid. 125.
37. Eleanor Hull, *The Poem-Book of the Gael* (London: Chatto & Windus, 1912), introduction, p. xxiv.
38. On the policy of translating classics into Irish, see Philip O'Leary, *The Prose Literature of the Gaelic Revival 1881–1921* (University Park: Pennsylvania State University Press, 1994), 355–99. On the general issue of translation, see Michael Cronin, *Translating Ireland: Translation, Languages, Cultures* (Cork: Cork University Press, 1996).
39. Among the earliest popular accounts, see the *Annual Register 1790* (London, 1793), 'History of Europe', 40–58; see also Hedva Ben-Israel, *English Historians on the French Revolution* (Cambridge: Cambridge University Press, 1968); among the classic French anti-revolutionary works that Taine drew on and deformed were Louis de Bonald, *Théorie du pouvoir politique et religieux* (1st pub. 1796: Paris, A. Leclerc, 1854); Joseph de Maistre, *Considérations sur la France* (Lyon: Rusand, 1829); C. F. Marie de Rémusat, *L'Angleterre au dix-huitième siècle*, 2 vols. (1st pub. 1856; New York: Arno, 1979); abbé de Montgaillard, *Histoire de France, depuis la fin de la règne de Louis XVI jusqu'à l'année 1825* (Paris: Montardier, 2nd edn. 1828). See also Maxime du Camp, *Les Convulsions de Paris* (Paris: Hachette, 1880); Todorov, *On Human Diversity*; Daniel Pick, *Faces of Degeneration: A European Disorder, c.1848–c.1918* (Cambridge: Cambridge University Press, 1989), 67–73. Taine's work, *Les Origines de la France contemporaine*, 6 vols. (Paris, 1876–94), has many English translations. See *The Origins of Contemporary France*, ed. and selected by Edward T. Gargan (Chicago: University of Chicago Press, 1974). In *L'Ancien Régime* (1878), Taine describes the Réveillon riots, the storming of the Bastille, and the October march on Versailles as sexual orgies of prostitutes and shameless women. See bk. I, ch. iv, 150–9:

> Two distinct currents again combine in one torrent to hurry the crowd onward to a common end. On the one hand are the cravings of the stomach, and women excited by famine . . . On the other hand, there is fanaticism, and men who are pushed by the lust for dominion . . . These are the premonitory symptoms of a crisis; a huge ulcer has formed in this feverish, suffering body, and it is about to break.
>
> But, as is usually the case, it is a purulent concentration of the most poisonous passions and the foulest motives. The vilest of men and women are engaged in it. Money was freely distributed . . . On the first day that the Flemish regiment goes into garrison at Versailles an attempt is made to corrupt it with money and women. Sixty abandoned women are sent from Paris for this

purpose . . . As to the attack, women are to be the advanced guard, because the soldiers will scruple to fire at them; their ranks, however, will be reinforced by a number of men disguised as women. No difficulty has been found in obtaining men and women among the prostitutes of the Palais-Royal and the military deserters who serve them as bullies. It is probable that the former lent their lovers the cast-off dresses they had to spare . . . Some appear to belong to the first rank in their calling, and to have tact and the manners of society—suppose, for instance, that Champfort and Laclos sent their mistresses. To these must be added washerwomen, beggars, barefooted women, and fishwomen . . . This is the first nucleus, and it keeps on growing; for . . . the troop incorporates into it . . . all the women it encounters—seamstresses, portresses, housekeepers, and even respectable females . . . Such is the foul scum which . . . rolls along with the popular tide . . . on leaving Paris, he [Maillard] has seven or eight thousand women with him, and, in addition, some hundreds of men; by dint of remonstrances, he succeeds in maintaining some kind of order among this rabble as far as Versailles.—But it is a rabble notwithstanding, and consequently so much brute force, at once anarchical and imperious. On the one hand, each, and the worst among them, does what he pleases . . . On the other hand, its ponderous mass crushes all authority and overrides all rules and regulations . . . Meanwhile, the scum has been bubbling up around the chateau; and the abandoned women of Paris are pursuing their calling. They slip through the lines of the regiment drawn up on the square, in spite of sentinels . . . Others lie sprawling on the ground, alluring the soldiers . . . Before the day is over, the regiment is seduced; the women have, according to their own idea, acted for a good motive. When a political idea finds its way into such heads, instead of ennobling them, it becomes degraded there; its only effect is to let loose vices which a remnant of modesty still keeps in subjection, and full play is given to luxurious or ferocious instincts under cover of the public good.—The passions, moreover, become intensified through their mutual interaction; crowds, clamour, disorder, longings, and fasting, end in a state of phrensy. from which nothing can issue but dizzy madness and rage . . . But it is especially against the Queen, who is a woman, and in sight, that the feminine imagination is the most aroused . . . Such is the new fraternity—a funeral procession of legal and legitimate authorities, a triumph of brutality over intelligence, a murderous and political Mardi-gras, a formidable masquerade which, preceded by the insignia of death, drags along with it the heads of France, the King,

the ministers, and the deputies, that it may constrain them to rule
according to its phrensy, that it may hold them under its pikes until
it is pleased to slaughter them.

40. The new system of national schools was directed towards that end,
especially by replacing 'rhetorical excess' with 'rational discourse'.
See Thomas A. Boylan and Timothy P. Foley, *Political Economy
and Colonial Ireland: The Propagation and Ideological Function of
Economic Discourse in the Nineteenth Century* (London: Routledge,
1992), 116–60. The Temperance Movement, although led by a
Catholic friar, Fr. Mathew, did not win the official support of
the Catholic Church. Desmond J. Keenan, in *The Catholic Church
in Nineteenth-Century Ireland* (Dublin: Gill & Macmillan, 1983),
points out that 'Temperance bands were distinctly pro-union
and loyal' (p. 154); the more effective Pioneer Total Abstinence
Society, founded by Fr. James Cullen in 1898, was more enduringly
successful.

41. Gabriel Tarde, *La Philosophie pénale* (1890); ET: *Penal Philosophy*, trans.
Rapelje Howell (Boston: Little, Brown, 1912), 325–6; see Robert E.
Park, *The Crowd and the Public and Other Essays* (1904), ed. Henry
Elsner (Chicago: University of Chicago Press, 1972); Ruth Harris,
Murders and Madness: Medicine, Law and Society in the Fin de Siècle
(Oxford: Clarendon Press, 1989); Robert A. Nye, *The Origins of Crowd
Psychology: Gustave Le Bon and the Crisis of Mass Democracy in the Third
Republic* (London: Sage Publications, 1975); id., *Crime, Madness and
Politics in Modern France: The Medical Concept of National Decline*
(Princeton: Princeton University Press, 1984); Susanna Barrows, *Dis-
torting Mirrors: Visions of the Crowd in Late Nineteenth-Century France*
(New Haven: Yale University Press, 1981); Serge Moscovici, *The Age
of the Crowd: A Historical Treatise on Mass Psychology* (1981), trans. J. C.
Whitehouse (Cambridge: Cambridge University Press, 1985); Nancy
Stepan, *The Idea of Race in Science: Great Britain 1800–1960* (Hamden:
Archon Books, 1982); Sander Gilman, *Difference and Pathology: Stereotypes of Sexuality, Race and Madness* (Ithaca: Cornell University Press,
1985); J. S. McClelland, *The Crowd and the Mob: From Plato to Canetti*
(London: Unwin Hyman, 1989); Jaap van Ginneken, *Crowds, Psychology, and Politics 1871–99* (Cambridge: Cambridge University Press,
1992).

42. See Marjorie Howes, *Yeats's Nations: Gender, Class and Irishness*
(Cambridge: Cambridge University Press, 1996); Elizabeth Butler
Cullingford, *Gender and History in Yeats's Love Poetry* (Cambridge:
Cambridge University Press, 1993); C. Lynn Innes, *Women and Nation
in Irish Literature and Society 1880–1935* (Athens: University of Georgia
Press, 1993), 75–108.

43. David Lloyd, *Nationalism and Minor Literature: James Clarence Mangan and the Emergence of Irish Cultural Nationalism* (Berkeley, Los Angeles, and London: University of California Press, 1987).

44. Lionel Johnson's preface to Mangan, *The Prose Writings of James Clarence Mangan*, ed. D. J. O'Donoghue (Dublin and London, 1904) was influential in establishing the literary-addiction links between Mangan and Lamb, Coleridge, De Quincey, and Maginn, and the 'Gothic' links with Godwin and Maturin (pp. vii–viii), and in identifying his 'two chief worlds' as those of 'the moonlit forests of German poetry' and 'the Eastern, the "Saracenic" world' (p. xiv). Most memorable of all is his description of Mangan himself: 'He wanders about the rotting alleys and foul streets, a wasted ghost, with the "Dark Rosaleen" on his lips, and a strange light in those mystical blue eyes which burn for us yet in the reminiscences of all who ever saw him and wrote of the unforgettable sight . . . Hard as it is to believe at all times, he was an intelligible, an explicable human being, and not some "twy-natured" thing, some city faun.' (p. xi). John D. Sheridan's *James Clarence Mangan* (Dublin: Talbot Press; London: Duckworth, 1937) extends the Mangan East–West myth to Joyce: 'East and West meet in that personality . . .' (p. 37); see also Ellen Shannon-Mangan, *James Clarence Mangan: A Biography* (Dublin: Irish Academic Press, 1996).

45. The full publication details are as follows: *The Poets and Poetry of Munster: A Selection of Irish songs by the poets of the last century, with poetical translations by the late James Clarence Mangan, now for the first time published, with the Original Music, and biographical sketches of the authors . . .* (Dublin: John O'Daly, 1849; 2nd edn. 1850; 3rd edn. 1885); 4th edn. published as *The Poets and Poetry of Munster: A Selection of Irish Songs by the Poets of the Eighteenth Century, with Poetical Translations by James Clarence Mangan* (Dublin: James Duffy, 1925). All citations are from the 1925 edn. unless otherwise indicated.

46. Ibid. 2.

47. Ibid. 5.

48. Ibid. 10.

49. Ibid. 11.

50. Ibid. 13.

51. Ibid.

52. Ibid. 21.

53. Ibid. 22.

54. Ibid.

55. Ibid. 43.

56. Ibid., p. xiv (1850 edn.).

57. Ibid., p. xvi.
58. Ibid., p. i (1925 edn.).
59. Ibid.
60. Daniel Corkery, *the Hidden Ireland: A Study of Gaelic Munster in the Eighteenth Century* (Dublin: Gill, 1924). See e.g. ch. 9 on Brian Merriman's 'more truly Gaelic' note (p. 125).
61. For a corrective to Corkery's view of the Gaelic literary tradition, see Brendán Ó Buachalla, 'Ó Corcora agus an Hidden Ireland', *Scríobh*, 4 (1978), 109–37; Michelle O'Ríordain, *The Gaelic Mind and the Collapse of the Gaelic World* (Cork: Cork University Press, 1990); see also Patrick Maume, *'Life that is Exile': Daniel Corkery and the Search for Irish Ireland* (Belfast: Institute for Irish Studies, 1993), 79–96; Louis M. Cullen, *The Hidden Ireland: Reassessment of a Concept* (Mullingar: Lilliput Press, 1988); Emmet Larkin, 'A Reconsideration: Daniel Corkery and his Ideas on Cultural Nationalism', *Eire-Ireland*, 8 (Spring 1973), 42–51; Lawrence McCaffrey, 'Daniel Corkery and Irish Cultural Nationalism', ibid. 35–41; Declan, Kiberd, *Inventing Ireland*, pp. 555–8; Seán Ó Tuama, *Repossessions: Selected Essays in the Irish Literary Heritage* (Cork: Cork University Press, 1995), 234–47.
62. Ibid., preface to 3rd edn., p. xvii.
63. Maurice Blanchot, *The Infinite Conversation*, trans. and with a foreword by Susan Hanson (Minneapolis: University of Minnesota Press, 1993), 359. On the fragment, see also Philippe Lacoue-Labarthe and Jean-Luc Nancy, *The Literary Absolute: The Theory of Literature in German Romanticism*, trans. Philip Barnard and Cheryl Lester (Albany: SUNY, 1988), 39–58.
64. 'Fragment of an Unfinished Autobiography', in *Poets and Poetry of Munster*, p. xxxiii.
65. Ibid., p. xli.
66. Ibid., pp. xxxvi–xxxvii.
67. Ibid., pp. xxxii–xxxiii.
68. Ibid., p. xxxiv.
69. Ibid., p. xxxiii.
70. Ibid., p. xlviii.
71. Ibid., p. xli.
72. Ibid., p. xlv.
73. Ibid., p. xxxvi.
74. Ibid., p. xxxi.
75. Ibid., p. xxxii.
76. Ibid.
77. Ibid.
78. Ibid., p. lv.
79. Ibid., p. lvi.

80. Ibid., preface to 3rd edn., p. xvi.
81. Ibid., p. ix.
82. Ibid., p. xxi.
83. Ibid., 'Autobiography', p. xliv.
84. Ibid., p. xliii.
85. Ibid., preface to 3rd edn., p. xxv.
86. Ibid., press notice, p. lvii.
87. Ibid.
88. Ibid., pp. lvii–lvii.
89. Ibid., p. lviii.
90. Ibid., 'Autobiography', p. xlv.
91. See Nigel Leask, *British Romantic Writers and the East: Anxieties of Empire* (Cambridge: Cambridge University Press, 1992), 170–228; John Barrell, *The Infection of Thomas De Quincey: A Psychopathology of Imperialism* (New Haven: Yale University Press, 1991).
92. *Poets and Poetry of Munster*, preface to 3rd edn., p. viii.
93. Ibid., 'Unfinished Autobiography', p. xxxix.
94. See Charles Benson, 'Printers and Booksellers in Dublin 1800–1850', in Robin Myers and Michael Harris (eds.), *Spreading the Word: The Distribution Networks of Print 1550–1850* (Winchester: St Paul's Bibliographies; Detroit: Omnigraphics Inc., 1990), 47–59; Mary M. Pollard, *Dublin's Trade in Books 1550–1800* (Oxford: Clarendon Press, 1989), 165–226; E. J. Riordan, *Modern Irish Trade and Industry* (London: Methuen, 1920), 160–4; Cormac Ó Gráda, *Ireland: A New Economic History 1780–1939* (Oxford: Clarendon Press, 1994), 305–6.
95. Mangan's position in relation to Moore was widely contested; in fact, John O'Daly's collaborator, Edward Walsh, was more than once offered as the truly Irish poet, with both Moore and Mangan dismissed as too commercial or too eccentric respectively. See the important anthology, directed at an Irish–American audience, *The Poets and Poetry of Ireland*, ed. James Hardiman, Samuel Lover, and D. F. McCarthy (New York: T. Farrell & Son, 1868), introductory remarks, 5–9; and the memoir of Moore and Mangan that precedes the selection of their work. 'How different from Clarence Mangan was Edward Walsh! This gifted, patient, long-suffering child of song was intensely Irish of the Irish. He spoke the native tongue: he knew it intimately. His originality suffered from the fact; but his soul of song shone out all the brighter' (p. 7).
96. *Poets and Poetry of Munster*, 'Autobiography', p. xxxv.
97. Ibid., press notice, p. lix.
98. Ibid., preface to 3rd edn., p. xi.
99. Emer Nolan, *James Joyce and Nationalism* (London and New York: Routledge, 1995).

100. *Poets and Poetry of Munster*, preface to 3rd edn., p. x.

101. Ibid., press notice, p. lviii.

102. Ibid., p. lx.

103. Ibid., introduction, pp. xxxix–xl.

104. Ibid., p. ii.

105. Yeats, *Explorations* (London: Macmillan, 1962), p. xx.

106. Jürgen Habermas, *The Structural Transformation of the Public Sphere: An Inquiry into a Category of Bourgeois Society*, trans. Thomas Burger with the assistance of Frederick Lawrence (Cambridge, Mass.: MIT Press, 1989), 181–235.

107. For a different reading of these issues in *Playboy*, see Declan Kiberd, *Inventing Ireland: The Literature of the Modern Nation* (London: Jonathan Cape, 1995), 166–88.

108. See Carol Coulter, *The Hidden Tradition: Feminism, Women, and Nationalism in Ireland* (Cork: Cork University Press, 1993); Angela Bourke, 'Reading a Woman's Death: Colonial Text and Oral Tradition in Nineteenth-Century Ireland' *Feminist Studies*, 21/3 (Fall 1995), 553–86.

Notes to Chapter Four

1. Cited in Margaret O'Callaghan, *British High Politics and a Nationalist Ireland: Criminality, Land and the Law under Forster and Balfour* (Cork: Cork University Press, 1994), 18.

2. Partha Chatterjee, *The Nation and its Fragments: Colonial and Postcolonial Histories* (Princeton: Princeton University Press, 1993), 223–39.

3. I take the formulation of this point from Elaine Scarry, *The Body in Pain: The Making and Unmaking of the World* (New York and Oxford: Oxford University Press, 1985), 12.

4. Cf. Ashis Nandy, 'The Discreet Charms of Indian Terrorism', in id., *The Savage Freud and Other Essays* (Princeton: Princeton University Press, 1995), 1–31.

5. Daniel Corkery, *Synge and Anglo-Irish Literature* (Cork: Cork University Press: London: Longman Green, 1931), 17.

6. Ibid.

7. Ibid. 18.

8. Ibid.

9. Ibid. 7–8.

10. Ibid. 7.

11. Ibid. 14.

12. Ibid. 16.

13. Ibid. 19.

14. Ibid. 12.

15. *The Hidden Ireland: A Study of Gaelic Munster in the Eighteenth Century* (Dublin: Gill, 1924), 169.

16. Ibid. 24.

17. Ibid. 12.

18. Wlad Godzich, *The Culture of Literacy* (Cambridge, Mass., and London: Harvard University Press, 1994), 58.

19. Homi K. Bhabha, *The Location of Culture* (London: Routledge, 1994), 157–60.

20. Corkery, *Synge*, 146.

21. Ibid. 44.

22. Ibid. 242.

23. Ibid. 243.

24. Tzvetan Todorov, *The Conquest of America*, trans. Richard Howard (New York: Harper and Row, 1982), 42.

25. On O'Brien, see Timothy O'Keefe (ed.), *Myles: Portraits of Brian O'Nolan* (London: Martin, Brian & O'Keefe, 1973); Anne Clissmann, *Flann O'Brien: A Critical Introduction to his Writings* (Dublin; Gill & Macmillan, 1975); Anne Clissmann and David Powell (eds.), *The Journal of Irish Literature*, 3 / 1 (Jan. 1974), special Flann O'Brien issue; Anthony Cronin, *Dead As Doornails* (Dublin: Dolmen, 1975); id., *No Laughing Matter: The Life and Times of Flann O'Brien* (London: Grafton, 1989); Rudiger Imhof (ed.), *Alive-Alive O! Flann O'Brien's At Swim-Two-Birds* (Dublin: Wolfhound, 1985); Brendan Ó Conaire, *Myles na Gaeilge* (Dublin: An Clóchomhar, 1986); Keith Hopper, *Flann O'Brien: A Portrait of the Artist as a Young Post-modernist* (Cork: Cork University Press, 1995).

26. Patrick Kavanagh, *Collected Pruse* (London: MacGibbon & Kee, 1967), 13–22, 223–31.

27. See Declan Kiberd, *Inventing Ireland: The Literature of the Modern Nation* (London: Jonathan Cape, 1995), 497–512.

28. Flann O'Brien, *At Swim-Two-Birds* (London: Longman, 1939; repr. MacGibbon & Kee, 1961), 26–40.

29. Ibid. 36.

30. See *The Various Lives of Keats and Chapman and the Brother,* ed. Benedict Kiely (London: Grafton, 1988).

31. Stanley Cavell, 'The Uncanniness of the Ordinary', in id., *In Quest of the Ordinary: Lines of Skepticism and Romanticism* (Chicago and London: University of Chicago Press, 1994), 153–78: 154.

32. See Robert Hariman, *Political Style: The Artistry of Power* (Chicago: Chicago University Press, 1995), 141.

33. Franco Moretti, *The Way of the World: The Bildungsroman in European Culture* (London: Verso, 1987), 192.

34. Hariman, *Political Style*, 168.

35. See Jacqueline Genet (ed.), *The Big House in Ireland: Reality and Repre-sentation* (Dingle: Brandon Press; Savage, Md.: Barnes & Noble, 1991); Otto Rauchbauer (ed.), *Ancestral Voices: The Big House in Anglo-Irish Literature* (Dublin: Lilliput Press, 1992).

36. See the analysis provided by David Lloyd, *Anomalous States: Irish Writing and the Post-Colonial Moment* (Dublin: Lilliput Press, 1993), 88–124.

37. W. B. Yeats, preface to the first edition of *The Well of the Saints*, in *Essays and Introductions* (London: Macmillan, 1961), 299: 'I said: "Give up Paris. You will never create anything by reading Racine, and Arthur Symons will always be a better critic of French literature. Go to the Aran Islands. Live there as if you were one of the people themselves; express a life that has never found expression."' This preface, along with the preface to the first edition of John M. Synge's *Poems and Translations* (pp. 306–10), and the essay 'John M. Synge and the Ireland of his Time' (pp. 311–42), form the prose nucleus of Yeats's creation of Synge as one of his heroic figures.

38. Stanley Weintraub, *Shaw: An Autobiography 1856–1898* (New York: Weybright & Talley, 1969), 75–6: 'London was the literary centre for the English language, and for such artistic culture as the realm of the English language (in which I proposed to be king) could afford. There was no Gaelic League in those days, nor any sense that Ireland had in herself the seeds of culture. Every Irishman who felt that his business in life was on the higher planes of the cultural professions felt that he must have a metropolitan domicile and an international culture: that is, he felt his first business was to get out of Ireland.' See Declan Kiberd, 'The London Exiles: Wilde and Shaw', in Seamus Deane, Andrew Carpenter, and Jonathan Williams (eds.), *The Field Day Anthology of Irish Writing*, 3 vols. (Derry: Field Day, 1991), ii. 372–515.

39. Patricia Meyer Spacks, *Boredom: The Literary History of a State of Mind* (Chicago and London: University of Chicago Press, 1995), 218–48.

40. Jean Ricardou, 'Time of the Narration, Time of the Fiction', *James Joyce Quarterly*, 16 (1979), 7–15. See also Derek Attridge, *Peculiar Language: Literature as Difference from the Renaissance to James Joyce* (London: Methuen, 1988), 210–38.

41. Spacks, *Boredom*, 164–90.

42. See John Kelly, 'The Fall of Parnell and the Rise of Irish Literature: An Investigation', *Anglo-Irish Studies*, 2 (1976), 1–23; R. F. Foster, 'Thinking from Hand to Mouth: Anglo-Irish Literature, Gaelic Nationalism and Irish Politics in the 1890s', in id., *Paddy and Mr. Punch: Connections in Irish and English History* (London: Penguin, 1995), 262–80; Herbert Howarth, *The Irish Writers 1880–1940: Literature under Parnell's Star*

(London: Rockliff, 1958); Malcolm Brown, *The Politics of Irish Literature from Thomas Davis to W. B. Yeats* (Seattle: University of Washington Press, 1972); William M. Murphy, *The Parnell Myth and Irish Politics 1891–1956* (New York: Peter Lang, 1986); Michael Steinman, *Yeats's Heroic Figures: Wilde, Parnell, Swift, Casement* (London: Macmillan, 1983); Seamus Deane, 'Parnell: The Lost Leader', in Donal MacCartney (ed.), *Parnell: The Politics of Power* (Dublin: Wolfhound Press, 1991), 183–91; James Fairhall, *James Joyce and the Question of History* (Cambridge: Cambridge University Press, 1993), 123–46. The outstanding account of Parnell's final crisis is Frank Callanan, *The Parnell Split 1890–91* (Syracuse: Syracuse University Press, 1992).

43. See Zeev Sternhell, with Mario Sznajder and Maia Asheri, *The Birth of Fascist Ideology: From Cultural Rebellion to Political Revolution*, trans. David Maisel (Princeton: Princeton University Press, 1994), 233–58. See also Elizabeth Cullingford, *Yeats, Ireland and Fascism* (New York and London: New York University Press, 1981); Conor Cruise O'Brien, 'Passion and Cunning: An Essay on the Politics of W. B. Yeats', in Norman Jeffares (ed.), *In Excited Reverie: A Centenary Tribute to W. B. Yeats, 1865–1939* (New York: St Martin's Press, 1965), 207–78; Grattan Freyer, *W. B. Yeats and the Anti-Democratic Tradition* (Dublin: Gill & Macmillan, 1981).

44. Yeats, 'The Fisherman', in *W. B. Yeats: The Poems*, ed. Richard J. Finneran (Dublin: Gill & Macmillan, 1984), 148. All references to Yeats's poems and his commentary upon them are to this volume.

45. This section is a revised version of the Judith Wilson Annual Lecture on Poetry, given at Cambridge University in March 1991, subsequently published as 'The Second Coming: Coming Second; Coming in a Second', *Irish University Review*, 20/1 (Spring/Summer 1992), 92–100.

46. See Gearóid Ó Tuathaigh, 'Nationalist Ireland 1912–1922: Aspects of Continuity and Change', in Peter Collins (ed.), *Nationalism and Unionism: Conflict in Ireland 1885–1921* (Belfast: Institute of Irish Studies, 1994), 47–73: 68; Tom Garvin, *Nationalist Revolutionaries in Ireland 1858–1928* (Oxford: Clarendon Press, 1987).

47. The poems of *Michael Robartes and the Dancer* are on pp. 175–90 of the 1984 Finneran Edition; Yeats's commentaries on these are on pp. 642–5 and pp. 646–8.

48. Patrick J. Keane, *Yeats's Interactions with Tradition* (Columbia: University of Missouri Press, 1987), 72–105.

49. Yeats, *Poems*, 647.

50. See Wlad Godzich, 'Emergent Literature and the Field of Comparative Literature', in id., *The Culture of Literacy*, 274–92.

51. Cited in R. W. Southern, 'The Shape and Substance of Academic History', in F. Stern (ed.), *The Varieties of History from Voltaire to the Present* (London: Macmillan, 2nd. edn. 1970), 409.

52. The section on power in Burke's *Enquiry* examines this relation between the 'godhead', the sublime and power. 'I know of nothing sublime which is not some modification of power' (p. 64).

53. The works most pertinent to my argument here are obviously Max Horkheimer and Theodor Adorno, *Dialectic of Enlightenment* (New York: Seabury Press, 1972), esp. the chapter 'Enlightenment as Mass Deception', in which they claim culture, consumerism, and boredom are lamentably interlocked. Of the vast literature concerning the relation between abstraction and domination, see esp. Alfred Sohn-Rethel, *Intellectual and Manual Labour* (London: Macmillan, 1978).

54. The phrase is from Aijaz Ahmad, *In Theory: Classes, Nations, Literatures* (London and New York: Verso, 1992), 11: 'I refuse to accept that nationalism is the determinate, dialectical opposite of imperialism . . . Nor do I accept that nationalism is some unitary thing, always progressive or always retrograde . . . So one struggles not against nations and states as such but for different articulations of class, nation and state. And one interrogates minority nationalisms, religious and linguistic and regional nationalisms, transnational nationalisms . . . neither by privileging some transhistorical right to statehood based upon linguistic difference or territorial identity, nor by denying, in the poststructuralist manner, the historical reality of the sedimentations which do in fact give particular collectivities of people real civilizational identities. Rather, one strives for a rationally argued understanding of social content and historic project for each particular nationalism. Some nationalist practices are progressive; others are not.'

55. For a pro-unionist account of the relations between Redmondite (post-Parnellite) nationalism and unionism, see Paul Bew, *Ideology and the Irish Question: Ulster Unionism and Irish Nationalism 1912–1916* (Oxford: Clarendon Press, 1994), esp. 71–90; see also Alvin Jackson, 'Irish Unionism, 1905–21', in Peter Collins (ed.), *Nationalism and Unionism: Conflict in Ireland 1885–1921* (Belfast: Institute of Irish Studies, 1994), 35–46; Dermot Nesbitt, *Unionism Restated: An Analysis of the Ulster Unionist Party's 'Statement of Aims'* (Belfast: Ulster Unionist Information Institute, issue no. 16, Dec. 1995).

56. See Richard Breen, Damian F. Hannan, David B. Rottman, and Christopher T. Whelan, *Understanding Contemporary Ireland: State, Class and Development in the Republic of Ireland* (Dublin: Gill & Macmillan, 1990); J. J. Lee, *The Modernisation of Irish Society 1848–1918* (Dublin: Gill & Macmillan, 1973); id., *Ireland 1912–85: Politics and*

Society (Cambridge: Cambridge University Press, 1990). For an account of 'the ideology of modernization' in Northern Ireland, see Paul Bew, Peter Gibbon, and Henry Patterson, *Northern Ireland 1921–94: Political Forces and Social Classes* (London: Serif, 1995), 111–44. For a more wide-ranging account of the modernization debate, see Luke Gibbons, *Transformations in Irish Culture* (Cork: Cork University Press, in association with Field Day, 1996).

57. *Hermathena*, 124 (Summer 1978), 7–28: 7; excerpted in Seamus Deane, Andrew Carpenter, and Jonathan Williams (eds.), *The Field Day Anthology of Irish Writing*, 3 vols. (Derry: Field Day, 1991), iii. 574–9.

58. 'Irish History and Irish Mythology', 23.

59. See Donal MacCartney, *W. E. H. Lecky: Historian and Politician 1838–1903* (Dublin: Lilliput Press, 1994), 109–13.

60. Among many discussions of the relationships between historical facts and structures and the position of the objective observer, see Roland Barthes, 'Le Discours de l'histoire', *Social Science Information*, 6 (1967), 65–75; Peter Novick, *That Noble Dream: The 'Objectivity Question' and the American Historical Profession* (Cambridge: Cambridge University Press, 1986); Stuart Clark, 'The *Annales* Historians', in Quentin Skinner (ed.), *The Return of Grand Theory in the Human Sciences* (Cambridge: Cambridge University Press, 1985), 179–98.

61. Dublin: R. Graisberry, 1830, 379.

62. Thomas D'Arcy McGee, *A Popular History of Ireland from the Earliest Period to the Emancipation of the Catholics*, 2 vols. (London and Glasgow: Cameron & Ferguson, 1862), ii. 384.

63. A charge made in Michael Hechter, *Internal Colonialism: The Celtic Fringe in British National Development, 1536–1966* (London: Routledge & Kegan Paul; Berkeley and Los Angeles: University of California Press, 1966); it was repeated in his 'Internal Colonialism Revisited', in Edward A. Tiryakian and Ronald Rogowski (eds.), *New Nationalisms of the Developed West: Toward Explanation* (London: Allen & Unwin, 1985), 17–25.

64. Louis Cullen, 'The Cultural Basis of Modern Irish Nationalism', in Rosalind Mitchison (ed.), *The Roots of Nationalism: Studies in Northern Europe* (Edinburgh: John Donald, 1980), 91–106: 105.

65. Seamus Deane, 'Wherever Green Is Read', in Máirín Ní Dhonncadha and Theo Dorgan (eds.), *Revising the Rising* (Derry: Field Day, 1991), 91–105.

66. For an account of these debates, see Ciaran Brady (ed.), *Ideology and the Historians* (Dublin: Lilliput Press, 1991); id. (ed.), *Interpreting Irish History: The Debate on Historical Revisionism 1938–1994* (Dublin: Irish Academic Press, 1994).

67. Jean-François Lyotard, *The Postmodern Condition; A Report on*

Knowledge, trans. Geoff Bennington and Brian Massumi (Minneapolis: University of Minneapolis Press, 1984), p. xxiv, where he defines postmodern as 'incredulity towards metanarratives'. However, as Fredric Jameson points out in *Postmodernism, or, The Cultural Logic of Late Capitalism* (Durham: Duke University Press, 1991), p. xi, 'everything significant about the disappearance of master narratives has itself to be couched in narrative form'.

68. See Kwame Anthony Appiah, 'Is the Post- in Postmodernism the Post- in Postcolonial?', *Critical Inquiry*, 17 (Winter 1991), 336–57.

69. Cf. Madhava Prasad, 'On the Question of a Theory of (Third World) Literature', *Social Text*, 10/2 and 3 (1992), 57–83.

70. *The Bell*, 9/3 (Dec. 1944); repr. in Seamus Deane, Andrew Carpenter, and Jonathan Williams (eds.), *The Field Day Anthology of Irish Writing*, 3 vols. (Derry: Field Day, 1991), iii. 569–73: 571.

71. For modernity is a condition in which the modern and the premodern uneasily coexist, as is evident in Yeats and Joyce. Cf. Fredric Jameson, 'An Unfinished Project', *London Review of Books*, 17/15 (Aug. 1995), 8–9: 'For modernity can be distinguished from our own post-modernity as a space of "unevenness" . . . in which the most modern uneasily coexists with what it has not yet superseded, cancelled, streamlined and obliterated. Only from the vantage-point of the Post-Modern, in which modernisation is at last complete, can this secret incompleteness of the modernisation process be detected as the source of modernity and Modernism alike' (p. 9).

72. Chatterjee, *The Nation and its Fragments*, 32.

73. F. S. L. Lyons, *Ireland since the Famine* (London and Glasgow: Collins, Fontana, rev. edn. 1973), 32–3.

Bibliography

ADORNO, THEODOR W., *Prisms*, trans. Samuel and Shierry Weber (Cambridge, Mass.: MIT Press, 1994).

AHMAD, AIJAZ, *In Theory: Classes, Nations, Literatures* (London and New York: Verso, 1992).

ANDERSON, BENEDICT, *Imagined Communities: Reflections on the Origin and Spread of Nationalism*, 2nd edn. (London: Verso, 1991).

ANDERSON, PERRY, *English Questions* (London and New York: Verso, 1992).

—— *A Zone of Engagement* (London and New York: Verso, 1992).

Annual Register 1790 (London: W. Otridge & Son, 1793).

ANON., *Prophecies of Pastorini Analyzed and Refuted and the powerful tendency of Inflammatory Prediction to excite Insurrection, satisfactorily demonstrated from incontrovertible Historical Records, with a Cursory View of the Dangerous State of Ireland, from an exclusively Popish Conspiracy, Humbly submitted to the Consideration of the Protestants of the British Empire by a Graduate of Trinity College* (Dublin, 1823).

APPIAH, KWAME ANTHONY, 'Is the Post- in Postmodernism the Post- in Postcolonial?', *Critical Inquiry*, 17 (Winter 1991), 336–57.

ARNOLD, MATTHEW, 'On the Study of Celtic Literature', in *The Complete Prose Works of Matthew Arnold*, ed. R. H. Super, vol. iii: *Lectures and Essays in Criticism* (Ann Arbor: University of Michigan Press, 1962).

ASTLE, RICHARD, 'Dracula as Totemic Monster: Lacan, Freud, Oedipus and History', *Sub-Stance*, 25 (1980), 98–105.

ATTRIDGE, DEREK, *Peculiar Language: Literature as Difference from the Renaissance to James Joyce* (London: Methuen, 1988).

BALIBAR, ETIENNE, and WALLERSTEIN, IMMANUEL, *Race, Nation, Class: Ambiguous Identities* (London: Verso, 1995).

BARKER, ERNEST, *National Character and the Factors in its Formation* (London: Methuen, 1927).

BARKER, FRANCIS, *The Culture of Violence: Tragedy and History* (Manchester: Manchester University Press, 1993).

BARRELL, JOHN, *Poetry, Language and Politics* (Manchester: Manchester University Press, 1988).

—— '"The Dangerous Goddess": Masculinity, Prestige, and the Aesthetic in Early Eighteenth-Century Britain', *Cultural Critique*, 12 (1989), 101–31.

—— *The Infection of Thomas De Quincey: A Psychopathology of Imperialism* (New Haven: Yale University Press, 1991).

BARRINGTON, JONAH, *Personal Sketches of His Own Times*, 2 vols. (London: Colburn, 1827).

BARROWS, SUSANNA, *Distorting Mirrors: Visions of the Crowd in Late Nineteenth-Century France* (New Haven: Yale University Press, 1981).

BARTHES, ROLAND, 'Le Discours de l'histoire', *Social Science Information*, 6 (1967), 65–75.

BARTLETT, THOMAS, *The Fall and Rise of the Irish Nation: The Catholic Question 1690–1830* (Dublin: Gill & Macmillan, 1992).

BATTEN, CHARLES, *Pleasurable Instruction: Form and Convention in Eighteenth-Century Travel Literature* (Berkeley: University of California Press, 1978).

BENEDICT, JULIUS, *The Lily of Killarney. Opera in Three Acts. The Words by Dion Boucicault and John Oxenford*, ed. J. Pittman (London and New York: Boosey & Co., 1861).

BEN-ISRAEL, HEDVA, *English Historians on the French Revolution* (Cambridge: Cambridge University Press, 1968).

BENSON, CHARLES, 'Printers and Booksellers in Dublin 1800-1850', in Robin Myers and Michael Harris (eds.), *Spreading the Word: The Distribution Networks of Print 1550–1850* (Winchester: St Paul's Bibliographies; Detroit: Omnigraphics Inc., 1990), 47–59.

BENTLEY, C. F., 'The Monster in the Bedroom: Sexual Symbolism in Bram Stoker's *Dracula*', *Literature and Psychology*, 22/1 (1972), 27–34.

BEW, PAUL, *Ideology and the Irish Question: Ulster Unionism and Irish Nationalism 1912–1916* (Oxford: Clarendon Press, 1994).

—— GIBBON, PETER, and PATTERSON, HENRY, *Northern Ireland 1921–1994: Political Forces and Social Classes* (London: Serif, 1995).

BHABHA, HOMI, *The Location of Culture* (London: Routledge, 1994).

BLAKEMORE, STEVEN, *Burke and the Fall of Language: The French Revolution as Linguistic Event* (Hanover and London: University Press of New England, 1988).

—— (ed.), *Burke and the French Revolution: Bicentennial Essays* (Athens and London: University of Georgia Press, 1992).

BLANCHOT, MAURICE, *The Infinite Conversation*, trans. and with a foreword by Susan Hanson (Minneapolis: University of Minnesota Press, 1993).

BONGIE, DAVID, *David Hume, Prophet of Counter-Revolution* (Oxford: Oxford University Press, 1965).

BOUCICAULT, DION, *The Colleen Bawn: or, The Brides of Garryowen* (1860).

—— *The Dolmen Boucicault*, ed. David Krause (Dublin: Dolmen Press; New York: Oxford University Press, 1984).

BOURDIEU, PIERRE, *Homo Academicus*, trans. Peter Collier (Stanford: Stanford University Press, 1988).

—— *The Field of Cultural Production*, ed. and introd. Randal Johnston (New York: Columbia University Press, 1993).

BOURKE, ANGELA, 'Reading a Woman's Death: Colonial Text and Oral Tradition in Nineteenth-Century Ireland', *Feminist Studies*, 21/3 (Fall 1995), 553–86.

BOVÉ, PAUL, *Mastering Discourse: The Politics of Intellectual Culture* (Durham and London: Duke University Press, 1992).

BOYCE, D. GEORGE, '"Trembling Solicitude": Irish Conservatism, Nationality and Public Opinion, 1833–86', in D. G. Boyce, R. Eccleshall, and V. Geoghegan (eds.), *Political Thought in Ireland since the Seventeenth Century* (London and New York: Routledge, 1993), 124–45.

BOYLAN, THOMAS A., and FOLEY, TIMOTHY P., 'John Elliot Cairnes, John Stuart Mill and Ireland: Some Problems for Political Economy', in *Economists and the Irish Economy from the Eighteenth Century to the Present Day*, ed. Antoin Murphy (Dublin: Irish Academic Press/Hermathena, 1984), 96–119.

———— *Political Economy and Colonial Ireland: The Propagation and Ideological Function of Economic Discourse in the Nineteenth Century* (London: Routledge, 1992).

BRADY, CIARAN (ed.), *Ideology and the Historians* (Dublin: Lilliput Press, 1991).

—— (ed.), *Interpreting Irish History: The Debate on Historical Revisionism 1938–1994* (Dublin: Irish Academic Press, 1994).

BRANTLINGER, PATRICK, *Rule of Darkness: British Literature and Imperialism 1830–1914* (Ithaca and London: Cornell University Press, 1988).

BREEN, RICHARD, HANNAN, DAMIAN F., ROTTMAN, DAVID B., and WHELAN, CHRISTOPHER T., *Understanding Contemporary Ireland: State, Class and Development in the Republic of Ireland* (Dublin: Gill & Macmillan, 1990).

BROMWICH, RACHEL, *Matthew Arnold and Celtic Literature: A Retrospect* (Oxford: Clarendon Press, 1965).

BROOKE, CHARLOTTE, *Reliques of Irish Poetry* (Dublin: George Bonham, 1789).

BROOKS, PETER, *The Melodramatic Imagination: Balzac, Henry James, Melodrama, and the Mode of Excess* (New Haven: Yale University Press, 1976; repr. 1984).

BROWN, MALCOLM, *The Politics of Irish Literature from Thomas Davis to W. B. Yeats* (Seattle: University of Washington Press, 1972).

—— *Sir Samuel Ferguson* (Lewisburg: Bucknell University Press, 1973).

BROWN, TERENCE, *Northern Voices: Poets from Ulster* (Dublin: Gill & Macmillan, 1975).

—— and HAYLEY, BARBARA (eds.), *Samuel Ferguson—A Centenary Tribute* (Dublin: Royal Irish Academy, 1987).

BROWN, VIVIENNE, *Adam Smith's Discourse: Canonicity, Commerce and Conscience* (London: Routledge, 1994).

BUNTING, EDWARD, *A General Collection of the Ancient Irish Music* (London: W. Power, 1796).

—— *A General Collection of the Ancient Music of Ireland* (London: Clementi, 1809).

—— *The Ancient Music of Ireland* (Dublin: Hodges & Smith, 1840).

BURKE, EDMUND, *A Philosophical Enquiry into the Origin of our Ideas of the Sublime and Beautiful* (1757), ed. J. T. Boulton (London: Routledge & Kegan Paul, 1958).

—— *Reflections on the Revolution in France* (1790), ed. J. G. A. Pocock (Indianapolis and Cambridge: Hackett Publishing Company, 1987).

—— *The Writings and Speeches of Edmund Burke*, gen. ed. Paul Langford: vol. viii: *The French Revolution 1790–1794*, ed. L. G. Mitchell (Oxford: Clarendon Press, 1989); vol. ix, pt. 1: *The Revolutionary War 1794–7*; vol. ix, pt. 2: *Ireland*, ed. R. B. McDowell (Oxford: Clarendon Press, 1991).

BUTLER, MARILYN, *Maria Edgeworth: A Literary Biography* (Oxford: Clarendon Press, 1972).

BUTT, ISAAC, *The Irish People and the Irish Land* (Dublin: Falconer; London: Ridgeway, 1867).

BUTTIMER, CORNELIUS G., 'Gaelic Literature and Contemporary Life in Cork, 1700–1840', *Cork: History and Society. Interdisciplinary Essays on the History of an Irish County* (Dublin: Geography Publications, 1993), 585–653.

BYRNE, FRANCIS JOHN, *A Thousand Years of Irish Script; An Exhibition of Irish Manuscripts in Oxford Libraries* (Oxford: Bodleian Library, 1979).

CAHALAN, J. M., *Great Hatred, Little Room: The Irish Historical Novel* (Syracuse: Syracuse University Press; Dublin: Gill & Macmillan, 1984).

CAIN, P. J., and HOPKINS, A. G., *British Imperialism: Crisis and Deconstruction 1914–1990* (London and New York: Longman, 1993).

CALLANAN, FRANK, *The Parnell Split 1890–91* (Syracuse: Syracuse University Press, 1992).

CALLEO, DAVID, *Coleridge and the Idea of the Modern State* (New Haven: Yale University Press, 1966).

CANETTI, ELIAS, *Crowds and Power* (1st pub. 1960; Harmondsworth: Penguin, 1984).

CAREY, DANIEL, 'Travel Narrative and the Problem of Human Nature in

Locke, Shaftesbury, and Hutcheson.' (D.Phil. thesis, Oxford University, 1994).

CARLSON, JULIE A., *In the Theatre of Romanticism: Coleridge, Nationalism, Women* (Cambridge: Cambridge University Press, 1994).

CAVELL, STANLEY, *In Quest of the Ordinary: Lines of Skepticism and Romanticism* (Chicago and London: University of Chicago Press, 1994).

CERTEAU, MICHEL DE, *Heterologies: Discourse on the Other*, trans. Brian Massumi (Minneapolis: University of Minnesota Press, 1986).

CHATTERJEE, PARTHA, *Nationalist Thought and the Colonial World: A Derivative Discourse* (Minneapolis: University of Minnesota Press, 1986).

—— *The Nation and its Fragments: Colonial and Postcolonial Histories* (Princeton: Princeton University Press, 1993).

CLARK, STUART, 'The *Annales* Historians', in Quentin Skinner (ed.), *The Return of Grand Theory in the Human Sciences* (Cambridge: Cambridge University Press, 1985), 179–98.

CLISSMANN, ANNE, *Flann O'Brien: A Critical Introduction to his Writings* (Dublin: Gill & Macmillan, 1975).

—— and POWELL, DAVID (eds.), *The Journal of Irish Literature*, 3/1 (Jan. 1974), special Flann O'Brien issue.

COBBAN, ALFRED, *Edmund Burke and the Revolt Against the Eighteenth Century: A Study of the Political and Social Thinking of Burke, Wordsworth, Coleridge and Southey* (London: Allen & Unwin, 1929).

COLLEY, LINDA, *Britons: Forging the Nation, 1707–1837* (New Haven and London: Yale University Press, 1992).

COLLINS, JIM, *Uncommon Cultures: Popular Cultures and Post-Modernism* (New York and London: Routledge, 1989).

COLLISON BLACK, R. D., 'Economic Policy in Ireland and India in the Time of J. S. Mill', *Economic History Review*, 2nd ser., 21 (1968), 321–36.

COLMER, JOHN, *Coleridge: Critic of Society* (Oxford: Clarendon Press, 1959).

CONNOLLY, S. J., *Religion, Law and Power: The Making of Protestant Ireland, 1660–1760* (Oxford: Clarendon Press, 1992).

COOK, ELIZABETH HECKENDORN, 'The Limping Woman and the Public Sphere', in Veronica Kelly and D. Von Mücke (eds.), *Body and Text in the Eighteenth Century* (Stanford: Stanford University Press, 1994), 23–44.

COOK, S. B., *Imperial Affinities: Nineteenth Century Analogies and Exchanges between India and Ireland* (New Delhi and Newbury Park, London: Sage Publications, 1993).

CORKERY, DANIEL, *The Hidden Ireland: A Study of Gaelic Munster in the Eighteenth Century* (Dublin: Gill, 1924).

—— *Synge and Anglo-Irish Literature* (Cork: Cork University Press; London: Longman Green, 1931).

CORNWELL, NEIL, *The Literary Fantastic: From Gothic to Postmodernism* (Hemel Hempstead: Harvester Wheatsheaf, 1990).

COULTER, CAROL, *The Hidden Tradition: Feminism, Women, and Nationalism in Ireland* (Cork: Cork University Press, 1993).

COURTNEY, C. P., *Montesquieu and Burke* (Oxford: Basil Blackwell, 1963).

COX, STEPHEN D., *The Stranger Within Thee: Concepts of the Self in Late Eighteenth-Century Literature* (Pittsburgh: University of Pittsburgh Press, 1980).

CRANNY-FRANCIS, ANNE, 'Sexual Politics and Political Repression in Bram Stoker's *Dracula*', in Clive Bloom, Brian Docherty, Jane Gibb, and Keith Shand (eds.), *Nineteenth-Century Suspense: From Poe to Conan Doyle* (New York: St Martin's Press, 1988), 64–79.

CROKER, JOHN WILSON, *A Sketch of the Present State of Ireland, Past and Present*, 2nd edn. (Dublin: M. N. Mahon, 1808).

CROKER, THOMAS CROFTON, *Fairy Legends and Traditions of the South of Ireland*, 3 vols. (London: Murray, 1825–8).

CRONIN, ANTHONY, *Dead As Doornails* (Dublin: Dolmen, 1975).

—— *No Laughing Matter: The Life and Times of Flann O'Brien* (London: Grafton, 1989).

CRONIN, JOHN, *Gerald Griffin 1803–40: A Critical Biography* (Cambridge: Cambridge University Press, 1978).

CRONIN, MICHAEL, *Translating Ireland: Translation, Languages, Cultures* (Cork: Cork University Press, 1996).

CROWE, EYRE EVANS, *Today in Ireland* (1825), introd. R. L. Wolff, 3 vols. (New York and London: Garland, 1979).

CULLEN, LOUIS M., *The Hidden Ireland: Reassessment of a Concept* (Mullingar: Lilliput Press, 1988).

—— 'The Cultural Basis of Modern Irish Nationalism', in Rosalind Mitchison (ed.), *The Roots of Nationalism: Studies in Northern Europe* (Edinburgh: John Donald, 1980), 91–106.

—— 'The Blackwater Catholics and County Cork: Society and Politics in the Eighteenth Century', in Patrick O'Flanagan and Cornelius G. Buttimer (eds.), *Cork: History and Society. Interdisciplinary Essays on the History of an Irish County* (Dublin: Geography Publications, 1993), 535–84.

CULLINGFORD, ELIZABETH BUTLER, *Yeats, Ireland and Fascism* (New York and London: New York University Press, 1981).

—— *Gender and History in Yeats's Love Poetry* (Cambridge: Cambridge University Press, 1993).

CURTIS, L. PERRY, *Apes and Angels: The Irishman in Victorian Caricature* (Washington: Smithsonian Institution Press, 1971).

D'ALTON, JOHN, *Essay on the History, Religion, Learning, Arts, and Government of Ireland, from the Birth of Christ to the English Invasion* (Dublin: R. Graisberry, 1830).

DALY, MARY E., *The Famine In Ireland* (Dundalk: Dundalgan Press, 1986).

DAVIS, GRAHAM, 'Making History: John Mitchel and the Great Famine', in Paul Hyland and Neil Sammels (eds.), *Irish Writing: Exile and Subversion* (London: Macmillan, 1991), 98–115.

DAVIS, RICHARD P., *The Young Ireland Movement* (Dublin: Gill & Macmillan, 1987).

DAVIS, THOMAS, *Prose Writings*, ed. T. W. Rolleston (London: W. Scott, 1890).

—— *Literary and Historical Essays*, ed. D. J. O'Donoghue (Dundalk: Dundalgan Press, 1914).

DAVITT, MICHAEL, *Some Suggestions for a Final Settlement of the Land Question* (Dublin: Gill & Son, 1902).

—— *The Fall of Feudalism in Ireland* (London: Harper & Brothers, 1904).

DEANE, SEAMUS, 'Lord Acton and Edmund Burke', *Journal of the History of Ideas*, 33/2 (Apr.–June 1972), 325–35.

—— 'The Reputation of the French *Philosophes* in the Whig Reviews between 1802 and 1824', *The Modern Language Review*, 70 (Apr. 1978), 271–90.

—— 'Swift and the Anglo-Irish Intellect', *Eighteenth-Century Ireland*, 1/1 (1987), 9–22.

—— 'Irish National Character, 1790–1900', in Tom Dunne (ed.), *The Writer As Witness: Literature as Historical Evidence* (Cork: Cork University Press, 1987), 90–113.

—— *The French Enlightenment and Revolution in England 1789–1832* (Cambridge, Mass., and London: Harvard University Press, 1988).

—— 'National Character and National Audience: Races, Crowds and Readers', in Michael Allen and Angela Wilcox (eds.), *Critical Approaches to Anglo-Irish Literature* (Gerrards Cross: Colin Smythe, 1989), 40–52.

—— 'Parnell: The Lost Leader', in Donal MacCartney (ed.), *Parnell: The Politics of Power* (Dublin: Wolfhound Press, 1991), 183–91.

—— 'Wherever Green Is Read', in Máirín Ní Dhonncadha and Theo Dorgan (eds.), *Revising the Rising* (Derry: Field Day, 1991), 91–105.

—— 'The Second Coming: Coming Second; Coming in a Second', *Irish University Review*, 20/1 (Spring/Summer 1992), 92–100.

—— (ed.), *Sale Catalogues of Libraries of Eminent Persons*, ix: *Politicians* (London: Mansell-Sotheby Parke-Bernet, 1973).

—— CARPENTER, ANDREW, and WILLIAMS, JONATHAN (eds.), *The Field Day Anthology of Irish Writing*, 3 vols. (Derry: Field Day, 1991).

DE BOLLA, PETER, *The Discourse of the Sublime: Readings in History, Aesthetics and the Subject* (Oxford: Basil Blackwell, 1989).

DE BONALD, LOUIS, *Théorie du pouvoir politique et religieux* (1st pub. 1796; Paris: A. Leclerc, 1854).

DE GENLIS, STEPHANIE FÉLICITÉ BRULART, *Précis de la conduite de Madame de Genlis depuis la révolution* (Hamburg: B. G. Hoffmann, 1796).

DE GENLIS, STEPHANIE FÉLICITÉ BRULART, *Les Dîners du Baron d'Holbach* (Paris: C. J. Trouve, 1822).

—— *Mémoires inédits de Madame la comtesse de Genlis sur le dix-huitième siècle*, 8 vols. (Pairs and London: Colburn, 1825).

DE MAISTRE, JOSEPH, *Considérations sur la France* (Paris, 1797; Lyon: Rusand, 4th edn. 1829).

DENMAN, PETER, *Samuel Ferguson: The Literary Achievement* (Gerrards Cross: Colin Smythe, 1990).

D'ÉPINAY, L. F. P., MARQUISE DE LA LIVE, *Mémoires et correspondance de Madame d'Épinay* 3 vols., (Paris: Didier, 1818).

DE RÉMUSAT, C. F. Marie, *L'Angleterre au dix-huitième siècle*, 2 vols. (1st pub. 1856; New York: Arno, 1979).

DU CAMP, MAXIME, *Les Convulsions de Paris* (Paris: Hachette, 1880).

DU DEFFAND, MARIE, *The Unpublished Correspondence of Mme. du Deffand*, trans. Mrs Meeke, 2 vols. (London: A. K. Newman, 1810).

—— *Letters of the Marquise du Deffand to the Hon. Horace Walpole . . . to which are added Letters of Madame du Deffand to Voltaire from 1759 to 1775*, ed. M. Berry, 4 vols. (London: Longman, Hurst, Lees & Orme, 1810).

DUNNE, TOM, *Maria Edgeworth and the Colonial Mind* (Cork: Cork University Press, 1984).

—— 'Haunted by History: Irish Romantic Writing, 1800–1850', in Roy Porter and M. Teich (eds.), *Romanticism in National Context* (Cambridge: Cambridge University Press, 1988), 68–91.

DWYER, JOHN, *Virtuous Discourse: Sensibility and Community in Late Eighteenth-Century Scotland* (Edinburgh: John Donald, 1987).

EAGLETON, TERRY, 'Aesthetics and Politics in Edmund Burke', in Michael Kenneally (ed.), *Irish Literature and Culture* (Savage, Md.: Barnes & Noble, 1989), 25–34.

—— *The Ideology of the Aesthetic* (Oxford: Basil Blackwell, 1990).

—— *Heathcliff and the Great Hunger: Studies in Irish Culture* (London and New York: Verso, 1995).

EDGEWORTH, MARIA, *Castle Rackrent* (1800), ed. and introd. George Watson (Oxford: Oxford University Press, 1981).

—— *Ennui* (1809), introd. Robert Lee Wolff (New York and London: Garland, 1978).

—— *The Absentee* (1812), ed. W. J. McCormack and Kim Walker (Oxford: Oxford University Press, 1988).

—— *Ormond* (1817), introd. Robert Lee Wolff (New York and London: Garland, 1978).

EHRENPREIS, IRVIN, *Swift: The Man, his Works and the Age*, 3 vols. (Cambridge, Mass.: Harvard University Press, 1962).

ELIAS, NORBERT, *The History of Manners*, trans. Edmund Jephcott (Oxford: Blackwell, 1978).

—— The Civilizing Process, trans. Edmund Jephcott (Oxford: Blackwell, 1982).

FABRICANT, CAROLE, Swift's Landscape (Baltimore: Johns Hopkins University Press, 1982).

FAIRHALL, JAMES, James Joyce and the Question of History (Cambridge: Cambridge University Press, 1993).

FAVERTY, FREDERICK, Matthew Arnold, the Ethnologist (Evanston: Northwestern University Press, 1951).

FERGUSON, MARY CATHARINE, Sir Samuel Ferguson in the Ireland of his Day, 2 vols. (Edinburgh: Blackwood, 1896).

FERGUSON, SAMUEL, 'Hardiman's Irish Minstrelsy', Dublin University Magazine, 3 (1834), 465–78; 4 (1834), 152–67, 447–67, 514–30.

FLANAGAN, THOMAS, The Irish Novelists 1800–1850 (New York: Columbia University Press, 1959).

FOSTER, ROY, Modern Ireland 1600–1972 (London: Penguin, 1988).

—— 'Protestant Magic: W. B. Yeats and the Spell of Irish History', Proceedings of the British Academy, 75 (1989), 234–66.

—— 'Thinking from Hand to Mouth: Anglo-Irish Literature, Gaelic Nationalism and Irish Politics in the 1890s', in id., Paddy and Mr. Punch: Connections in Irish and English History (London: Penguin, 1995), 262–80.

FOUCAULT, MICHAEL, 'What Is an Author?', The Foucault Reader, ed. P. Rabinow (Harmondsworth: Penguin, 1984), 101–20.

FREYER, GRATTAN, W. B. Yeats and the Anti-Democratic Tradition (Dublin: Gill & Macmillan, 1981).

FURNISS, TOM, Edmund Burke's Aesthetic Ideology: Language, Gender and Political Economy in Revolution (Cambridge: Cambridge University Press, 1993).

GALTON, FRANCIS, Hereditary Genius: An Inquiry into its Laws and Consequences (London: Macmillan & Co., 1869).

GARNETT, RHYS, 'Dracula and The Beetle: Imperial and Sexual Guilt and Fear in Late Victorian Fantasy', in Rhys Garnett and R. J. Ellis (eds.), Science Fiction Roots and Branches: Contemporary Critical Approaches (New York: St Martin's Press, 1988), 30–54.

GARVIN, TOM, Nationalist Revolutionaries in Ireland 1858–1928 (Oxford: Clarendon Press, 1987).

GELLNER, ERNEST, Nations and Nationalism (Ithaca, NY: Cornell University Press, 1983).

—— Culture, Identity and Politics (Cambridge: Cambridge University Press, 1987).

GENET, JACQUELINE (ed.), The Big House in Ireland: Reality and Representation (Dingle: Brandon Press; Savage, Md.: Barnes & Noble, 1991).

GIBBONS, LUKE, 'Constructing the Canon: Versions of the National Identity', in Seamus Deane, Andrew Carpenter, and Jonathan Williams (eds.), *The Field Day Anthology of Irish Writing*, 3 vols. (Derry: Field Day, 1991), ii. 950–1223.

—— ' "A Shadowy Narrator": History, Art and Romantic Nationalism in Ireland 1750–1850', in Ciaran Brady (ed.), *Ideology and the Historians* (Dublin: Lilliput Press, 1991), 99–127.

—— *Transformations in Irish Culture* (Cork: Cork University Press, in association with Field Day, 1996).

—— ' "The Stranger Within": Adam Smith, Edmund Burke and the Colonial Sublime', forthcoming in id., *The Colonial Sublime: Edmund Burke and the Politics of Irish Culture*.

GILMAN, SANDER, *Difference and Pathology: Stereotypes of Sexuality, Race and Madness* (Ithaca: Cornell University Press, 1985).

GLOVER, DAVID, ' "Dark Enough fur Any Man": Bram Stoker's Sexual Ethnology and the Question of Irish Nationalism', in Roman de la Campa, E. Ann Kaplan, and Michael Sprinker (eds.), *Late Imperial Culture* (London: Verso, 1995), 53–71.

GODZICH, WLAD, *The Culture of Literacy* (Cambridge, Mass., and London: Harvard University Press, 1994).

GOODMAN, DENA, *The Republic of Letters: A Cultural History of the French Enlightenment*, (Ithaca and London: Cornell University Press, 1994).

GRAFTON, ANTHONY, *Defenders of the Text: The Traditions of Scholarship in an Age of Science, 1450–1800* (Cambridge, Mass., and London: Harvard University Press, 1991).

GREEN, MARTIN, *Dreams of Adventure, Deeds of Empire* (New York: Basic Books, 1979).

GRIFFIN, GERALD, *The Collegians: A Tale of Garryowen*, introd. John Cronin (Dublin: Appletree Press, 1992).

HABERMAS, JÜRGEN, *The Structural Transformation of the Public Sphere: An Inquiry into a Category of Bourgeois Society*, trans. Thomas Burger with the assistance of Frederick Lawrence (Cambridge, Mass.: MIT Press, 1989).

HALBERSTAM, JUDITH, 'Technologies of Monstrosity: Bram Stoker's *Dracula*', *Victorian Studies*, 36 (1993), 333–52; repr. in Sally Ledger and Scott McCracken (eds.), *Cultural Politics at the Fin De Siècle* (Cambridge: Cambridge University Press, 1995), 248–66.

HARDIMAN, JAMES, *Irish Minstrelsy, or Bardic Remains of Ireland with English Poetical Translations*, 2 vols. (London: Robins, 1831).

—— LOVER, SAMUEL, and McCARTHY, D. F. (eds.), *The Poets and Poetry of Ireland* (New York: T. Farrell & Son, 1868).

HARDWICK, JOAN, *The Yeats Sisters* (London: Pandora, 1996).

HARIMAN, ROBERT, *Political Style: The Artistry of Power* (Chicago: Chicago University Press, 1995).

HARRIS, RUTH, *Murders and Madness: Medicine, Law and Society in the Fin de Siècle* (Oxford: Clarendon Press, 1989).

HARTH, PHILLIP, *Swift and Anglican Rationalism* (Chicago: University of Chicago Press, 1961).

HARVEY, DAVID, *The Condition of Postmodernity: An Enquiry into the Origins of Cultural Change* (Oxford, and Cambridge, Mass.: Blackwell, 1990; repr. 1994).

HARVIE, CHRISTOPHER, *Scotland and Nationalism: Scottish Society and Politics 1707–1994* (London and New York: Routledge, 2nd. edn. 1994).

HECHTER, MICHAEL, *Internal Colonialism: The Celtic Fringe in British National Development, 1536–1966* (London: Routledge & Kegan Paul; Berkeley and Los Angeles: University of California Press, 1966).

—— 'Internal Colonialism Revisited', in Edward A. Tiryakian and Ronald Rogowski (eds.), *New Nationalisms of the Developed West: Toward Explanation* (London: Allen & Unwin, 1985), 17–25.

HIGGINS, IAN, *Swift's Politics: A Study in Disaffection* (Cambridge: Cambridge University Press, 1994).

HOBSBAWM, ERIC, *Nations and Nationalism since 1750: Programme, Myth, Reality* (Cambridge: Cambridge University Press, 1990).

HOME, HENRY (Lord Kames), *Loose Hints upon education, chiefly concerning the culture of the heart* (Edinburgh: John Bell & John Murray, 1781).

HONE, J. M., *Thomas Davis* (London: Duckworth, 1934).

HONT, ISTVAN, and IGNATIEFF, MICHAEL (eds.), *Wealth and Virtue: The Shaping of Political Economy in the Scottish Enlightenment* (Cambridge: Cambridge University Press, 1983).

HOPPER, KEITH, *Flann O'Brien: A Portrait of the Artist as a Young Post-modernist* (Cork: Cork University Press, 1995).

HORKHEIMER, MAX, and ADORNO, THEODOR, *Dialectic of Enlightenment* (New York: Seabury Press, 1972).

HOWARTH, HERBERT, *The Irish Writers 1880–1940: Literature under Parnell's Star* (London: Rockliff, 1958).

HOWES, MARJORIE, 'The Mediation of the Feminine: Bisexuality, Homoerotic Desire, and Self-Expression in Bram Stoker's *Dracula*', *Texas Studies in Literature and Language*, 30/1 (Spring 1988), 104–19.

—— *Yeats's Nations: Gender, Class and Irishness* (Cambridge: Cambridge University Press, 1996).

HULL, ELEANOR, *The Poem-Book of the Gael* (London: Chatto & Windus, 1912).

HUME, DAVID, *Political Essays*, ed. Knud Haakonssen (Cambridge: Cambridge University Press, 1994).

HUNT, LYNN (ed.), *Eroticism and the Body Politic* (Baltimore: Johns Hopkins University Press, 1990).

HURST, MICHAEL, *Maria Edgeworth and the Public Scene: Intellect, Fine Feeling and Landlordism in the Age of Reform* (London: Macmillan, 1969).

HUTCHINSON, JOHN, *The Dynamics of Cultural Nationalism: The Gaelic*

Revival and the Creation of the Irish Nation State (London: Allen & Unwin, 1987).

HYDE, DOUGLAS, *'An Craoibhin Aoibhinn': Language, Lore and Lyrics. Essays and Lectures*, ed. Brendan Ó Conaire (Dublin: Irish Academic Press, 1986).

IMHOF, RUDIGER (ed.), *Alive-Alive O! Flann O'Brien's At Swim-Two-Birds* (Dublin: Wolfhound, 1985).

INNES, C. LYNN, *Woman and Nation in Irish Literature and Society 1880–1935* (Athens: University of Georgia Press, 1993).

JACKSON, ALVIN, 'Irish Unionism, 1905–21', in Peter Collins (ed.), *Nationalism and Unionism: Conflict in Ireland 1885–1921* (Belfast: Institute of Irish Studies, 1994), 35–46.

JAMESON, FREDRIC, *The Political Unconscious: Narrative as a Socially Symbolic Act* (Ithaca and London: Cornell University Press, 1981).

—— *Postmodernism, or, The Cultural Logic of Late Capitalism* (Durham: Duke University Press, 1991).

—— 'An Unfinished Project', *London Review of Books*, 17/15 (3 Aug. 1995), 8–9.

JOYCE, JAMES, *A Portrait of the Artist as a Young Man*, ed. Seamus Deane (London: Penguin, 1993).

KAVANAGH, PATRICK, *Collected Pruse* (London: MacGibbon & Kee, 1967).

KEANE, PATRICK J., *Yeats's Interactions with Tradition* (Columbia: University of Missouri Press, 1987).

KEENAN, DESMOND J., *The Catholic Church in Nineteenth-Century Ireland* (Dublin: Gill & Macmillan, 1983).

KELLEHER, JOHN V., 'Matthew Arnold and the Celtic Revival', in Harry Levin (ed.), *Perspectives of Criticism* (Cambridge, Mass.: Harvard University Press, 1950), 197–221.

KELLY, JOHN, 'The Fall of Parnell and the Rise of Irish Literature: An Investigation', *Anglo-Irish Studies*, 2 (1976), 1–23.

KENEALY, CHRISTINE, *This Great Calamity: The Irish Famine, 1845–52* (Dublin: Gill & Macmillan, 1994).

KEOGH, DÁIRE, *The French Disease: The Catholic Church and Radicalism in Ireland 1790–1800* (Dublin: Four Courts Press, 1993).

KERR, DONAL E., *'A Nation of Beggars'? Priests, People and Politics in Famine Ireland, 1846–1852* (Oxford: Clarendon Press, 1994).

KIBERD, DECLAN, 'The London Exiles: Wilde and Shaw', in Seamus Deane, Andrew Carpenter, and Jonathan Williams (eds.), *The Field Day Anthology of Irish Writing*, 3 vols. (Derry: Field Day, 1991), ii. 372–515.

—— *Inventing Ireland: The Literature of the Modern Nation* (London: Jonathan Cape, 1995).

KOHN, HANS, *The Age of Nationalism* (New York: Harper, 1962).

LACOUE-LABARTHE, PHILLIPPE, and NANCY, JEAN-LUC, *The Literary Absolute: The Theory of Literature in German Romanticism*, trans. Philip Barnard and Cheryl Lester (Albany: SUNY, 1988).

LALOR, JAMES FINTAN, *Collected Writings*, ed. Nathaniel Marlowe (Dublin: Maunsel, 1918).

LANDA, LOUIS, *Swift and the Church of Ireland* (Oxford: Clarendon Press, 1954).

LARKIN, EMMET, 'A Reconsideration: Daniel Corkery and his Ideas on Cultural Nationalism', *Eire-Ireland*, 8 (Spring 1973), 42–51.

LAUGHLIN, JAMES, 'Some Comparative Aspects of Irish and English Nationalism in the Late Nineteenth Century', in Myrtle Hill and Sarah Barber (eds.), *Aspects of Irish Studies* (Belfast: Institute of Irish Studies, 1990), 9–15.

LEASK, NIGEL, *British Romantic Writers and the East: Anxieties of Empire* (Cambridge: Cambridge University Press, 1992).

LE BON, GUSTAVE, *La Psychologie des foules* (Paris: Flammarion, 1895).

—— *La Révolution française et la psychologie des révolutions* (1912); ET: *The Psychology of Revolution*, trans. Bernard Miall (London: Unwin, 1913).

LEE, JOSEPH J., *The Modernisation of Irish Society 1848–1918* (Dublin: Gill & Macmillan, 1973).

—— *Ireland 1912–85: Politics and Society* (Cambridge: Cambridge University Press, 1990).

LEERSSEN, JOEP TH. 'On the Edge of Europe: Ireland in Search of Oriental Roots, 1650–1850', *Comparative Criticism*, 8 (1986), 91–112.

—— *Mere Irish and fíor-Gael; Studies in the Idea of Irish Nationality, its Development and Literary Expression Prior to the Nineteenth Century* (Amsterdam and Philadelphia: John Benjamins, 1988).

—— *Remembrance and Imagination: Patterns in the Historical and Literary Representation of Ireland in the Nineteenth Century* (Cork: Cork University Press/Field Day, 1996).

LEIGHTON, C. D. A., *Catholicism in a Protestant Kingdom: A Study of the Irish Ancien Régime* (Dublin: Gill & Macmillan, 1994).

LENEMAN, LEAH, 'Ossian and the Enlightenment', *Scotia*, 11 (1987), 13–29.

LEO XII, POPE, *The Encyclical Letter of Pope Leo XII. Annexed to Pastoral Instructions by the Roman Catholic Archbishops and Bishops* (Dublin: Richard Coyne, 1824).

LLOYD, DAVID, 'Arnold, Ferguson, Schiller: Aesthetic Culture and the Politics of Aesthetics', *Cultural Critique*, 2 (Winter 1985/6), 139–52.

—— *Nationalism and Minor Literature: James Clarence Mangan and the Emergence of Irish Cultural Nationalism* (Berkeley, Los Angeles, and London: University of California Press, 1987).

—— *Anomalous States: Irish Writing and the Post-Colonial Moment* (Dublin: Lilliput Press, 1993).

Lock, F. P., *Swift's Tory Politics* (London: Duckworth, 1983).

Lombroso, Cesare, *L'Uomo Delinquente* (1876); ET: *Criminal Man* (New York and London: G. P. Putnam, 1911).

Lukács, Georg, *Goethe and his Age*, trans. Robet Anchor (London: Merlin Press, 1968).

Lynam, Edward W., *The Irish Character in Print 1571–1923* (Oxford: Oxford University Press offprint, 1924; Shannon: Irish University Press, 1968).

Lyons, F. S. L., *Ireland since the Famine* (London and Glasgow: Collins, Fontana, rev. edn. 1973).

Lyotard, Jean-François, *The Postmodern Condition: A Report on Knowledge*, trans. Geoff Bennington and Brian Massumi (Minneapolis: University of Minneapolis Press, 1984).

McCaffrey, Lawrence, 'Daniel Corkery and Irish Cultural Nationalism', *Eire-Ireland*, 8 (Spring 1973), 35–41.

MacCartney, Donal, 'The Writing of History in Ireland, 1800–50', *Irish Historical Studies*, 10/40, (Sept. 1957), 347–62.

—— *W. E. H. Lecky: Historian and Politician 1838–1903* (Dublin: Lilliput Press, 1994).

McClelland, J. S., *The Crowd and the Mob: From Plato to Canetti* (London: Unwin Hyman, 1989).

McClure, John, *Late Imperial Romance* (London: Verso, 1994).

McCormack, W. J., *Sheridan Le Fanu and Victorian Ireland* (Oxford: Clarendon Press, 1980).

—— *Ascendancy and Tradition in Anglo-Irish Literary History from 1789 to 1939* (Oxford: Clarendon Press, 1985).

—— 'French Revolution . . . Anglo-Irish Literature . . . Beginnings? The Case of Maria Edgeworth', in Hugh Gough and David Dickson (eds.), *Ireland and the French Revolution* (Dublin: Irish Academic Press, 1990), 229–43.

—— 'Maria Edgeworth', in Seamus Deane, Andrew Carpenter, and Jonathan Williams (eds.), *The Field Day Anthology of Irish Writing*, 3 vols. (Derry: Field Day, 1991), i. 1011–52.

—— 'The Intellectual Revival (1830–50)', ibid. ii. 1173–200.

—— 'Irish Gothic and After, 1820–1945', ibid. 831–949.

—— *Dissolute Characters: Irish Literary History through Balzac, Sheridan le Fanu and Bowen* (Manchester: Manchester University Press, 1993).

—— *From Burke to Beckett: Ascendancy, Tradition and Betrayal in Literary History* (Cork: Cork University Press, 1994).

McCracken, J. L., 'Protestant Ascendancy and the Life of Colonial Nationalism, 1714–60', in T. W. Moody, F. X. Martin, and F. J. Byrne (eds.), *A New History of Ireland*, vol. iv (Oxford: Clarendon Press, 1986).

MacDonagh, Oliver, *States of Mind: A Study of Anglo-Irish Conflict 1780–1980* (London: George Allen & Unwin, 1983).

—— O'Connell. *The Life of Daniel O'Connell 1775–1847* (London: Weidenfeld & Nicolson, 1991).

McGANN, JEROME, *Social Values and Poetic Acts: The Historical Judgment of Literary Work* (Cambridge, Mass., and London: Harvard University Press, 1988).

—— *Black Riders: The Visible Language of Modernism* (Princeton: Princeton University Press, 1993).

McGEE, THOMAS D'ARCY, *A Popular History of Ireland from the Earliest Period to the Emancipation of the Catholics*, 2 vols. (London and Glasgow: Cameron & Ferguson, 1862).

McGUINNE, DERMOT, *Irish Type Design: A History of Printing Types in the Irish Character* (Dublin: Irish Academic Press, 1992).

MAHONY, ROBERT, *Jonathan Swift: The Irish Identity* (New Haven and London: Yale University Press, 1995).

MANGAN, JAMES CLARENCE, *see* O'Daly, John.

MARSHALL, DAVID, *The Figure of Theater: Shaftesbury, Defoe, Adam Smith and George Eliot* (New York: Columbia University Press, 1986).

MARTIN, BON LOUIS HENRI, *Histoire de France depuis les temps les plus reculés jusqu'en 1789*, 17 vols. (Paris: Furne, 4th edn. 1855–60). Trans. and abridged as *Martin's History of France: The Decline of the French Monarchy*, by M. C. Booth, 2 vols. (Boston: Walker, Fuller & Co., 1866).

MARX, KARL, and ENGELS, FRIEDRICH, *Ireland and the Irish Question*, ed. R. Dixon (London: Lawrence & Wishart, n.d.).

MAUME, PATRICK, *'Life that is Exile': Daniel Corkery and the Search for Irish Ireland* (Belfast: Institute for Irish Studies, 1993).

MICHAELS, WALTER BENN, 'Race into Culture: A Critical Genealogy of Cultural Identity', in Kwame Anthony Appiah and Henry Louis Gates, Jr. (eds.), *Identities* (Chicago: University of Chicago Press, 1995), 32–62.

MILLS, SARA, *Discourses of Difference: An Analysis of Women's Travel Writing and Colonialism* (London and New York: Routledge, 1991).

MITCHEL, JOHN, *The Last Conquest of Ireland (perhaps)* (Dublin: The Irishman Office, 1861).

—— *History of Ireland, from the Treaty of Limerick to the Present Day*, (Dublin: James Duffy, 2nd edn. 1869).

—— *Jail Journal; or, Five Years in British Prisons* (New York: Office of 'The Citizen', 1854; Dublin: M. H. Gill, 1913).

MOLONY, JOHN N., *A Soul Came into Ireland: Thomas Davis 1814–45. A Biography* (Dublin: Geography Publications, 1996).

MONTAG, WARREN, *The Unthinkable Swift: The Spontaneous Philosophy of a Church of England Man* (London: Verso, 1994).

MONTGAILLARD, G. H. R., ABBÉ DE, *Histoire de France, depuis la fin de la règne de Louis XVI jusqu'à l'année 1825* (Paris: Moutardier, 2nd edn. 1827).

MOODY, T. W., 'Irish History and Irish Mythology', *Hermathena*, 124 (Summer 1978), 7–28.

—— and MARTIN, F. X., *The Course of Irish History* (Dublin and Cork: Mercier, 1967).

MOORE, THOMAS, *Irish Melodies* (London: Longman, 1810).

—— *Memoirs of Captain Rock, the Celebrated Irish Chieftain, with some account of his Ancestors* (London: Longman, 1824).

—— *The Life and Death of Lord Edward Fitzgerald*, 2 vols. (London: Longman, Rees, Orme, Brown and Green, 1831).

—— *Irish Melodies and Miscellaneous Poems with a Melologue upon National Music* (Dublin: W. Power, 1833).

MORASH, CHRIS, ' "Ever under some unnatural condition": Bram Stoker and the Colonial Fantastic', in Brian Cosgrove (ed.), *Literature and the Supernatural* (Dublin: Columba Press, 1995), 95–119.

—— *Writing the Irish Famine* (Oxford: Clarendon Press, 1995).

MORETTI, FRANCO, *The Way of the World: The Bildungsroman in European Culture* (London: Verso, 1987).

—— *Signs Taken for Wonders*, trans. S. Fischer, D. Forgacs, and D. Miller (London: Verso, rev. edn. 1988).

MORROW, JOHN, *Coleridge's Political Thought* (London: Macmillan, 1990).

MOSCOVICI, SERGE, *The Age of the Crowd: A Historical Treatise on Mass Psychology* (1981), trans. J. C. Whitehouse (Cambridge: Cambridge University Press, 1985).

MOYNAHAN, JULIAN, *Anglo-Irish: The Literary Imagination in a Hyphenated Culture* (Princeton: Princeton University Press, 1995).

MURPHY, WILLIAM M., *The Parnell Myth and Irish Politics 1891–1956* ((New York: Peter Lang, 1986).

NANDY, ASHIS, *The Savage Freud and Other Essays* (Princeton: Princeton University Press, 1995).

NASH, CATHERINE, 'Landscape, Body and Nation: Cultural Geographies of Irish Identities' (Ph.D. thesis, University of Nottingham, 1995).

NESBITT, DERMOT, *Unionism Restated: An Analysis of the Ulster Unionist Party's 'Statement of Aims'* (Belfast: Ulster Unionist Information Institute, issue no. 16, Dec. 1995).

NEWMAN, GERALD, *The Rise of English Nationalism: A Cultural History, 1720–1830* (New York: St Martin's Press, 1987).

NOLAN, EMER, *James Joyce and Nationalism* (London and New York: Routledge, 1995).

NORDAU, MAX, *Entartung* (1892); ET: *Degeneration* (London: Heinemann, 1895).

NOVICK, PETER, *That Noble Dream: The 'Objectivity Question' and the American Historical Profession* (Cambridge: Cambridge University Press, 1986).

NYE, ROBERT A., *The Origins of Crowd Psychology: Gustave Le Bon and the Crisis of Mass Democracy in the Third Republic* (London: Sage Publications, 1975).

—— *Crime, Madness and Politics in Modern France: The Medical Concept of National Decline* (Princeton: Princeton University Press, 1984).

O'BRIEN, CONOR CRUISE, 'Passion and Cunning: An Essay on the Politics of W. B. Yeats', in Norman A. Jeffares (ed.), *In Excited Reverie: A Centenary Tribute to W. B. Yeats, 1865–1939* (New York: St Martin's Press, 1965), 207–78.

O'BRIEN, FLANN (pseud. Brian O'Nolan), *At Swim-Two-Birds* (London: Longman, 1939; repr. MacGibbon & Kee, 1961).

—— *An Béal Bocht nó an milleanac* [le Myles na Copaleen] (Dublin: An Press Naisiunta, 1941).

—— *The Hard Life: An Exegesis of Squalor* (London: MacGibbon & Kee, 1961).

—— *The Dalkey Archive* (London: MacGibbon & Kee, 1964).

—— *The Third Policeman* (London: MacGibbon & Kee, 1967).

—— *The Best of Myles: A Selection from 'Cruiskeen Lawn'*, ed. Kevin O'Nolan (London: MacGibbon & Kee, 1968).

—— *The Poor Mouth: A Bad Story about the Hard Life*, trans. Patrick C. Power (New York: Seaver Books, 1981).

—— *The Various Lives of Keats and Chapman and the Brother*, ed. Benedict Kiely (London: Grafton, 1988).

Ó BUACHALLA, BRENDÁN, 'O Corcora agus an Hidden Ireland', *Scríobh*, 4 (1979), 109–37.

O'CALLAGHAN, MARGARET, *British High Politics and a Nationalist Ireland: Criminality Land and the Law under Forster and Balfour* (Cork: Cork University Press, 1994).

Ó CATHÁIN, DIARMUID, 'An Irish Scholar Abroad: Bishop John O'Brien of Cloyne and the Macpherson Controversy', in Patrick O'Flanagan and Cornelius G. Buttimer (eds.), *Cork: History and Society. Interdisciplinary Essays on the History of an Irish County* (Dublin: Geography Publications, 1993), 499–533.

Ó CÍOSÁIN, NIALL, 'Printed Popular Literature in Irish 1750–1850: Presence and Absence', in Mary Daly and David Dickson (eds.), *The Origins of Popular Literacy in Ireland: Language Change and Educational Development 1700–1920* (Dublin: Trinity College and University College, 1990), 45–57.

Ó CONAIRE, BRENDAN, *Myles na Gaeilge* (Dublin: An Clóchomhar, 1986).

O'CONOR, CHARLES, *Dissertation on the First Migrations, and Final Settlement of the Scots in North-Britain; with occasional Observations on the poems of Fingal and Temora* (Dublin: Geroge Faulkner, 1766).

—— *Rerum Hibernicarum Scriptores Veteres*, 4 vols. (London: T. Payne, 1814–26).

O'Conor, Charles, *The Letters of Charles O'Conor of Belnagare*, ed. Catherine Coogan Ward and Robert E. Ward, 2 vols. (University Microfilms International, 1980).

O'Daly, John, *The Poets and Poetry of Munster: A Selection of Irish songs by the poets of the last century. with poetical translations by the late James Clarence Mangan, now for the first time published, with the Original Music, and biographical sketches of the authors* . . . (Dublin: John O'Daly, 1849; 2nd edn. 1850; 3rd edn. 1885).

—— *The Irish Language Miscellany; being a selection of poems by the Munster bards of the last century* (Dublin: John O'Daly, 1876).

—— *The Poets and Poetry of Munster: A Selection of Irish Songs by the Poets of the Eighteenth Century, with Poetical Translations by* JAMES CLARENCE MANGAN (Dublin: James Duffy, 4th edn. 1925).

O'Driscoll, Robert, *An Ascendancy of the Heart; Ferguson and the Beginnings of Irish Literature in English* (Dublin: Dolmen Press, 1976).

Ó Dúill, Greagóir, *Samuel Ferguson: Beatha agus Saothar* (Dublin: Clóchomhar, 1993).

O'Faolain, Sean, *King of the Beggars: A Life of Daniel O'Connell, the Irish Liberator, in a Study of the Rise of Irish Democracy* (London: Nelson, 1938).

—— 'The Gaelic Cult', *The Bell*, 9/3 (Dec. 1944); repr. in Seamus Deane, Andrew Carpenter, and Jonathan Williams (eds.), *The Field Day Anthology of Irish Writing*, 3 vols. (Derry: Field Day, 1991), iii. 569–73.

O'Flanagan, Theophilus, *Advice to a Prince, by Thaddy Mac Brody or Mac Brodin, Son of Dary; being the inauguration ode of Donach O'Brien, Fourth earl of Thomond, when elected prince of his nation, according to ancient Irish Usage* . . . , from *Transactions of the Gaelic Society of Dublin, established for the investigation and revival of Ancient Irish Literature* (Dublin: J. Barlow, 1808).

—— *Deirdri, or The lamentable Fate of the Sons of Usnach, An Ancient Dramatic Irish Tale, one of the three tragic stories of Erin* (Dublin: J. Barlow, 1808).

Ó Gráda, Cormac, *The Great Irish Famine* (Houndmills: Macmillan, 1989).

—— *Ireland: A New Economic History, 1780–1939* (Oxford: Clarendon Press, 1994).

O'Grady, Standish, *History of Ireland*, i: *The Heroic Period* (London: Sampson Low, Searle, Marston and Rivington; Dublin: E. Ponsonby, 1878).

—— *History of Ireland*, ii: *Cuculain and his Contemporaries* (London: Sampson Low, Searle, Marston and Rivington; Dublin: E. Ponsonby, 1880).

—— *The Crisis in Ireland* (Dublin: E. Ponsonby, 1882).

—— *Toryism and the Tory Democracy* (London: Chapman and Hall, 1886).

—— *Selected Essays and Passages*, introd. Ernest Boyd (Dublin: Talbot, 1917).

O'Keefe, Timothy (ed.), *Myles: Portraits of Brian O'Nolan* (London: Martin, Brian & O'Keefe, 1973).

O'LEARY, PHILIP, *The Prose Literature of the Gaelic Revival 1881–1921* (University Park: Pennsylvania State University Press, 1994).

Ó RÍORDAIN, MICHELLE, *The Gaelic Mind and the Collapse of the Gaelic World* (Cork: Cork University Press, 1990).

Ó TUAMA, SEÁN, *Repossessions: Selected Essays in the Irish Literary Heritage* (Cork: Cork University Press, 1995).

Ó TUATHAIGH, GEARÓID, 'Nationalist Ireland 1912–1922: Aspects of Continuity and Change', in Peter Collins (ed.), *Nationalism and Unionism: Conflict in Ireland 1885–1921* (Belfast: Institute of Irish Studies, 1994), 47–73.

PARIS, MARK S., 'From Clinic to Classroom while Uncovering the Evil Dead in *Dracula*: A Psychoanalytic Pedagogy', in James M. Cahalan and David B. Downing (eds.), *Practicing Theory in Introductory College Courses* (Urbana, Ill.: National Council of Teachers of English, 1991), 47–56.

PARK, ROBERT E., *The Crowd and the Public and Other Essays* (1904), ed. Henry Elsner (Chicago: University of Chicago Press, 1972).

'Pastor Fido', *Pastorini Proved to be a Bad Prophet and a Worse Divine in an Address to the Roman Catholics of Ireland. Earnestly recommended to their Serious Perusal* (Dublin: M. Goodwin, 1823).

PETRIE, GEORGE, *The Ecclesiastical Architecture of Ireland, anterior to the Anglo-Norman invasion; comprising an essay on the origin and uses of the round towers of Ireland . . .* (Dublin: Hodges & Smith, 1845).

—— *The Petrie Collection of the Ancient Music of Ireland: Arranged for the Pianoforte*, 2 vols. (Dublin: Dublin University Press, 1855–82).

PICK, DANIEL, 'Terrors of the Night: *Dracula* and "Degeneration" in the Late Nineteenth Century', *Critical Quarterly*, 30/4 (Winter 1988), 72–87.

—— *Faces of Degeneration: A European Disorder, c.1848–c.1918* (Cambridge: Cambridge University Press, 1989).

PITTOCK, MURRAY G. H., *Poetry and Jacobite Politics in Eighteenth-Century Britain and Ireland* (Cambridge: Cambridge University Press, 1994).

POCOCK, J. G. A., 'Burke and the Ancient Constitution: A Problem in the History of Ideas', in id., *Politics, Language and Time: Essays on Political Thought and History* (New York: Atheneum, 1971), 202-32.

—— 'Edmund Burke and the Redefinition of Political Enthusiasm: The Context as Counter-Revolution', in F. Furet and M. Ozouf (eds.), *The French Revolution and the Creation of Modern Political Culture*, iii: *The Transformation of Political Culture 1789–1848* (Oxford: Pergamon, 1989), 19–35.

—— 'Empire, Revolution and the End of Early Modernity', in id. (ed.), assisted by G. J. Schochet and L. G. Schwoerer, *The Varieties of British Political Thought, 1500–1800* (Cambridge: Cambridge University Press, 1993), 283–320.

POIRTÉIR, CATHAL (ed.), *The Great Irish Famine* (Cork: Mercier Press, 1995).

POLLARD, MARY M., *Dublin's Trade in Books 1550–1850* (Oxford: Clarendon Press, 1989).

POOVEY, MARY, *The Proper Lady and the Woman Writer: Ideology as Style in the Works of Mary Wollstonecraft, Mary Shelley, and Jane Austen* (Chicago: University of Chicago Press, 1984).

PORTER, DENNIS, *Haunted Journeys: Desire and Transgression in European Travel Writing* (Princeton: Princeton University Press, 1991).

PRASAD, MADHAVA, 'On the Question of a Theory of (Third World) Literature', *Social Text*, 10/2 and 3 (1992), 57–83.

PRATT, MARY LOUISE, *Imperial Eyes: Travel Writing and Transculturation* (London: Routledge, 1992).

PRICE, LEAH, 'Vies privées et scandaleuses: Marie Antoinette and the Public Eye', *The Eighteenth Century: Theory and Interpretation*, 33 (Summer 1992), 176–92.

RAUCHBAUER, OTTO (ed.), *Ancestral Voices: The Big House in Anglo-Irish Literature* (Dublin: Lilliput Press, 1992).

REGAN, STEPHEN, 'W. B. Yeats and Irish Cultural Politics', in Sally Ledger and Scott McCracken (eds.), *Cultural Politics at the Fin de Siècle* (Cambridge: Cambridge University Press, 1995), 66–84.

RENAN, ERNEST, *'The Poetry of the Celtic Races' and Other Essays*, trans. W. G. Hutchinson (London: W. Scott, 1896).

—— *Souvenirs d'enfance et de jeunesse* (1883); ET: *Recollections of My Youth*, trans. C. B. Pitman (Boston: Houghton Mifflin, 1929).

RICARDOU, JEAN, 'Time of the Narration, Time of the Fiction', *James Joyce Quarterly*, 16 (1979), 7–15.

RICHARDS, SHAUN, and CAIRNS, DAVID, *Writing Ireland: Colonialism, Nationalism and Culture* (Manchester: Manchester University Press, 1988).

RIGNEY, ANN, *The Rhetoric of Historical Representation* (Cambridge: Cambridge University Press, 1991).

RIORDAN, E. J., *Modern Irish Trade and Industry* (London: Methuen, 1920).

ROUSSEAU, JEAN-JACQUES, *Emile, or, On Education*, trans. Allan Bloom (New York: Basic Books, 1979).

SAID, EDWARD W., *The World, The Text, and the Critic* (London: Faber & Faber, 1984).

—— *Orientalism* (1st pub. 1978; London and Harmondsworth: Penguin, 1985).

—— *Culture and Imperialism* (New York: Knopf, 1993).

SAMUEL, RAPHAEL (ed.), *Patriotisms: The Making and Unmaking of British National Identity*, 3 vols. (London: Routledge, 1989).

SCARRY, ELAINE, *The Body in Pain: The Making and Unmaking of the World* (New York and Oxford: Oxford University Press, 1985).

SCHILLER, FRIEDRICH, *On the Aesthetic Education of Man in a Series of Letters* (1801), ed. Elizabeth M. Wilkinson and L. A. Willoughby (Oxford: Clarendon Press, 1967).

SCHMITT, CANNON, 'Mother Dracula: Orientalism, Degeneration, and Anglo-Irish National Subjectivity at the Fin de Siècle', in John S. Richard (ed.), *Irishness and (Post)Modernism* (Lewisburg: Bucknell University Press; London: Associated University Presses, 1994), 25–43.

SENF, CAROL A., ' "Dracula": Stoker's Response to the New Woman', *Victorian Studies*, 26/1 (Autumn 1982), 33–49.

SHANNON-MANGAN, ELLEN, *James Clarence Mangan: A Biography* (Dublin: Irish Academic Press, 1996).

SHERIDAN, JOHN D., *James Clarence Mangan* (Dublin: Talbot Press; London. Duckworth, 1937).

SIGHELE, SCIPIO, *La Folla Delinquente* (1891).

SIMMS, J. G., *Colonial Nationalism: 1692–1776* (Cork: Mercier Press, 1976).

—— 'Protestant Ascendancy, 1691–1714', in T. W. Moody, F. X. Martin, and F. J. Byrne (eds.), *A New History of Ireland*, vol. iv (Oxford: Clarendon Press, 1986).

SIMPSON, DAVID, *Romanticism, Nationalism and the Revolt against Theory* (Chicago and London: University of Chicago Press, 1993).

SKINNER, ANDREW S., and WILSON, THOMAS (eds.), *Essays on Adam Smith* (Oxford: Clarendon Press, 1975).

SLOAN, BARRY, *The Pioneers of Anglo-Irish Fiction, 1800–50* (Gerrards Cross: Colin Smythe; Totowa, NJ: Barnes & Noble, 1986).

SMITH, ANTHONY D., *The Ethnic Origins of Nations* (Oxford: Blackwell, 1987).

SMYTH, JIM, *The Men of No Property: Irish Radicals and Popular Politics in the Late Eighteenth Century* (Basingstoke: Macmillan, 1992).

SNYDER, EDWARD, *The Celtic Revival in English Literature, 1760–1800* (Cambridge, Mass.: Harvard University Press, 1923).

SOHN-RETHEL, ALFRED, *Intellectual and Manual Labour* (London: Macmillan, 1978).

SOUTHERN, R. W., 'The Shape and Substance of Academic History', in F. Stern (ed.), *The Varieties of History from Voltaire to the Present* (London: Macmillan, 2nd edn. 1970).

SPACKS, PATRICIA MEYER, *Boredom: The Literary History of a State of Mind* (Chicago and London: University of Chicago Press, 1995).

SPENCER, KATHLEEN L., 'Purity and Danger: *Dracula*, The Urban Gothic, and the Late Victorian Degeneracy Crisis', *English Literary History*, 59 (1992), 197–225.

—— *The Spirit of the Nation* (Dublin: J. Duffy, 1843–4).

STAFFORD, FIONA, *The Sublime Savage* (Edinburgh: Edinburgh University Press, 1988).

STAFFORD, FIONA, and GASKILL, HOWARD (eds.), *Ossian Revisited* (Edinburgh: Edinburgh University Press, 1991).

STEEVES, HARRISON R., *Before Jane Austen: The Shaping of the English Novel in the Eighteenth Century* (London: Allen & Unwin, 1966).

STEINMAN, MICHAEL, *Yeats's Heroic Figures: Wilde, Parnell, Swift, Casement* (London: Macmillan, 1983).

STEPAN, NANCY, *The Idea of Race in Science: Great Britain 1800–1960* (Hamden: Archon Books, 1982).

STERNHELL, ZEEV, with SZNAJDER, MARIO, and ASHERI, MAIA, *The Birth of Fascist Ideology: From Cultural Rebellion to Political Revolution*, trans. David Maisel (Princeton: Princeton University Press, 1994).

STEWART, SUSAN, *Crimes of Writing: Problems in the Containment of Representation* (Durham and London: Duke University Press, 1994).

STOKER, BRAM, *Dracula* (Dingle: Brandon Books, 1992).

STOKES, ERIC, *The English Utilitarians and India* (Oxford: Clarendon Press, 1959).

SYNGE, JOHN MILLINGTON, *Collected Works,* iii and iv: *Plays,* ed. Anne Saddlemyer (London and Oxford: Oxford University Press, 1968).

TAINE, HIPPOLYTE, *Les Origines de la France contemporaine,* 6 vols. (Paris, 1876–94); ET: *The Origins of Contemporary France,* ed. and selected by Edward T. Gargan (Chicago: University of Chicago Press, 1974).

TARDE, JEAN GABRIEL, *La Philosophie pénale* (1890); ET: *Penal Philosophy,* trans. Rapelje Howell (Boston: Little, Brown, 1912).

TAYLOR, CHARLES, *Sources of the Self: The Making of Modern Identity* (Cambridge, Mass.: Harvard University Press, 1989).

THOM, MARTIN, *Republics, Nations and Tribes* (London and New York: Verso, 1995).

THOMAS, CHANTAL, *La Reine scélérate: Marie-Antoinette dans les pamphlets* (Paris: Éditions du Seuil, 1989).

THOMSON, DERICK, 'Macpherson's *Ossian*: Ballads to Epics', in Bo Almquist, Séamus ó Catháin, and Padraig O Héaláin (eds.), *The Heroic Process: Form, Function and Fantasy in Folk Epic* (Dun Laoghaire: Glendale Press, 1987), 243–64.

THUENTE, MARY HELEN, *W. B. Yeats and Irish Folklore* (Dublin: Gill & Macmillan, 1980).

TODOROV, TZVETAN, *The Conquest of America,* trans. Richard Howard (New York: Harper & Row, 1982).

—— *On Human Diversity: Nationalism, Racism, and Exoticism in French Thought,* trans. Catherine Porter (Cambridge, Mass.: Harvard University Press, 1993).

TOMPKINS, J. M. S., *The Popular Novel in England, 1770–1800* (London: Constable, 1932; repr. Methuen, 1961).

TRACY, ROBERT, 'The Mobbed Queen: Marie Antoinette as Victorian Ikon', *LIT,* 4 (1993), 275–90.

TRUMPENER, KATE, 'National Character, Nationalist Plots: National Tale and the Historical Novel in the Age of *Waverley*, 1806–1830', *English Literary History*, 60/3 (Fall 1993), 685–731.

TURNER, MICHAEL, 'Rural Economies in Post-Famine Ireland, c.1850–1914', in Brian J. Graham and Lindsay J. Proudfoot (eds.), *An Historical Geography of Ireland* (London: Academic Press, 1993), 293–337.

VALLANCEY, CHARLES, *Collectanea de Rebus Hibernicis*, 6 vols. (Dublin: L. White *et al.*, 1786–1804).

VANCE, NORMAN, 'Celts, Carthaginians and Constitutions; Anglo-Irish Literary Relations, 1780–1820', *Irish Historical Studies*, 22/87 (Mar. 1981), 216–38.

VAN GINNEKEN, JAAP, *Crowds, Psychology, and Politics 1871–99* (Cambridge: Cambridge University Press, 1992).

VON HUMBOLDT, WILHELM, *Über die Verschiedenheit des menschlichen Sprachbaues* (1st pub. 1836; Bonn: F. Dummler, 1960).

WALKER, JOSEPH COOPER, *Historical Memoirs of the Irish Bards* (1st edn. 1786; 2nd edn., 2 vols., Dublin: J. Christie, 1818).

WALL, GEOFFREY, ' "Different from Writing": *Dracula* in 1897', *Literature and History*, 10/1 (Spring 1984), 15–24.

WALMESLEY, CHARLES, *The General History of the Christian Church from her birth to her final triumphant state in heaven chiefly deduced from the apocalypse of St. John The Apostle and Evangelist* (1771) (Dublin: P. Wogan, 5th edn. 1813).

WALSH, EDWARD, *Irish Popular Songs; with English metrical translations, and introductory remarks and notes* (Dublin: McGlashan, 1847; 2nd edn., rev. and corr., Gill, 1883).

—— *Reliques of Irish Jacobite Poetry; with biographical sketches of the authors* (Dublin: part 1, S. J. Machen; part 2, John Cumming, 1844; 2nd edn. John O'Daly, 1866).

WARWICK, ALEXANDRA, 'Vampires and the Empire: Fears and Fictions of the 1890s', in Sally Ledger and Scott McCracken (eds.), *Cultural Politics at the Fin De Siècle* (Cambridge: Cambridge University Press, 1995), 202–20.

WASSON, RICHARD, 'The Politics of *Dracula*', *English Literature in Translation*, 9 (1966), 24–7.

WEIL, SIMONE, *The Need for Roots: Prelude to a Declaration of Duties towards Mankind*, trans. A. F. Wills (London: Routledge & Kegan Paul, 1952).

WEINTRAUB, STANLEY, *Shaw: An Autobiography 1856–98* (New York: Weybright & Talley, 1969).

WELCH, ROBERT, *History of Verse Translation from the Irish 1789–1897* (Gerrards Cross: Colin Smythe, 1987).

WHELAN, KEVIN, 'Catholics, Politicisation and the 1798 Rebellion', in Reamoinn O Muirí (ed.), *Irish Church History Today* (Armagh: Cumann Seancháis Ard Macha, 1990), 63–84.

—— 'Ireland in the World-System, 1600–1800', in Hans-Jurgen Nitz (ed.),

The Early-Modern World-System in Geographical Perspective (Stuttgart: Franz Steiner, 1993), 204–18.

—— 'Settlement Patterns in the West of Ireland in the Pre-Famine Period', in Timothy Collins (ed.), *Decoding the Landscape* (Galway: Social Sciences Research Centre, 1994), 60–78.

—— 'The Republic in the Village: The United Irishmen, the Enlightenment and Popular Culture', in id., *The Tree of Liberty: Radicalism, Catholicism and the Construction of Irish Identity 1760–1830* (Cork: Cork University Press, in association with Field Day, 1996), 59–98.

WHITE, HAYDEN, *Tropics of Discourse: Essays in Cultural Criticism* (Baltimore and London: Johns Hopkins University Press, 1978; 1985).

WOOD, NEAL, 'The Aesthetic Dimension of Burke's Political Thought', *Journal of British Studies*, 4/1, (1964), 41–64.

YEATS, W. B., *Mythologies* (London: Macmillan, 1959).

—— *Essays and Introductions* (London: Macmillan, 1961).

—— *Explorations* (London: Macmillan, 1962).

—— *W. B. Yeats: The Poems*, ed. Richard J. Finneran (Dublin: Gill & Macmillan, 1984).

YOUNG, ROBERT, *Colonial Desire: Hybridity in Theory, Culture and Race* (New York: Routledge, 1995).

YOUNGS, TIM, *Travellers in Africa: British Travelogues, 1850–1900* (Manchester: Manchester University Press, 1994).

ZERILLI, LINDA M. G., 'Text/Woman as Spectacle: Edmund Burke's 'French Revolution', *The Eighteenth Century: Theory and Interpretation*, 32 (Spring 1992), 47–72.

ZEUSS, JOHANN KASPAR, *Grammatica Celtica* (Lipsiae: Weidmannos, 1853).

Index